G000038887

Pocket Book of
British Ceramic Marks

Also by J. P. Cushion
(in collaboration with W. B. Honey)

HANDBOOK OF POTTERY AND
PORCELAIN MARKS

Pocket Book of
British
Ceramic Marks

★

including
Index to Registered Designs
1842–83

★

compiled by
J. P. CUSHION
lately Senior Research Assistant of the
Department of Ceramics
Victoria and Albert Museum, London

FABER AND FABER
3 Queen Square
London

First published in 1959
by Faber and Faber Limited
as Pocket Book of English Ceramic Marks
Second edition 1965
Second impression 1967
Third impression 1969
Fourth impression 1970
Fifth impression 1972
Third enlarged edition, revised and reset 1976
Printed in Great Britain at
the Alden Press, Oxford
All rights reserved

ISBN 0 571 04869 2

© 1959, 1976 John Patrick Cushion

Acknowledgements

The author wishes to express his gratitude to the many officers and colleagues at the Victoria and Albert Museum, numerous collectors, English Ceramic Circle members and ceramic dealers, all of whom have assisted him in the recording of elusive marks for the guidance of future seekers.

Thanks are also recorded to Mr. Murray Fieldhouse, editor of *Pottery Quarterly*, and to the members of The Craftsmen Potters Association, who have assisted him in the collection of the marks and particulars of the present-day studio potters. The author is indebted to Mr. Geoffrey Godden for information concerning the dates of nineteenth-century factories and potters.

Thanks for information concerning recently established factories, closures, take-overs etc. are due to the proprietors of *Tableware International* (formerly *Pottery Gazette and Glass Trade Review*, established 1877), and to Mr. Terence Woolliscroft of Milton, Stoke-on-Trent, who so generously carried out the research concerning the recent, and often very complicated, changes of proprietorship of many Staffordshire factories. Mr. Woolliscroft noted that by January 1972 only one hundred and forty-four factories (individual producing units) remained in the Stoke area, employing thirty-four thousand workers.

Contents

Preface: Scope and Arrangement
of the Book

This pocket-book of ceramic marks has been produced especially to answer the requirements of the collector and dealer who has long needed such a guide when on 'pot-hunting' expeditions. In order to restrict the bulk of this volume the marks shown here have been confined to those of Great Britain and Ireland; Continental and Far Eastern marks are dealt with in the *Handbook of Pottery and Porcelain Marks*.

The marks recorded here are restricted to true factory marks and those others which by their frequent occurrence, or in other ways are of actual use in helping to identify the place and period of manufacture of a piece.

The arrangement is in alphabetical order of towns, subdivided into names of factories or owners, again alphabetically. The pottery centre of Staffordshire is treated in a separate section from the rest of England.

As far as practicable the marks are shown in facsimile (space has not permitted full-scale reproduction in all cases), the chief exception being those numerous modern marks consisting of the names or initials of the maker, or of the place of manufacture, which are reproduced by using printers' type, as has so often been done in the marks themselves on the actual wares.

The scope of this book has been extended to include many nineteenth- and twentieth-century marks not hitherto recorded, and brought right up-to-date by showing the marks of modern studio-potters.

To help the enquirer, an approximate date or period

is given for every mark together with the name of the principal proprietor where of interest, and a word or so of description of the type of ware on which the mark is generally found.

*   *   *

This enlarged and revised new edition of the *Pocket Book of English Ceramic Marks*, includes that part of the Class IV Design Index which relates to pottery and porcelain (Appendix B, page 288). It is included by the kind permission of the Public Record Office and will enable readers not only to date their wares by using the tables on pages 284–287, but also to determine the name of the manufacturer or person or firm, who initially registered the design to protect it from 'piracy' for a period of three years, by consulting the Index (i.e. Appendix B).

Historical Note and Methods
of Marking

The practice of marking ceramic wares as a guide to the manufacturer is a very old one and was carried out by the Romans on their red-wares, but it is not until the sixteenth century in Europe that the soft-paste Italian 'Medici' porcelain appears with a fully developed factory-mark, i.e. the sketch of the dome of Florence Cathedral in underglaze blue.

It was not until 1723 that the Meissen (Dresden) factory in Saxony adopted as a regular factory-mark the crossed swords of the arms of Saxony; this mark was invariably painted in underglaze blue on the base of the article in the Chinese manner. Other European porcelain and faience factories quickly followed the lead of Meissen and in 1766 the porcelain makers of France were required by law to use a mark which had been previously registered with the police authorities.

The practice of marking was never regularized throughout the eighteenth century with the result that factories which were proud of their reputation used a recognized mark, whilst the less important factories either left their wares unmarked in the hope that they would be mistaken for those factories whose style they were copying, or alternatively, used a mark similar enough to a famous one to be mistaken for genuine. The crossed swords of Meissen were used on numerous imitations and quite openly copied on Bow, Derby, Worcester and Lowestoft.

Many of the marks encountered on ceramics are

merely those of painters or workmen and are not a sure guide to the place of manufacture even when identified, for these people were of a very nomadic nature and often worked in many different factories in the course of their career. The throwers and 'repairers' (a term used for the workers who assembled the various parts of figures, etc.) invariably used a mark scratched in the body prior to the biscuit firing. These marks when under the glaze can safely be treated as genuine, but otherwise they should be closely examined for the burr or raised edge which is unavoidable when scratching soft clay, to ensure the mark has not been ground in after firing in order to deceive.

Painters and gilders generally used one of the colours in their palette or gilt, to mark the wares upon which they worked, this information was probably solely for the benefit of the management and for purposes of payment, which was often on a piecework basis.

Not to be confused with the names of potters are those of London dealers, who during the eighteenth and nineteenth centuries had goods made and decorated to their specific orders.

The marks used on English wares were applied in several different ways, including the incising (or scratching) on the unfired clay we have mentioned above. The other marks impressed in the body at this stage are also a reliable guide and usually were names of the factory, place or proprietor, made up of printers' type and stamped in one operation.

Painting or transfer-printing under the glaze in blue (also in green after 1850) was a most common method of marking wares and may be accepted as genuine, at least as far as knowing the piece was marked at the time of manufacture.

The practice of marking by painting, transfer-printing, or stencilling over the glaze in enamel-colours, are methods which are always liable to be fraudulent, as it is possible to add these type of marks at any time after the piece has been made.

The beginner should approach all marks with caution and it is important to learn to detect the difference between the various materials, (i.e. earthenware, hard-paste porcelain, soft-paste porcelain and bone-china, etc.); this would enable him to immediately realize that a neat gold anchor on a Chelsea-type figure cannot possibly be of that factory if the body is a hard continental paste and not the soft-paste as used at Chelsea. Finally do remember that many nineteenth-century factories include the date of their establishment in their mark and those early dates do not signify that the piece in question was made at that date, and also, that grandmother, who died at the ripe old age of one hundred and one, did not necessarily acquire the piece of china she has passed down to you at her birth.

Notes on Wares Made in
Great Britain and Ireland

The English late-medieval wares are not only of great artistic interest, but historically important as the direct ancestors of the Staffordshire wares. Little is known of the places of their production, the finer specimens perhaps being made in monasteries, and though of coarse materials the jugs and pitchers are often of great beauty of form and bear simple but effective decoration.

In the fifteenth and sixteenth centuries smaller neater jugs appear with a rich copper-green glaze together with a hard red pottery with dark brown or black glaze sometimes decorated with trailed white slip or with applied pads of white clay.

A rare and distinct class of sixteenth-century English pottery comprises cisterns, stove-tiles and candle-brackets finely moulded in relief and covered with a green or yellow glaze.

English pottery tradition before the industrial period was rooted in the medieval use of lead-glazed earthenware. The sixteenth-century Cistercian pottery was the immediate forerunner of the Tickenhall and Staffordshire slip-wares, and the tradition of the last in turn gave vitality to the 'Astbury' and 'Whieldon' wares made in the same district in the eighteenth century.

The impulse towards refinement, which had been inspired by the Elers brothers (who made fine red wares in the Chinese style) and by the vogue of porcelain, also led to the making of a fine white salt-glazed stoneware in Staffordshire, where the industrializing process was finally carried through by Josiah Wedgwood. His cream-coloured ware was immediately imitated at numerous neighbouring potteries as well as at Leeds, Liverpool, Bristol, Swansea, Sunderland, Newcastle, Portobello and elsewhere, quickly securing a world-wide market.

Aside from the main English tradition are the decorative stonewares of Wedgwood, products of the neo-Classical enthusiasm.

Tin-glazed ware, largely inspired by Italian, Dutch and Chinese models, was made at London, Bristol, Liverpool, Dublin and Glasgow, but had little effect on the main current of the English tradition as represented by the wares of Staffordshire, where delftware (as this is called) was never made. English delftware was painted in high-temperature colours; overglaze enamels were used only on very rare examples and were probably the work of Dutch independent enamellers.

The seventeenth-century stoneware of Fulham, inspired at first by the Rhenish and Chinese wares, produced the isolated phenomenon of Dwight's admirable figures; that of Nottingham, though typically English, was of minor importance, reflecting latterly something of the Staffordshire style.

English porcelain of the eighteenth century is remarkable for its variety of composition. Soft-pastes of French type ware made at Chelsea, Derby and Longton Hall; soapstone pastes at Worcester, Caughley and Liverpool; and hard-paste at Plymouth and Bristol. From about 1750 onwards for several decades Derby was a most productive factory and a large proportion of the surviving English porcelain figures were made there. At Bow the use of bone-ash from 1747 heralded the type of porcelain which towards the end of the eighteenth century became and still remains the English standard body; this last was a hybrid porcelain in which some part of the kaolin was replaced by bone-ash. At Nant-garw and Swansea a belated soft-paste was made in the period 1813–22.

None of the factories enjoyed royal or princely pro-tection or subsidy and most were short-lived. Chelsea, and possibly Worcester, alone reached the standard set by the chief manufacturers of France or the many establishments supported by the rulers of small states in Germany; the porcelain of the first-named, however, ranks with the best ever made in Europe. The unsophis-ticated charm of Bow and Lowestoft is of a different order and typically English.

From the absence of marks, the English porcelains are difficult to identify. The chief factories were those named above, but other early manufacturers may have existed in Limehouse, Lambeth, Kentish Town, Vauxhall and Greenwich.

The ceramic art of the nineteenth century suffered no less than others from misdirected effort and mistaken enthusiasms. While the early part of the century lived largely on the artistic capital of the preceding period, the later part was chiefly occupied with the deliberate revival of former styles.

Yet in spite of unfavourable conditions the native genius of the English potters did succeed in producing wares which are both beautiful and of permanent value; the simple 'cottage china' and lustre wares of the New Hall type and its kindred earthenware; Worcester, Derby, Spode, Coalport and other porcelains which were its opulent contemporaries and successors, the charming blue-printed ware, and the entirely English brown stonewares of the Midlands and Lambeth. A singular use of glazed Parian is to be noted in the wares of Belleek in Co. Fermanagh, Ireland, where a pottery was started in 1863. Vases in naturalistic shell-forms were especially characteristic.

At the end of the century the revival of handicraft makes its appearance with De Morgan and the Martin Brothers, heralding the studio pottery of the present day.

AMESBURY (Wiltshire)
    Zillwood, W., late 18th-
    early 19th centuries
    pottery

                    W.Z.
                    incised

ASHBY-DE-LA-ZOUCH
(Leicestershire)
    Thompson, J., *c.* 1815–56
    general pottery

              JOSEPH THOMPSON
               WOODEN BOX
                POTTERY
              DERBYSHIRE
               impressed
and other printed marks

    Wilson & Proudman
    Coleorton Pottery
    1835–42, general pottery

              WILSON &
              PROUDMAN
              impressed

ASHTEAD (Surrey)
    Ashtead Potters Ltd.
    1926–36, earthenware

AYLBURTON (Gloucestershire)
    Leach, Margaret, 1946–56
    Taena Community, 1951–56
    and Upton St. Leonards, Glos.
    where L. A. Groves also
    used mark. Studio-pottery

              impressed

BARNSTAPLE (Devon)
    Baron, W. L., 1899–1939
    Rolle Quay Pottery
    earthenware

             BARON. BARNSTAPLE
              incised

20

Brannam, Ltd., C. H.,
Litchdon Pottery, 1879–
earthenwares

C. H. BRANNAM
BARUM
incised

as from 1913–

C. H. BRANNAM LTD.
impressed

printed or impressed, 1929–

impressed, 1930–

C. H. BRANNAM
BARUM DEVON

BELPER (Derbyshire)
Belper Pottery 1809–34
stonewares
(transferred to Denby 1834)

BELPER
impressed

BENTHALL (Salop)
Pierce & Co., W., *c.* 1800–18
earthenwares

W. PIERCE & CO.

Salopian Art Pottery Co.
1882–*c.* 1912 earthenwares,

SALOPIAN
impressed

BILLINGHAM (Cleveland) and
elsewhere
Dunn, Constance, 1924–
studio-pottery

incised

BIRKENHEAD (Merseyside)
  Della Robbia Co. Ltd.
  earthenwares, *c.* 1894–1901

DELLA ROBBIA
impressed or incised

  top initial that of decorator

BISHOPS WALTHAM
(Hampshire)
  Bishops Waltham Pottery
  decorative earthenwares
  only from 1866–7 in
  Greek revival form

BISHOPS
WALTHAM
printed

BOVEY TRACEY (Devon)
  Bovey Tracey Pottery Co.
  earthenwares, 1842–94
  Bovey Pottery Co. Ltd.
  1894–1957
  also
  'Blue Waters Pottery'
  c. 1954–57

B.T.P. CO.
printed or impressed

c. 1937–49   1949–56

  Devonshire Potteries Ltd.
  earthenwares. 1947–
  also
  'Trentham Art Wares'
  1959–

TRENTHAM
ART WARE

Ehlers, A. W. G.
  Lowerdown Cross, 1946–55
  studio-potter

incised or painted

Leach, David, 1956–
(also at St. Ives *c.* 1932–56)
  'LD' for Lowerdown
  Pottery

LD
impressed

BOW (London)
(Stratford High St., Essex)
c. 1747– *c.* 1776
soft-paste porcelain
  early marks, *c.* 1750

incised

  presumably 'repairers'
  marks 1750–60

R AF

incised

impressed **B**

probably mark of
'repairer'
Mr. Tebo (Thibaud?)
marks on blue-painted
wares 1750–70

T⁰ T
impressed

underglaze blue

on figures and other late pieces
and
'anchor and dagger'
period, *c.* 1762–76

⚓ †
in red

in underglaze
blue and red

in red

in underglaze blue

in underglaze
blue and red

in underglaze
blue

on blue-and-white
cups, in underglaze
blue

in underglaze blue

BRADFORD (W. Yorkshire)
  Booth, Frederick, *c.* 1881
earthenware

     F.B.

BRAMPTON (Derbyshire)
  Knowles & Son, Matthew
stonewares, *c.* 1835–1911

     KNOWLES

Oldfield & Co., *c.* 1838–88
earthenware

     J. OLDFIELD

     OLDFIELD & CO.
       impressed

Pearson Ltd., James
Oldfield and London
Potteries. stonewares
19th century—1939
1920–

     J.P. LTD.
  impressed or printed
    from 1907

Bramfield Ware

BRAUNTON (N. Devon)
Braunton Pottery Co. Ltd.
earthenwares, 1910–
    mark of *c.* 1947–
(moved or finished by 1972)

BRAUNTON
POTTERY
DEVON

printed or impressed

BRISTOL (Avon)
(Lund & Miller's factory)
soft-paste (soapstone)
porcelain 1748–52, then
transferred to Worcester

BRISTOL
BRISTOLL
in relief

(Cookworthy & Champion's factory)
hard-past porcelain
1770–81, transferred
from Plymouth

4

underglaze blue,
blue enamel, red or
gold

early mark during
Cookworthy's
ownership (also used
at Plymouth)

X   6
    X

in blue enamel

underglaze blue
and blue enamel

+X   ×B

blue
enamel

tin-glazed earthenware
(delftware) *c.* 1650–

mark of John Bowen,
painter, apprenticed
1734

yf. 1st : Sept:
1761
Bowen - fecit,

in blue

25

initials of Michael Edkins,
delft-painter and his wife
on plate dated 1760

in blue

Bristol Pottery
c. 1785–1825
earthenwares

BRISTOL POTTERY
impressed or painted

Coombes, a china-mender
c. 1775–1805
in pale brown lustre

Fifield, William (*b.* 1777,
d. 1857) painter on
Bristol pottery
c. 1810–55

W.F.
W.F.B.
W. FIFIELD

Pardoe, Thomas (*d.* 1823)
painter at Derby,
Worcester, Cambrian
Pottery, Swansea,
factories, independent
decorator of pottery and
porcelain in Bristol
c. 1809–20

Pardoe
28 Bath St.,
Bristol
Warranted

Pardoe, Bristol
painted

Pardoe, William Henry
(son), decorator at
Cardiff and elsewhere
c. 1820–35

PARDOE, CARDIFF

Patience, Thomas
18th century stoneware

PATIENCE
impressed

26

Pountney & Allies Bristol Pottery *c.* 1816– 35, earthenware	P. P. & A. P.A. B.P.
printed, impressed or painted	P.A. BRISTOL POTTERY
impressed	
Pountney & Goldney Bristol Pottery, 1836–49	POUNTNEY & GOLDNEY (or as above)
impressed Pountney & Co., 1849– Bristol Victoria Pottery	BRISTOL POTTERY P. & CO.
1849–89	POUNTNEY & CO.
1889–	POUNTNEY & CO. LTD.

c. 1954–
now Cauldon Bristol
Potteries Ltd.

Bristol
founded ✕ in 1652
England

Powell, William (& Sons)
Temple Gate Pottery
c. 1830–1906, stoneware

POWELL
BRISTOL

BRISTOL TEMPLE
GATE POTTERY

impressed *c.* 1830–

Ring, Joseph 1785–
(*d.* 1788), cream
coloured earthenware
continued by partners
until 1812

RING & CO.
impressed

BROSELEY (Salop)
Maw & Co. Ltd., 1850–
tiles and art pottery
from *c.* 1875
c. 1880–

MAW & CO.

FLOREAT MAW
SALOPIA

BURTON-ON-TRENT (Derbyshire)
Bretby Art Pottery, Woodville
Tooth & Ault 1883–87
Tooth & Co. 1887–
earthenwares
Henry Tooth *c.* 1883–1900

c. 1914–

CLANTA
WARE

Woodward, James
Swadlincote Pottery
'Majolica' earthenware
1859–88

printed or impressed

CASTLE HEDINGHAM (Essex)
Hedingham Art Pottery
Bingham, Edward
1864–1901
reproduction of medieval
and Tudor type wares

applied in relief

28

incised signature
1864–1901

E. BINGHAM
CASTLE HEDINGAM
ESSEX

early 20th century

ROYAL ESSEX ART
POTTERY WORKS

CASTLEFORD (W. Yorkshire)
  Clokie & Masterson
  earthenware, 1872–81

C. & M.
CLOKIE &
MASTERMAN
printed or impressed

Clokie & Co., 1888–1961
earthenware
(Ltd. after 1940)
  printed

Dunderdale & Co., David
Castleford Pottery,
c. 1790–1820
earthenware and
stoneware

D.D. & CO.

D.D. & CO.
CASTLEFORD

Gill, William (& Sons)
Providence Pottery
1880–1932

printed

Hartley's (Castleford)
Ltd., Phillips Pottery
c. 1898–1960
stoneware and earthenware;
decorative art wares
from 1953

HARTROX

Nicholson & Co., Thomas earthenware, *c.* 1854–71	T.N. & CO. printed with name of pattern
Robinson Bros. Castleford & Allerton Potteries stoneware, 1897–1904	R.B. printed or impressed
Robinson & Son, John stoneware, 1905–33	J.R. & S. impressed

CAUGHLEY (Salop)
Turner, Thomas
c. 1772–1799 (then taken over by John Rose
of Coalport factory)
soft-paste porcelain and
black basaltes
(*see also* 'Benthall')

SALOPIAN
Salopian
impressed

printed or painted in
underglaze blue *c.* 1772–95

printed or painted
c. 1772–95

printed mark usually
Worcester
open printed crescent
also on Coalport

printed

Chinese type mark

CHEAM (Surrey)
  Clark, Henry, 1869–80
  earthenware

                 HENRY CLARK
                CHEAM POTTERY
            impressed or incised

CHELSEA (London)
  c. 1745–1784 soft-paste porcelain
  (1770–84 known as 'Chelsea-Derby'
  period under William Duesbury)

    rare incised mark on
    'triangle' period
    1745–*c.* 1749

    usual triangle mark

                  incised

    rare mark of 'crown
    and trident', 1745–*c.*
    1750 in underglaze blue

    'raised-anchor' mark
    c. 1749–52, latterly
    picked out in red

                in applied relief

    'red-anchor' mark
    1752–*c.* 1758
    occasionally painted in
    blue or purple

                painted in red

31

c. 1750–56
painted in underglaze blue

'gold anchor' mark
c. 1756–69
(also seen on Chelsea-
Derby wares as late
as 1775)

in gold

rare 'repairers' mark
(not Roubiliac)

impressed

Chelsea Pottery, 1952–
(Rawnsley Academy Ltd.)
impressed or
incised, 1952–

CHELSEA POTTERY
incised

Vyse, Charles, 1919–c. 63
studio-potter

C.V.   C.V.
CHELSEA

painted mark with
year-date added

19 $\mathbb{V}$ 34
CHELSEA

CHESTERFIELD
(Derbyshire)
Pearson & Co., 1805–
Whittington Moor
Potteries
1805–c. 1880

P. & CO.

PEARSON & CO.
WHITTINGTON
MOOR
impressed

32

1880–

from *c.* 1925 renamed as
Pearson & Co. (Chesterfield) Ltd.

Barker Pottery Co.
1887–1957
stoneware
   printed or impressed
   mark 1928–1957

CHURCH GRESLEY (Derbyshire)
Green & Co. Ltd., T.G.
c. 1864– earthenware
and stoneware
   printed mark *c.* 1888–

GRESLEY

   mark of *c.* 1930, numerous
   other late marks all
   include 'T. G. Green
   & Co., Ltd.'

GRESLEY
MADE IN
ENGLAND

CLEVEDON (Avon)   1879–1920
   Elton, Sir Edmund
   Sunflower Pottery
   1879–1930   1920–30

Elton

Holland, William Fishley
studio-potter, 1921–
earthenware

W H Holland

WH   FH

                         incised

33

Holland, Isabel Fishley
pottery figures, 1929–42

I. HOLLAND

Holland, George Fishley
earthenware, 1955–

CLIFTON JUNCTION
(nr. Manchester)
Pilkington Tile & Pottery
Co. Ltd., earthenwares
and tiles, (decorative
pottery, 1897–1938,
1948–57)

P
early incised mark

factory mark, VIII for
1908

VIII

c. 1914–38

'ROYAL LANCASTRIAN'

marks of notable designers:

Lewis F. Day Walter Crane C. E. Cundall R. Joyce

Jessie Jones G. M. Forsyth Gladys Rodgers W. Mycock

COALPORT (Salop)
John Rose, *c.* 1796–
(transferred to Stoke-on-Trent
c. 1926)

rare early mark in red

COALBROOKDALE

impressed

1815–25 on many wares
decorated in Swansea
style

c. 1810–25, in underglaze
blue

c. 1810–25, in underglaze
blue

underglaze blue mark
c. 1810–20

C. B. DALE

marks used from *c.* 1820

1830–50

JOHN ROSE & CO.
COALBROOKDALE
SHROPSHIRE

c. 1851–61, painted or gilt

c. 1861–75, 'C'
Coalport, 's',
Swansea, 'N', Nantgarw

painted or gilt

printed mark *c.* 1870–80
incorporating Patent
Office Registration
mark

c. 1875–81, printed or   COALPORT A.D. 1750
painted
late marks *c.* 1881–
'England' added 1891
'Made in England'
c. 1920

wares made for London
dealer A. B. & R. P.
Daniell *c.* 1860–1917

large size anchor mark
on Coalport copies of
Chelsea, also on
Continental wares
without 'C'

CODNOR PARK   W. BURTON
(Derbyshire)   CODNOR PARK
  Burton, William,   impressed
  c. 1821–32, stoneware

CROWBOROUGH (Sussex) & REDHILL (Surrey)
  Walford, J. F., 1948–
  studio-potter

DARTINGTON (S. Devon)
  Trey, Marianne de
  studio-potter, 1947–
  Shinners Bridge Pottery

incised or painted

  Haile, T. S., *c.* 1936–43,
  1945–8, studio-potter

impressed

DENBY (Derbyshire)   BOURNES
  Bourne & Son Ltd.,   WARRANTED
  Joseph, *c.* 1809–
  stoneware

                 J. BOURNE & SON
  Joseph Bourne, 1833–60   PATENTEES
  'Son' added 1850   DENBY POTTERY
                 NEAR DERBY
                 impressed

DENHOLME (W. Yorkshire)   N. Taylor
  Taylor, Nicholas   Denholme
  1893–1909   incised
  earthenware

DERBY (Derbyshire)
  c. 1750–1848
  soft-paste porcelain
    early marks of Planché
    period *c.* 1750–56

Derby

incised *1750*

Derby Porcelain Works
1756–1848
  'William Duesbury &
  Co.' *c.* 1760

incised

'N' seen on dishes, etc.
c. 1770–80

incised

'Chelsea-Derby' marks
c. 1770–84

in gold

c. 1770–82, in blue or
purple

incised model numbers
on figures, *c.* 1775–
early 19th century

No 314

No 195

common Derby mark
1782–, incised, purple,
blue or black
c. 1800–25 in red
enamel

mark of Isaac
Farnsworth 'repairer'

mark of Joseph Hill
'repairer'

'size' mark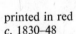

'Duesbury & Kean',
c. 1795
in blue, crimson or purple

blue-painted mark in
imitation of Meissen
c. 1785–1825

Robert Bloor Period

printed in red
c. 1820–40

printed in red
c. 1830–48

mark in imitation of
Sèvres, *c.* 1825–48
in blue enamel

Locker & Co., King Street factory
c. 1849–59

similar marks used also
by:
Stevenson Sharp & Co.
1859–61
'Courtney late Bloor'
1849–63

Stevenson & Hancock
1861–1935, this mark
also used after 1935
when King St. factory
was taken over by Royal Crown Derby
Porcelain Co. Ltd.

Derby Crown Porcelain Co. Ltd. Est. 1876
c. 1878–90, together
  with year mark as
  shown in table on next
  page

Derby

printed   impressed

Royal Crown Derby Porcelain Co. Ltd.
1890–
  printed mark of *c.* 1890
  'England' from 1891
  'Made in England'
  added from *c.* 1920
  together with year
  mark

(Part of Royal Doulton Tableware Ltd. from 1973)

TABLE OF DERBY YEAR-MARKS,
1882–

1882	1883	1884	1885	1886	1887	1888
—	⊥	H	∽	∾	☾	⊢◡⊣

1889	1890	1891	1892	1893	1894	1895
		◠				◯

1896	1897	1898	1899	1900	1901	1902
⊖	⊕	◇				✕

1903	1904	1905	1906	1907	1908	1909
		V	⋁	M	⋀	⋀

1910	1911	1912	1913	1914	1915	1916
	⊓	□			⊞	∧

1917	1918	1919	1920	1921	1922	1923
△					⊥	I

1924	1925	1926	1927	1928	1929	1930
	⊙	⊙	⊙	⊙	⊙	↓

1931	1932	1933	1934	1935	1936	1937

1938	1939	1940	1941	1942	1943	1944
I	II	III	IV	V	VI	VII

1945	1946	1947	1948	1949	1950	1951
VIII	IX	X	XI	XII	XIII	etc.

41

Derby Pot Works
creamwares, *c.* 1750–80

T. RADFORD SC.
DERBY

Thomas Radford,
engraver of prints
found on some
Cockpit Hill wares

RADFORD fecit
DERBY POT WORKS

Potts, W. W.
St. George's Works, *c.*
1831–, earthenware
(also at Burslem)

marks indicating
patent printing
processes, 1831 & 1835

DONYATT (Somerset)
Rogers, James, 19th century
(with descendants)
sgraffiato slipwares

Jas Rogers
Maker Octr 10th
1848

impressed on jug
dated 1864

ROGERS & SONS
CROCK STRETT
POTTERY

EAST HENDRED (Oxfordshire)
Thompson, Pauline
studio-potter, 1950–

incised or painted

EAST HORSLEY (Surrey)
Moore, Denis & Michael
Buckland
Green Dene Pottery
1953–
    (initials also used)

impressed or painted

42

FARNHAM (Surrey)
  Hammond, Henry
  studio-potter, 1934–40,
  1946–

incised impressed

  Barron, Paul
  studio-potter, 1948–

impressed

FELIXSTOWE (Suffolk)
  Kemp, Dorothy, 1939–
  studio-potter

incised or impressed

FERRYBRIDGE (Yorkshire)
  Ferrybridge Pottery, 1792–
  known as Knottingley Pottery, 1792–1804

  1792–6, *c.* 1801–34

TOMLINSON & CO.
impressed or printed

  Wedgwood, Ralph, *c.*
  1796–1801

WEDGWOOD & CO.

  c. 1804–

FERRYBRIDGE
impressed

Reed & Taylor, *c.* 1843–56   R. & T.   R.T. & CO.
Woolf & Sons, L., *c.*   L.W.   L.W. & S.
  1856–83
Poulson, Bros., Ltd.   P.B.   P.BROS
  1884–97
Sefton & Brown, *c.*   S.B.
  1897–1919

Brown & Sons, T., *c.*   T.B & S.
  1919–

FREMINGTON (Devon)
  Fishley, Edwin Beer
  1861–1906, earthenware

               E. B. FISHLEY
               FREMINGTON
               N. DEVON
               incised

FULHAM (London)
  Dwight, John, 1671–
  salt-glazed stoneware

               no certain
               marks

De Morgan, William
  c. 1872–1907
  decorator of earthenwares made to order
  from other factories, and own wares
    impressed mark, 1882–
    '& Co.' added after 1888

  marks used at Merton Abbey, 1882–88
  made own tiles from *c.*
  1879, and wares from 1882

    impressed or painted
    1882–

  Sands End Pottery, 1888–97
  (period of partnership with
  Halsey Ricardo)

1898–1907, partnership with
Frank Iles, Charles & Fred
Passenger at Fulham

decoration continued
until 1911, four years
after De Morgan retired

all impressed

earthenwares were decorated
in De Morgan style at
Mrs. Ida Perrin's studio,
Bushey Heath, 1921–33
by Fred Passenger

Fulham Pottery & Cheavin Filter Co. Ltd.
vases & commercial pottery
1889–present

FULHAM POTTERY
LONDON
impressed

1948–

GATESHEAD (Tyne and Wear)
Durham China Co. Ltd.
general ceramics, 1947–57

printed or impressed

HENLEY-ON-THAMES
(Berkshire)
Hawkins, John & Son
china and glass dealers
closed about 1935

'FAMOUS HENLEY CHINA'
EST. 1867
HAWKINS
HENLEY-ON-THAMES

HEREFORD
  Godwin & Hewitt, tiles
  1889–1910, mark printed
  or impressed

HONITON (Devon)
  Honiton Art Potteries
  Ltd., earthenware, *c.*
  1881–, printed or
  impressed *c.* 1915

THE HONITON
LACE ART POTTERY
CO.

  Collard, C., 1918–1947
  printed or impressed

COLLARD HONITON
ENGLAND

  Hull, N. T. S., 1947–1955

N.T.S. HULL

  1947–

HONITON POTTERY
DEVON

  Hull, Norman
  Norman Hull Pottery
  1947–55

NORMAN HULL
POTTERY

HORNSEA (Humberside)
  Hornsea Pottery Co. Ltd.
  earthenware, *c.* 1951
  printed or impressed, 1962–

HULL (Humberside)
  Longbottom, Samuel
  earthenware, late 19th
  century, closed 1899

S.L.
impressed

IPSWICH (Suffolk)
  Balaam, W., 1870–81
  Rope Lane Pottery
  slipwares

W. BALAAM
ROPE LANE POTTERY
IPSWICH
impressed

ISLEWORTH (London)
  earthenware, *c.* 1760–
  1825, Shore, J.
  Shore & Co.
  Shore & Goulding
  (*Note:* S. & G. seen on Wedgwood type wares
  are Schiller & Gerbing, Bodenbach, Bohemia.
  See Pocket-Book of German Ceramic Marks)

SHORE & CO.
S. & CO.
S. & G.
ISLEWORTH

JACKFIELD (Salop)
  Craven Dunnill & Co.
  Ltd., tiles, 1872–1951

CRAVEN & CO.

JACKFIELD

KEW (Surrey)
  Duckworth, Ruth
  studio-potter, 1956–

painted or incised

KILMINGTON MANOR (Wiltshire)
  Pleydell-Bouverie, Katharine
  stoneware, 1925–
  studio-potter
  (also at other addresses)

incised or stamped

LAMBETH (London)   'Coade Lambeth'
Coade & Sealy, 1769–
1811, artificial stoneware

Doulton & Watts
stoneware and earthenware
c. 1815–1858
  c. 1826–1838
  on early brown salt-
  glazed wares

  c. 1826–1858

  all marks impressed
  moulded or incised

Doulton & Co.
Lambeth, *c.* 1858–1956   **DOULTON**
Burslem, *c.* 1882–   **LAMBETH**
  c. 1869–77, decorated
coloured wares, year often
appears in centre after 1872

'4D' mark on decorated
salt-glaze

Note: 'England' added
after 1891   *c.* 1877–80   *c.* 1880–1902

mark on mural tiles
c. 1879–1900

on wares decorated with
coloured clays
c. 1887–1900

underglaze decorated
earthenware

c. 1872–73

c. 1873–1908

underglaze decorated
earthenware, *c.* 1881–1910

'Carrara' ware, stoneware
covered with translucent
crystalline enamel
c. 1888–1898

'Silicon' ware, unglazed
stoneware, *c.* 1882–1912

fine earthenware and china,
made at Burslem
c. 1882–1902

standard impressed mark
c. 1902–22
c. 1927–36

Lambeth stoneware
c. 1922–

Burslem factory marks   DOULTON
c. 1882–1902

          DOULTON
                              & SLATERS
                              PATENT
c. 1900–   ROYAL   ROYAL
                  DOULTON DOULTON
                  FLAMBE   KALON
c. 1960–   ENGLISH
                  TRANSLUCENT
                  CHINA

selection of initials used
by Doulton decorators:
Atkins, Elizabeth, *c.* 1876–82   *EA*
Banks, Eliza, *c.* 1876–84
Barlow, Arthur B., 1871–8   *E/B*
Barlow, Florence E., *c.* 1873–1909   FℰB

Barlow, Hannah B., *c.* 1872–1906   ℰℋℬ

Barnard, Harry, *c.* 1880–90   ℬ

Butler, Frank A., *c.* 1872–1911

Butterton, Mary, *c.* 1874–94	
Capes, Mary, *c.* 1876–83	
Dewsberry, David, 1889–1919	D.Dewsberry
Dunn, William, E., *c.* 1883–95	
Lee, Frances E., *c.* 1875–90	FEL
Marshall, Mark V., 1879–1912	M·V·M
Pope, Frank C., 1880–1923	F·C·P
Raby, Edward J., 1892–1911	E.Raby
Rowe, William, 1883–1939	WR
Simeon, Henry, 1894–1936	H8
Simmance, Eliza, *c.* 1873–1928	S
Tinworth, George, 1886–1913	

A full-list of painters, modellers and designers are shown in *Royal Doulton* 1815–1965 by Desmond Eyles, London, 1965, together with full guides, etc. to precise dating

Green, Stephen
Imperial Pottery
stoneware, *c.* 1820–58

impressed marks

STEPHEN GREEN
IMPERIAL
POTTERIES
LAMBETH

Stiff, James
London Pottery, *c.* 1840–
1913 stonewares
  c. 1863

J. STIFF

J. STIFF & SONS
impressed

LANGLEY MILL (Nottingham)
Lovatt & Lovatt, 1895–
stoneware and earthenware
printed or impressed marks
                    c. 1900–

now Langley
Pottery Ltd. (1967) *c.* 1900–   *c.* 1931–62

LEEDS (W. Yorkshire)
c. 1770–1881
creamware, earthenware and stoneware

Green Bros., 1770–

LEEDS *POTTERY
impressed

Humble, Green & Co., 1774–76

Humble, Hartley, Greens   LEEDS POTTERY
& Co., 1776–1780

LEEDS *POTTERY

Hartley, Greens & Co.   LEEDS *POTTERY
1781–1830

1800–1830   LEEDS.POTTERY

HARTLEY   GREENS & Co   LEEDS *POTTERY.
LEEDS * POTTERY   LEEDS *POTTERY

all marks impressed

1780–1810   **LP**
impressed or enamelled

Britton & Son, Richard   R.B. & S.
1872–8, earthenware   printed
    initials found on variety
    of transfer-printed wares

Rainforth & Co. 1800–17   RAINFORTH & CO.
Petty's Pottery, 1817–46   PETTYS & CO. LEEDS
earthenware & creamware

        printed or impressed

Burmantofts   BURMANTOFTS
art-pottery, 1882–1904   FAIENCE
  marks impressed

Leeds Fireclay Co. Ltd.   L.
earthenware, *c.* 1904–14   F.C.

decorative wares, made   LEFICO
up until 1914, after
which only commercial   GRANITOFTS
& utility wares were
produced

Yates, William, *c.* 1840–76   YATES
(retailer only)   LEEDS
               printed or painted

LETCHWORTH   ICENI WARE
(Hertfordshire)   impressed
  Cowlishaw, W. H.
  1908–14, earthenwares

LIVERPOOL (Merseyside)
  Chaffers, Richard, 1743–65
  tin-glazed earthenware
  and soft-paste porcelain
    dated example referring
    to son: *Richard Chaffers ~1769~*

  Christian, Philip   'CHRISTIAN'
  c. 1765–1776   impressed

  Billinge, Thomas   *Billinge Sculp*
  engraver, *c.* 1760–80   *Liverpool*

Sadler, John & Green, Guy, printers only, their work seen on tiles, Wedgwood's creamware, Longton Hall, etc., 1756–1799

J. Sadler, Liverpool

Green, Liverpool

Abbey, Richard engraver and printer 1773–80, potter from 1790

ABBEY
LIVERPOOL

R. Abbey, sculp.

Johnson, Joseph engraver, second half 18th century

'I. JOHNSON,
LIVERPOOL'

Herculaneum Pottery earthenware and procelain *c.* 1793–1841 Worthington, Humble & Holland, 1794–1806

HERCULANEUM

impressed or printed marks, *c.* 1796–1833

1822–41

HERCULANEUM POTTERY
impressed or printed
in blue

Case, Thomas & Mort,
John, 1833–1836

printed, usually in red

Mort & Simpson

'Liver' bird printed or
impressed, *c.* 1836–41

Gibson, John &
Solomon, earthenware,
early 19th century

JOHN GIBSON
LIVERPOOL
1813

VARIOUS RETAILERS OF POTTERY & PORCELAIN

Allsup, John, 1832–58
printed

JOHN ALLSUP
ST. PAUL'S CHURCH-
YARD, LONDON

Blades, John
c. 1800–30

BLADES LONDON

Bradley & Co., J.
decorators and retailers
c. 1813–20

J. BRADLEY & CO.

Brameld, J. W.
c. 1830–50
partner of
Rockingham Works

I. W. BRAMELD

at various
London addresses

56

Daniell, A. B. & R. P.
c. 1825–1917
    printed mark on wares
    of Coalport, etc. made
    to order for Daniell's

Dreydel & Co., Henry
late 19th century
    mark of wares made
    to order both in England
    and on Continent

Goode & Co. (Ltd.), Thomas
c. 1860–present
'Ltd' from 1918
now in South Audley St.

Green & Co., J.
1834–42 at St. Paul's
Churchyard, elsewhere
until *c.* 1874

Haines, Batchelor & Co.
1880–90

    H.B.
    printed

Hales, Hancock &
Goodwin, Ltd., 1922–60
(Hales, Hancock & Co.
Ltd., and Hales Bros.)

    H.H. & G. LTD.
    printed

Hart & Son 1826–69	H. & S. printed
Howell & James *c.* 1820–1922 (also retailers of materials for amateur decorators)	HOWELL & JAMES

Mortlock, J.
1746–*c.* 1930
  many marks used
  including name of such
  manufacturers as
  Mintons
	MORTLOCK
	
	MORTLOCKS
	OXFORD STREET

Pearce, Alfred B. 1866–1940	ALFRED B. PEARCE 39 LUDGATE HILL LONDON
Pellatt & Co., Apsley *c.* 1789– (also glass retailers)	APSLEY PELLATT & CO.
Pellatt & Green *c.* 1805–30	PELLATT & GREEN LONDON
Pellatt & Wood *c.* 1870–90	PELLATT & WOOD

Phillips, *c.* 1799–1929
  c. 1858–97
  c. 1897–1906
  c. 1908–29
	
	W. P. & G. PHILLIPS
	PHILLIPS & CO.
	PHILLIPS LTD.

Walker, William   WALKER MINORIES
c. 1795–1800

MINOR FACTORIES AND STUDIO-POTTERS IN LONDON

Benham, Tony, 1958
  mark written or incised
  with year, studio-potter
(now at Wateringbury, Kent),
Billington, Dora
studio-potter, 1912–

incised or painted

Briglin Pottery Ltd.   BRIGLIN
earthenware, 1948–   impressed

Dalton, William B.
stoneware and porcelain
studio-potter, 1900–
c. 1955
(In U.S.A. from 1941)

incised or painted

Eeles, David   D.E.
studio-potter, 1955
Shepherd's Well Pottery
London, then in 1962
to Mosterton, Dorset

Fine Arts Porcelain Ltd.
earthenwares, 1948–52

printed

59

Fry, Roger, Omega
Workshops *c.* 1913–19,
studio-potter

Groves, Lavender
studio-potter, 1952–

Leach, Jeremy
studio-potter, *c.* 1959

J.L.   J.L.

D.S.

Martin Bros. (Robert Wallace, Walter, Edwin
and Charles), studio-potters, stoneware,
1873–1914

    1873–5   R. W. Martin fecit

    1873–4

    1874–8

    1878–9

    SOUTHALL   MARTIN
    MARTIN   SOUTHALL
    POTTERY   POTTERY

    1879–82

    1882–

all marks either incised or impressed together
with month and year

Mills, Donald
studio-potter, 1946–55

Donald Mills

Murray, William Staite
studio-potter, 1919–62
in S. Rhodesia from 1940

W. S. MURRAY
(date)
LONDON

Northen & Co., W.
Union Potteries,
Lambeth, stoneware,
1847–92, '& Co.'
added 1887

W. NORTHEN
POTTER
VAUXHALL
LAMBETH

O'Malley, Peter
studio-potter, 1953–

Parnell, Gwendolen
studio-potter, 1916–36

CHELSEA CHEYNE
(date)
G.P.

Parr, Harry
studio-potter, *c.* 1919–
c. 1948

HY PARR
CHELSEA (date)

Powell, Alfred & Louise
decorators of Wedgwood
earthenwares, *c.* 1904–39

Powell, John
painter and retailer
c. 1810–30

Powell
91, Wimpole St.

Richards, Frances E.
studio-potter, 1922–31
  mark incised

Rie, Lucie
studio-potter, *c.* 1938–
  mark impressed

Samuel, Audrey
studio-potter, 1949–

A S

Smith & Co., Thomas
stonewares, 1879–93

T. SMITH & CO.
OLD KENT ROAD
LONDON

Stabler, Harold &
Phoebe, earthenware
designers and potters
b. 1872–*d.* 1945 (wife
d. 1955)

Phoebe Stabler
(date)

Stabler (date)

Vergette, Nicholas
studio-potter, 1946–58

Walters, Helen
studio-potter, 1945–
(now Helen Swain,
mark 'HWS')

1945–53   1953–

62

White, William J.
Fulham Pottery
stoneware, *c.* 1750–1850

    incised dated marks

W.W.
(date)

W. J. WHITE
(date)

LOWER DICKER (Sussex)
U. Clark & Nephews,
1843–1946, earthenware
1933–
Dicker Potteries Ltd. 1946–59

U.C. & N.
THE DICKER
SUSSEX
DICKER WARE

LOWESBY (Leicestershire)
Lowesby Pottery
Fowke, Sir Frederick
c. 1835–40
earthenwares

LOWESBY

LOWESTOFT (Suffolk)
soft-paste porcelain
c. 1757– *c.* 1800
    decorators numbers,
    to approx. 17, painted
    on inner wall of foot-
    rim, *c.* 1760–75
copies of Worcester

1 3 5

7 9 13

and Meissen marks
c. 1775–1790

Allen, Robert, *b.* 1744, *d.* 1835
decorator at Lowestoft factory
and independent enameller
from *c.* 1800

*Allen
Lowestoft*
painted

MADELEY (Salop)
Randall, Thomas M.
c. 1825–40, decorator of
English and Sèvres porcelain;
with factory at Madeley
for production of soft-paste
imitations of Sèvres

T MR
Madeley
S
painted

MALVERN (Worcestershire)
Woods, Richard, *c.* 1850–
retailer only

R. WOODS
printed

MANCHESTER
Sutcliffe & Co., *c.* 1885–1901
decorative tiles

printed or impressed

MANSFIELD
(Nottinghamshire)
Billingsley, William
1799–1802
painter and gilder

BILLINGSLEY
MANFIELD
painted

MEXBOROUGH
(S. Yorkshire)
Emery, James
earthenware, 1837–61

J. EMERY
MEXBRO

incised

64

Rock Pottery
Reed, James, *c.* 1839–49

REED
impressed

Mexbro Pottery
Reed, John, *c.* 1849–73

Sowter & Co., *c.* 1795–
1804, Mexborough Old
Pottery
  marks impressed

SOWTER & CO.
MEXBRO

S. & CO.

Wilkinson & Wardle
Denaby Pottery, 1864–6
earthenware

Wardle & Co., John,
Denaby Pottery
earthenwares (including creamware)
1866–70
  printed mark

JOHN WARDLE & CO.

MIDDLESBROUGH
(Cleveland)
  Linthorpe Pottery, 1879–90
earthenware (art pottery type)

LINTHORPE
impressed

  incised, impressed or
  painted signature of Dresser

Chr. Dresser

  Tooth, Henry, manager
  1879–1882

Ħ H T

Middlesbrough Pottery Co.
1834–44
earthenware and
creamware

M.P. CO.

MIDDLESBRO'
POTTERY CO.

Middlesbrough   M.E. & CO.
Earthenware Co.
1844–52, earthenware
   initials used with various
   printed or impressed marks

                 MIDDLESBRO POTTERY
                   (with anchor)
Wilson & Co., Isaac   I.W. & CO.
Middlesbrough Pottery   MIDDLESBRO'
1852–87   impressed

MORTLAKE (London)   KISHERE
   Mortlake Pottery, *c.*
   1800–43, Kishere,   I.K.
   Joseph   impressed
   salt-glazed stoneware

NEW BARNET (Hertfordshire)   D.A.
   Arbeid, Dan, 1956–
   Abbey Art Centre   ARBEID
   studio-potter   painted or impressed
   (now at Saffron Walden, Essex)

NEWCASTLE UPON TYNE   DAVIES & CO.
(Tyne and Wear)   impressed
   Davies & Co., 1833–51
   Tyne Main Pottery
   earthenware

   Fell, Thomas, 1817–90   FELL
   St. Peter's Pottery   impressed
   earthenware and creamware
   1817–30

                  impressed

Fell & Co., *c.* 1830–90	F. & CO.
initials used with	T.F. & CO.
various marks:	T. FELL & CO.

Ford & Patterson	FORD & PATTERSON
Sheriff Hill Pottery	Sheriff Hill
c. 1820–*c.* 1830	Pottery
earthenware	impressed
Jackson & Patterson	J. & P.
1830–45	
Maling, Robert	MALING
Ouseburn Pottery	M
1817–59, earthenware	impressed

Maling, C. T.	MALING
Ford Pottery, 1859–90	C. T. MALING
earthenware, often	C.T.M.
with lustre decoration	

Maling & Sons, Ltd.
1890–1963
earthenwares, mark of
  c. 1875–1908

1890–

c. 1908   *c.* 1949–63

Patterson & Co.
Sheriff Hill Pottery,
1830–1904, earthenware

PATTERSON & CO.
printed or
impressed

Sewell, 1804– *c.* 28
St. Anthony's Pottery, *c.* 1780–1878
earthenware (including creamwares)
1780–1820
Sewell & Donkin
1828–52
Sewell & Co., 1852–78

SEWELL

ST. ANTHONY'S
SEWELL & DONKIN

SEWELL & CO.
all impressed or printed

Taylor & Co., *c.* 1820–5
Tyne Pottery
earthenware

TAYLOR & CO.
printed

Wallace & Co., J.
Newcastle or Forth Bank
Pottery, 1838–93, earthenware

WALLACE & CO.
impressed

Warburton, John, &
family, Carr's Hill
Pottery, earthenware, *c.* 1750–1817

J. WARBURTON
N. ON TYNE

NEWTON ABBOT (Devon)
Phillips & Co., John
Aller Pottery, 1868–87

ɎIΛΕꞶ IIꞀIꞀON

printed or impressed

Aller Vale Art Potteries
earthenware, 1887–1901

ALLER VALE
impressed

Royal Aller Vale &
Watcombe Pottery Co.
(Torquay) *c.* 1901–62
  impressed or printed
  1901–

ROYAL ALLER VALE

ROYAL   DEVON
TORQUAY MOTTO
POTTERY WARE

Candy & Co. Ltd.
Great Western Potteries
earthenwares, 1882–

CANDY WARE
C
N A

NORTH SHIELDS
(Tyne and Wear)
  Carr, John
  earthenware, *c.* 1845–1900

J. CARR & CO.

NOTTINGHAM
  (Nottinghamshire)
  Lockett, William
  stoneware, *c.* 1740–80

'Wm. and Ann Lockett,
1755'

OXFORD (Oxfordshire)
  Blackman, Audrey
  studio-potter, 1949–
  'Astbury-type' figures

A. BLACKMAN

OXSHOTT (Surrey)
  Oxshott Pottery, 1919
  Wren, Henry, *c.* 1919–47

HW hw

  Wren, Denise, *c.* 1919–

DKW

  Wren, Rosemary, *c.* 1945–
69

OXSHOTT

PINXTON (Derbyshire)
Pinxton Works, *c.* 1796–1813
John Coke, William Billingsley
soft-paste porcelain
(Billingsley, *c.* 1796–93)
(Cutts, *c.* 1803–1813)

in red   in purple
from arms of Coke

    marks found on late
    pieces

PLYMOUTH (Devon)
Plymouth Porcelain Works
Cookworthy, William
hard-paste porcelain, 1768–70
(transferred to Bristol in 1770)
  workman's mark also seen
  on Bow, Worcester, Bristol
  and Wedgwood

underglaze-blue,
blue enamel,
red or gold

Plymouth Pottery Co. Ltd.
earthenware, 1856–63

P.P. COY.L
STONE CHINA

POOLE (Dorset)
Carter & Co.
earthenware, 1873–1921

CARTER & CO.
CARTER POOLE

Carter, Stabler & Adams
1921–
  'Ltd.' added 1925
  1956–
  1963– Poole Pottery Ltd.

POOLE
ENGLAND

printed

PRAZE (Cornwall)
  Crowan Pottery, 1946–62
  Davis, Harry & May
  studio-potters

impressed

PRESTBURY (Cheshire)
  Nowell, C. D., *c.* 1946–59
  studio-potter
  (at Disley *c.* 1946–51)

C D Nowell

PRESTBURY

PRESTWOOD (Buckinghamshire)
  Newland, William
  studio-potter, 1948–

WN

(date)

  Casson, Michael & Sheila
  studio-potters, 1953–
    Sheila Casson, 1951–59

CM M
          W
          S

RAINHAM (Kent)
  Upchurch Pottery, 1913–61
  Baker, W. & J.
    'Seeby', name of agent
    1945–61

UPCHURCH

UPCHURCH
SEEBY

  Rainham Pottery Ltd.
  earthenware, 1948–
  Wilson, Alfred, now
  E. J. Baker

Rainham
impressed or painted

RAMSBURY (Wiltshire)
  Holdsworth Potteries
  Holdsworth, Peter, 1945–

71

READING (Berkshire)
Collier Ltd., S. & E.
terra-cotta, *c.* 1848–1957

RICHMOND (Surrey)   Steven Sykes
Sykes, Steven, 1948–55   (signature)
studio-potter

ROCKINGHAM (Yorkshire)
Rockingham Works
(nr. Swinton) earthenware
c. 1750–1842 (porcelain
also made from about 1826)
c. 1778–87   BINGLEY
     impressed

Brameld & Co., 1806–42   BRAMELD
     impressed

    c. 1826–30   ROCKINGHAM ROCKINHGAM
     WORKS,   BRAMELD
     BRAMELD

    c. 1830–42   ROYAL
     ROCKINGHAM
     WORKS
     BRAMELD

'griffin-mark', *c.* 1826–30
from crest of Earl Fitzwilliam,
Marquis of Rockingham

from *c.* 1830–42
  'Royal' added to title
of factory
mark in red *c.* 1826–30, puce 1830–42
'Manufacturer to the King' added to mark
in 1830–37 (William IV)

Baguley, Alfred & Isaac
Rockingham Works
decorator only of
porcelain in Rockingham
style, *c.* 1842–65 (Mexborough)
   c. 1865–91

'Griffin mark'
with
'Baguley'

printed

ROLVENDEN (Kent)
Watson, Dorothy
Bridge Pottery 1921–

impressed or printed

ROTHERHAM (S. Yorkshire)
  Holmes Pottery, 1870–87
Jackson & Co., J.
earthenware
Shaw & Sons, Ltd., G.
1887–1948

J.J. & CO.

J. & CO.

G.S. & S.
printed

Northfield Pottery
earthenware
Hawley, W. & G., 1863–8,
Hawley Bros Ltd.,
1868–1903, 'Ltd'. added 1897

W. & G. HAWLEY

H.B.
HAWLEY BROS.

Northfield Hawley Pottery Co. Ltd.
earthenware, 1903–19

  impressed or printed
  mark introduced about
  1898 by Hawley Bros.

Walker & Son
earthenware, *c.* 1772–

WALKER

RUSTINGTON (Sussex)
Champion, G. H. & E. E.
studio-potters, 1947–

RYE (Sussex)
  1869– mark of *c.* 1900
  pottery (including tin-glaze)
  c. 1869–1920
  (Sussex Rustic Ware)
  'S.A.W.' Sussex Art Ware
  c. 1920–39
  J. C. Cole & W. V.
  Cole, 1947–
    various marks including
    name 'RYE'
  Walter V. Cole, 1957–

SUSSEX WARE

RYE

Cadborough Pottery,
  1807–71, earthenware

OLD SUSSEX WARE
RYE

Mitchell, William, *c.*
1840–, W. Mitchell &
Sons, 1859–69,
Mitchell, F. & H., 1869–71

MITCHELL
M

Iden Pottery, 1961–
Townsend, D. & Wood, J. H.
studio-potters
(moved from Iden to Rye
in 1963)

Everett, Raymond, 1963–
studio-potter

ST. IVES (Cornwall)
  Leach, Bernard, 1921–
    Leach Pottery marks
  studio-pottery
    personal marks of B. Leach

Hamada, Shoji
1920–23, 1929–*c.* 30

Leach, Janet, 1956–

Leach, John, *c.* 1950–8
(at Langport, Somerset since 1964)

Marshall, William, 1954–   impressed

incised

Mc. Kenzie, Warren, 1950–2

(at Dartington from 1963–)
  mark used at Dartington

Quick, Kenneth, 1945–63
(at St. Ives 1945–*c.* 55 and
1960–63)
  mark used at Tregenna Hill Pottery
  c. 1955–60

ST. MARY CHURCH (Devon) WATCOMBE
Watcombe Pottery Co.   TORQUAY
1867–1901

                            WATCOMBE
                            POTTERY

   printed mark, 1875–1901

Royal Aller Vale &
Watcombe Pottery Co.   ROYAL
c. 1901–62   TORQUAY
                      POTTERY

SALISBURY (Wiltshire)   PAYNE SARUM
Payne, retailer only   printed
c. 1834–41

SMETHWICK   TAYLOR
(nr. Birmingham)   impressed
  Ruskin Pottery, 1898–1935
  earthenware
  Taylor, W. Howson, c. 1898–

  painted or incised

  impressed mark, c. 1904–15
  with added date

STANMORE (London)   E.C./(date)
  Collyer, Ernest & Pamela
  studio-potters, 1950–

  Collyer-Nash   P.N. (Pamela Nash)

STEDHAM (Sussex)   Ray Marshall
  Marshall, Ray   (date)
  studio-potter, 1945–
  impressed mark   signature

STOCKTON-ON-TEES (Cleveland)
Ainsworth, W. H. & J. H.
1865–1901, earthenware

impressed

Harwood, J.
Clarence Pottery, 19th
century earthenware
  impressed mark, *c.* 1849–77

HARWOOD
STOCKTON

Skinner & Co., George
Stafford Pottery
earthenware, *c.* 1855–70

G.S. & CO.
printed

Skinner & Walker
1870–80

S. & W.
QUEEN'S WARE
STOCKTON

Smith & Co.,   W.S. & CO.   W.S. & CO.
William, *c.* 1825–55   STAFFORD
Stafford Pottery   W.S. & CO'S   POTTERY
                      WEDGWOOD

Smith, George F.   G.F.S.
North Shore Pottery
c. 1855–60, earthenware

Smith (Junr), William   W. S. JUNR. & CO.
c. 1845–84   all printed or impressed

STOURBRIDGE (West Midlands)
Sunfield Pottery, 1937–
earthenware and stoneware

SUNDERLAND   ATKINSON & CO.
(Tyne and Wear)   impressed or
  Southwick Pottery,   printed
1788–99, Atkinson & Co., earthenware

  Deptford Pottery,   COPYRIGHT BALL
1857–1918   BROS.
Ball, William,   SUNDERLAND
earthenware, Ball Bros., 1884–

  Wear Pottery   J. BRUNTON
Brunton, John,   printed
1796–1803, earthenware

  South Hylton &   DAWSON   I. DAWSON
Ford Potteries
Dawson, John, *c.* 1799–1864
c. 1799–1848, earthenware
Thomas Dawson & Co.,   DAWSON & CO.
c. 1837–48, earthenware
  printed marks   FORD POTTERY   J. DAWSON
                                 SOUTH HYLTON

  Garrison or   J. PHILLIPS
Sunderland Pottery   SUNDERLAND
earthenware, *c.* 1807–65   POTTERY
  c. 1807–12

  c. 1813–19   PHILLIPS & CO. DIXON & CO.
                        DIXON, AUSTIN
  c. 1820–26   & CO.
                        DIXON, AUSTIN
  c. 1827–40   PHILLIPS & CO.

  c. 1840–65   DIXON, PHILLIPS
                      & CO.

Wear Pottery, 1803–74   MOORE & CO.
Moore & Co., Samuel   SUNDERLAND
earthenware

North Hylton   MALING
Pottery, 1762–67,   impressed
earthenware, Maling, William, 1762–, continued
by family until 1815

Phillips & Co.,   JOHN PHILLIPS
John, 1815–67   HYLTON POT
(Phillips &   WORKS
Maling, 1780–1815)

Southwick Pottery, *c.* 1800–97
    c. 1800–29   A. SCOTT & CO.
                       SCOTT, SOUTHWICK
    c. 1829–44   A. SCOTT & SONS
                              S. & SONS
    c. 1844–54   S.B. & CO.
                      SCOTT BROTHERS
    c. 1854–97   A. SCOTT & SON
                              S. & S.

Union Pottery,   UNION POTTERY
c. 1802   printed

SWADLINCOTE (S. Derbyshire)
Ault, William, 1887–1923
earthenware
    The wares of this
    pottery sometimes
    bear the signature
    of the designer
    Christopher Dresser
    and date from
    1891–6

                   printed or   printed
                   impressed

Ault & Tunnicliffe Ltd.
1923–37
(*see* Ashby Potter's Guild)

Ault Potteries Ltd., 1937–
(now Pearson & Co., Group)
  marks impressed or printed

SWINTON (Yorkshire)
Don Pottery, earthenware
1790–1893
  1800–34   DON POTTERY

                                       GREEN
                                       DON POTTERY

  1820–34, impressed or
  printed

Barker, Samuel, 1834–93

  '& Son' or '& Sons'   BARKER
  added 1851–93   DON POTTERY

Bingley & Co., Thomas   BINGLEY
earthenware, 1778–87   impressed

Twigg, Joseph & brothers
Kilnhurst Pottery & Newhill Pottery, *c.* 1822–81
earthenware
  impressed or   J.T.
  printed, *c.* 1822–
  impressed, *c.*   TWIGG
  1822–66   NEWHILL
  impressed, *c.*   TWIGG
  1839–81   K.P.

TONBRIDGE (Kent)
　Slack & Brownlow
　earthenware, *c.* 1928–34

TONBRIDGE WARE
printed or impressed

TORQUAY (Devon)
　Torquay Terra-Cotta Co. Ltd.
　Dr. Gillow, 1875–1909
　earthenware figures, busts, etc.

impressed or printed

TRING (Hertfordshire)
　Pendley Pottery, 1949–
　Fieldhouse, Murray
　studio-potter (now at
　Northfields Studio)

incised or printed

TRURO (Cornwall)
　Chapel Hill Pottery,
　1872–, Lake & Son Ltd.,
　W. H., earthenware

LAKE'S CORNISH
POTTERY TRURO
printed or impressed

WAREHAM (Dorset)
　Sibley Pottery Ltd., 1922–
　62, earthenware and
　stoneware

SIBLEY POTTERY LTD
DORSET
ENGLAND
impressed or printed

WATTISFIELD (Suffolk)
　Watson Potteries Ltd., Henry
　earthenware and stoneware
　c. 1800–; mark of about
　　1948, early wares unmarked

WELWYN GARDEN CITY (Hertfordshire)
　Coper, Hans, 1947–
　studio-potter

81

WENFORD BRIDGE (nr. Bodmin, Cornwall)
Wenford Bridge Pottery
c. 1939–42; 1949–
    impressed mark
(*see also* WINCHCOMBE)

WESTON-SUPER-MARE (Avon)
Matthews, John
terra-cotta, 1870–88
    impressed mark with
    Royal Arms

JOHN MATTHEWS
LATE PHILLIPS
ROYAL POTTERY
WESTON-SUPER-MARE

WHITTINGTON (Derbyshire)
Walton Pottery Co. Ltd.
1946–56
Gordon, William
salt-glazed stoneware

WINCANTON Somerset)
Ireson, Nathaniel
c. 1730–50
tin-glazed earthenware

IRESON
WINCANTON

WINCHCOMBE (Gloucestershire)
c. 1926–39
Cardew, Michael A.
also at Wenford Bridge
c. 1939–42
studio-potter

mark impressed

82

Finch, Raymond, 1939–
studio-potter, impressed
mark used from *c.* 1926

WITHERNSEA (Humberside)
Eastgate Potteries, Ltd.
earthenware, 1955–

EASTGATE
ENGLAND
(on a gate)

WOODVILLE (Derbyshire)
Ashby Potters' Guild
earthenware, 1909–22

impressed

Mansfield Bros., Ltd.
Art Pottery Works, *c.* 1890–
1957

M.B.
impressed

WORCESTER (Worcestershire)
Worcester Porcelain Factory
1751 (Lund & Miller's Bristol factory
est. 1748, taken over in 1752)
soft-paste porcelain (soapstone)

workmen's marks
in underglaze blue

'open' crescent on painted
wares, 1755–83

crescent-mark with
crossed-hatched lines
on printed wares

in underglaze blue

any crescents in gilt or enamel colour
probably indicate outside decorator or
reproduction
on painted and printed
wares

painted in blue

marks on wares decorated
with 'Japan patterns'
c. 1760–75

in blue

'fretted square' mark
usually on heavily decorated
wares with scale-blue ground
c. 1755–75 (frequently seen
on reproductions)

in blue

Worcester imitation of Meissen
crossed-swords mark
c. 1760–70

in blue

printed numerals disguised as Chinese
characters, numbers 1–9, until recent
excavations at Worcester factory site these were
thought to be marks of Caughley (Salop)

'Flight' period, 1783–92
  'small crescent', 1783–92

  mark in blue, 1783–92

  mark in blue, 1788–92

'Flight & Barr' period
1792–1807

F. & B.

'Barr', *c.* 1792–1807

B incised   **B✗**

'Barr Flight & Barr' period
1807–13

BFB
impressed

Barr, Flight & Barr   BARR, FLIGHT
Worcester   & BARR
Flight & Barr   ROYAL PORCELAIN
Coventry Street,   WORKS
London   WORCESTER
Manufacturers to their   LONDON HOUSE
Majesties and   NO. 1
Royal Family   COVENTRY STREET

85

'Flight, Barr & Barr' period
1813–40

impressed

(factory taken over by Chamberlains, 1840–52)

Kerr & Binns, 1852–62

Kerr & Binns, '54' = 1854
    mark on outstanding
    examples, including decorator's
    initials (bottom left)

standard mark, printed or
impressed, *c.* 1852–62
Note: crown added
in 1862

'Worcester Royal Porcelain Company Ltd.'
(Royal Worcester) 1862–present

    standard mark, 1862–present
    early version, with 'C'
    in centre replacing crescent
    in Kerr & Binn's version
    numbers below = last 2 years
    of date

From 1867 a letter indicating the year of
manufacture was printed under the factory mark
according to the following table:

A 1867	G 1872	M 1877	T 1882	Y 1887
B '1868	H 1873	N 1878	U 1883	Z 1888
C 1869	I 1874	P 1879	V 1884	O 1889
D 1870	K 1875	R 1880	W 1885	
E 1871	L 1876	S 1881	X 1886	

'a' in Old English script in 1890; date letter
omitted in 1891.
'Royal Worcester England' written around mark
from 1891, after which, dots, stars and other
letters and forms were added to the mark each
year as listed below until 1963 when the year in
full is added.

1892, dot to left of crown, 1893 dot either side of
crown; dots were then added to either side of
crown until 1915, thus:

1894 3 dots	1900 9 dots	1906 15 dots	1912 21 dots
1895 4 dots	1901 10 dots	1907 16 dots	1913 22 dots
1896 5 dots	1902 11 dots	1908 17 dots	1914 23 dots
1897 6 dots	1903 12 dots	1909 18 dots	1915 24 dots
1898 7 dots	1904 13 dots	1910 19 dots	
1899 8 dots	1905 14 dots	1911 20 dots	

In 1916 the dots alongside the crown were
replaced by a star under the mark, dots were then
added to either side of this star until 1927:

1916 1 star	1922 star & 6 dots
1917 star & 1 dot	1923 star & 7 dots
1918 star & 2 dots	1924 star & 8 dots
1919 star & 3 dots	1925 star & 9 dots
1920 star & 4 dots	1926 star & 10 dots
1921 star & 5 dots	1927 star & 11 dots

then as follows:

1928 ▢   1929 ◇   1930 ÷

1931 ∞   1932 ∞∞   1933 ∞∞·

further dots were then added to three interlaced circles as follows:

1934 circles & 2 dots	1938 circles & 6 dots
1935 circles & 3 dots	1939 circles & 7 dots
1936 circles & 4 dots	1940 circles & 8 dots
1937 circles & 5 dots	1941 circles & 9 dots

from 1941 to 1948 inclusive there were no changes in the year-mark

1949 V	1953 W and 3 dots
1950 W	1954 W and 4 dots
1951 W and 1 dot	1955 W and 5 dots
1952 W and 2 dots	

1956 R in place of W with 6 dots	1960 R and 10 dots
	1961 R and 11 dots
1957 R and 7 dots	1962 R and 12 dots
1958 R and 8 dots	1963 R and 13 dots
1959 R and 9 dots	

From 1963 all new patterns have the year in full.

(*By courtesy of the Worcester Royal Porcelain Co. Ltd.*)

Hancock, Robert, *b.* 1730, *d.* 1817
engraver of transfer-prints
c. 1756–65

Rᶠ. Worcester

(Hancock associated with   initials of Hancock
Turner of Caughley in   and rebus of Richard
1776)   Holdship on prints

Chamberlain, *c.* 1786–1852
decorators from *c.* 1786–*c.* 1790, then
manufacturers of soft-paste porcelain
  c. 1790–1810

*Chamberlains
Worcs No276*
in red

written or printed   *Chamberlain's*
c. 1811–40   *Worcester,*
(under crown)   *& 155*
New Bond Street
London,
Royal Porcelain
Manufactory

c. 1814–16   *Chamberlain's*
Worcester,
& 63 Piccadilly,
London

written or printed

incised, *c.* 1815–25

CHAMBERLAINS
ROYAL PORCELAIN
WORCESTER

printed mark under
crown, *c.* 1840–5
('& Co.' from this
date)

CHAMBERLAIN & CO.
WORCESTER
155 New Bond St.
& No. 1
COVENTRY ST.
LONDON

written or printed
c. 1846–50

CHAMBERLAIN & CO.
WORCESTER

impressed or printed
c. 1847–50

CHAMBERLAINS

printed *c.* 1850–52

(then Kerr & Binns, p. 86)

Doe and Rogers,
c. 1820–40
porcelain decorators

Doe & Rogers
Worcester

Grainger, Wood & Co.
c. 1801–12, porcelain
  rare mark

Grainger Wood & Co.
Worcester, Warranted

Grainger, Lee & Co.
c. 1812–*c.* 39
porcelain

Grainger, Lee & Co.
Worcester
painted

c. 1820–30 painted	New China Works Worcester
c. 1812–30 painted	Royal China Works Worcester

Grainger, George *c.* 1839–1902 porcelain	GEO. GRAINGER CHINA WORKS WORCESTER
painted or printed mark *c.* 1839–60	
'& Co.' added *c.* 1850	G. GRAINGER & CO. WORCESTER

's.p.' for 'Semi-Porcelain', *c.* 1850–	G.G. & CO. S.P. S.P. G.G.W.
initials included in printed marks, 1850–60	impressed or printed G.W.
1850–89	G. & CO. W.
printed mark on copies of 'Dr. Wall' period wares *c.* 1860–80	⊠ GRAINGER & CO. WORCESTER
printed or impressed *c.* 1870–89	

c. 1889–1902 ('England' added in 1891)

letters added under mark to indicate year of
manufacture from 1891–1902:

A 1891	D 1894	G 1897	J 1900
B 1892	E 1895	H 1898	K 1901
C 1893	F 1896	I 1899	L 1902

George Grainger & Co. was taken over by
Worcester Royal Porcelain Co. Ltd. in 1889 and
closed down in 1902.

Hadley & Sons, James
porcelain and earthenware
1896–1905

    signature on work   incised or impressed
    modelled by Hadley for
Worcester Royal Porcelain Co.
    c. 1875–94
    printed or impressed
    1896–97
    1897–1902,
    impressed

FINE ART
HADLEY'S
TERRA-COTTA

    printed mark 1897–1902
    (centre ribbon omitted
    from 1900)

    printed mark, 1902–5

Locke & Co., porcelain   LOCKE & CO.
1895–1904   WORCESTER

'globe-mark', *c.* 1895–1904
'Ltd,' added in *c.* 1900

Sparks, George, *c.*
1836–54, decorator of
Worcester and Coalport porcelain

Sparks Worcester
written mark

WROTHAM (Kent)
Greene, John
slipware potter, *c.* 1670

I.G.

Hubble, Nicholas
slipware potter, second
half of 17th century

N.H.

Ifield, Thomas, Henry
& John
slipware potters whose
   initials are found on wares
   dating from *c.* 1620–75

T.I.
H.I.   I.I.

Livermore, John
(*d.* 1658) slipware potter,
wares dated from 1612–49

I.L.

Richardson, George
slipware potter, wares
dated from 1642–77

G.R.

all above slip-trailed

Wells, Reginald,
(1877–1951)
studio-potter

WELLS
incised

c. 1909	COLDRUM
	WROTHAM
c. 1910–24 (at	COLDRUM
Chelsea)	CHELSEA
c. 1910	R. F. WELLS
c. 1918–51 (at Storrington, Sussex, *c.* 1925–51)	SOON impressed or incised

YARMOUTH (Norfolk)
  Absolon, William, 1784–1815
  independent enameller of
  the wares of various
  earthenwares and glass

painted in brown

STAFFORDSHIRE

Since the early seventeenth century the area in,
and around, Stoke in Staffordshire has been the
centre of the English ceramic industry.
Manufacture was first confined to earthenwares,
but later included salt-glazed stonewares,
jasperwares, bone-china and the mass of various
hybrid pottery and porcelain bodies introduced
about 1800 and later. The smaller pottery towns
are today grouped together to form
Stoke-on-Trent.
  In this section of the book, the various

Staffordshire potters are listed alphabetically under the names of the towns in which they potted.

Many of the more recent factories have often changed their mark many times and the following general aids to dating are often sufficient enough as a guide.

Few serious collectors seek pieces which include 'ENGLAND' in the mark, for this implies the piece was made in, or after, 1891 in order to comply with the American McKinley Tariff, which called for the country of origin to be marked on imported wares. The term 'MADE IN ENGLAND' suggests a date of about 1920.

The mass of blue-printed earthenwares are difficult to attribute if unmarked. Many have just a Royal Arms as a mark; this is a sure indication of a 19th-century date, whereas often similar marks, or 'back-stamps', include the name of the design and the initials of the potter. These initials may well be included in the index at end of the book. Versions of the Royal Arms used after 1837 lack the small inescutcheon on the quartered shield which is present on arms previous to this date.

In addition to factory marks, many wares will be found to bear the well-known 'diamond' or 'lozenge'-mark (see Appendix A, page 284). This mark was applied by either printing, impressing, or applying as a relief medallion and indicates that the design of the form or decoration had been registered with the London Patent Office and was protected against 'piracy' for a period of three years. If the numbers and letters in the four corners of this 'diamond-mark' can be accurately read, the reader should consult the key diagrams and tables on pages 284–7 to check the day, month and year the design was initially registered between 1842 and 1883. After this year wares bear only a registered number (e.g. Rd. 12345), which can be dated to the year, up until 1909.

Appendix B in this book is an abbreviated copy of the Class IV (pottery, porcelain, etc.) Index, giving the name and whereabouts of the firms registering ceramic designs between 1842 and 1883. This list is reproduced with the kind permission of the Public Record Office.

BILSTON (Staffs., now West Midlands)
  Myatt Pottery Co., *c.* 1850–94
  earthenware, mark of 1880   MYATT

BURSLEM (Staffs, now West Midlands.)
  Albert Potteries Ltd.
  earthenware, 1946–54   printed or impressed

  Allman, Broughton & Co.,   A.B. & CO.
  earthenware, 1861–8   printed or impressed

  Baggaley, Jacob   J.B.
  earthenware, 1880–6   impressed

  Bagshaw & Meir   B. & M.
  earthenware, 1802–8   printed or impressed

  Ball, Izaac   I.B.
  slipware, *c.* 1700

  Bancroft & Bennett
  earthenware, 1846–50

  Barker & Son   B. & S.
  earthenware, *c.* 1850–60   printed
                  BARKER & SON
                printed or impressed

  Barker, Sutton & Till   B.S. & T.
  earthenware, 1834–43

  Bates, Elliott & Co.   B.E. & CO.
  general ceramics, 1870–5

97

Bates, Gildea & Walker,
general ceramics, 1878–81

B.G. & W.
printed

Bates, Walker & Co.
general ceramics, 1875–78

B.W. & CO.
printed

Bathwell & Goodfellow
earthenware, 1818–23
(also Tunstall 1820–2)

BATHWELL &
GOODFELLOW
impressed

Beech, James
earthenware, 1877–89
Swan Bank Works (also
at Tunstall)

J.B.
printed

Blackhurst & Bourne
earthenware, 1880–92

B. & B.
printed

Blackhurst & Tunnicliffe
earthenware, *c.* 1879

B. & T.
printed

Bodley & Co.
earthenware, 1865

Bodley & Co., E. F.
earthenware, *c.* 1862–81

E.F.B. & CO.

SCOTIA POTTERY

Bodley & Son
bone-china, 1874–5

BODLEY
B. & SON
printed

Bodley, E. J. D.
general ceramics, 1875–92

E.J.D.B.
printed,
impressed or as
monogram

Bodley & Harrold
Scotia Pottery
1863–5, earthenware

B. & H.
Bodley & Harrold
printed

Boote, Ltd., T. & R.
Waterloo Pottery
general ceramics and
tiles, 1842–*c.* 1966

T. & R.B.   T.B. & S.

T. & R. BOOTE
printed or impressed

printed mark
1890–1906
'England' added
from 1891

Booth & Co., Thomas
(also at Tunstall)
earthenware, 1868–72

T.B. & CO.
printed

Bridgwood & Clarke
(also at Tunstall)
earthenware, 1857–64

BRIDGWOOD &
CLARKE
impressed
B. & C.   B. & C.
BURSLEM
printed

Brown & Steventon, Ltd.
earthenware, 1900–23

B. & S.
printed
'sun-face' mark
from 1920–

Buckley, Heath & Co.
earthenware, 1885–90

printed or impressed

Buckley, Wood & Co.
earthenware, 1875–85

B.W. & CO.
printed or impressed

Burgess, Henry
earthenware, 1864–92

H.B.
impressed or printed
under Royal Arms

Burgess & Leigh
earthenware, *c.* 1862–

B. & L.
impressed or printed

'Ltd.' added to marks
from *c.* 1919, large
variety of printed
marks from 1880,
'England' added from
1891

printed

monogram mark
1862–

impressed or printed

Burslem Pottery Co. Ltd.
earthenware, 1894–1933

    printed

ENGLAND

Burslem School of Art
earthenware, figures, etc.
in 'Astbury' style
1935–41

impressed

Clarke & Co., Edward   EDWARD CLARKE
earthenware, *c.* 1880–87
(also at Tunstall, *c.* 1865–   EDWARD CLARKE &
77, and Longport, *c.*   CO.
1878–80)   printed

Clowes, William   W. CLOWES
general ceramics   impressed
c. 1783–96

Collinson & Co.,   C. COLLINSON & CO.
Charles, earthenware,   printed
1851–73

Cooper & Co., J.   J. COOPER & CO.
earthenware, 1922–5   ENGLAND
printed or impressed   DUCAL WORKS
    in circle
Cooper Pottery, Susie   *Susie Cooper*
('Ltd.' from *c.* 1961)   CROWN WORKS
general ceramics   BURSLEM
  c. 1930–   ENGLAND

printed mark, 1932–

Cooper China Ltd., Susie
(also at Longton, *c.* 1950–9)
china, *c.* 1959–
Member of the
Wedgwood Group

Cork & Edge
earthenware,
1846–60

C. & E.
printed with a
variety of designs

Cork, Edge & Malkin
earthenware, 1860–71

C.E. & M.
printed with varying
'backstamps' often
including pattern-name

Dale, John
'Staffordshire
figures', early 19th century

J. DALE
BURSLEM

I. DALE
BURSLEM

Daniel & Cork
earthenware, 1867–9

DANIEL & CORK
printed

Davison & Son, Ltd.
earthenware,
c. 1898–1952

mark of 1948–

printed

Dean, S. W.
earthenware, 1904–10

  printed mark

Deans (1910) Ltd.
earthenware, 1910–19
  printed mark

DEANS (1910) LTD.
BURSLEM
ENGLAND

Doulton & Co.
earthenware and
porcelain, *c.* 1882
(Doulton Fine China Ltd.
from 1955 and Royal
Doulton Tableware Ltd., 1973–)
  impressed name of
  new material from
  1960

see under
LAMBETH
for major
marks

ENGLISH
TRANSLUCENT
CHINA

Duke & Nephews, Sir James
various hybrid porcelains
c. 1860–3

  impressed hand

Dunn, Bennett & Co.
earthenware, 1875–
('Ltd.' added from 1907–)
(now Royal Doulton Group)
  marks 1875–1907

D.B. & CO.
printed

printed mark, 1937–	DUNN BENNETT & CO. LTD. *BURSLEM* ENGLAND
added to mark on 'Ironstone' from 1955–	'Vitreous Ironstone'
Edge, Malkin & Co. earthenware, 1871–1903	E.M. & CO.
'LTD.' added from 1899	E.M. & CO. B printed
Edwards & Son, James various pottery, 1851–82	J.E. & S.
'Dale Hall', Burslem	EDWARDS D.H. printed or impressed
Edwards, James & Thomas earthenware, 1839–41	J. & T.E.
printed or impressed	J. & T. EDWARDS B
Ellgreave Pottery Co. Ltd. earthenware, 1921– (Wood & Sons Ltd.)	'Lottie Rhead Ware'
and other fully named marks	'Heatmaster'
Elton & Co. Ltd., J. F. earthenware, 1901–1910 (also in monogram)	J.F.E. CO. LTD. BURSLEM printed or impressed

Emery, Francis J.
earthenware, *c.* 1878–93

F. J. EMERY
printed

Evans & Booth
earthenware, 1856–69

E. & B.
printed

Ford & Co., Samuel
earthenware, 1898–1939
(*see* Smith & Ford)

S & F.

'F. & CO.' alternative to
'S. & F.'

printed

c. 1936–9

'Samford Ware'

Ford & Riley
earthenware, 1882–93

F. & R.
B

Ford & Sons ('Ltd.'
added 1908),
earthenware, *c.* 1893–1938

F. & S.
B

also 'CROWN
FORD', 'NEWCRAFT'

F. & SONS, LTD.
printed

Ford & Sons (Crownford)
earthenware, 1938–

printed, 1961–

Gibson & Sons, Ltd.
earthenware, 1885–

G. & S. LTD.
B

Gibson & Sons, Ltd.
'Harvey Pottery'
   printed, *c.* 1904–9

'Royal Harvey', *c.* 1950–5
   large variety of fully named marks, 1909–

Gildea & Walker, 1881–5
earthenware

G. & W.

c. 1881–5:
$$\frac{4}{82} = APRIL, 1882$$

Gildea, James
earthenware, 1885–8

   printed mark includes
   a pattern-name

Godwin, B. C.
earthenware, *c.* 1851–

B.C.G.
printed

Godwin, Thomas &
Benjamin, general
ceramics, *c.* 1809–34

T. & B.G.
T.B.G.
printed

Godwin, Thomas
earthenware, 1834–54

THOS GODWIN
BURSLEM
STONE CHINA

Godwin, Rowley & Co. earthenware, 1828–31	G.R. & CO. printed
Hall & Sons, John earthenware, 1814–32	I. HALL HALL
c. 1822–32	I. HALL & SONS impressed or printed
Hammersley & Son, Ralph, earthenware, 1860–1905	R.H.
'& Son' added 1884–	R.H. & S. printed
Hancock, Whittingham & Co., earthenware, 1863–72	H.W. & CO. printed
Harding, Joseph earthenware, 1850–1	J. HARDING printed
Harrison & Phillips earthenware, 1914–15	H. & P. BURSLEM printed
Heath & Son earthenware, *c.* 1800	HEATH & SON impressed
Heath, John general ceramics, 1809–23	HEATH impressed
Heath, Thomas earthenware, 1812–35	T. HEATH impressed or printed

Heath & Blackhurst & Co.,
earthenware, 1859–77

H. & B.
H.B. & CO.

Heath & Greatbatch
earthenware, 1891–3

H. & G.
B
printed or impressed

Hill Pottery Co. Ltd.
general ceramics, *c.* 1861–7

J.S.H.
printed
(also as monogram)

Hobson, Charles
earthenware, 1865–80
  's' added 1873–5

C.H.
C.H. & S.
impressed or printed

Hobson, G. & J.
earthenware, 1883–1901

HOBSON'S
printed

Hobson, George
earthenware, 1901–23
  printed or impressed

Holdcroft & Co., Peter
earthenware, 1846–52

P.H. & CO.
printed

Holdcroft, Hill & Mellor,
earthenware,
1860–70

H.H. & M.
printed

Hollinshead & Griffiths
earthenware, 1890–1909

CHELSEA ART POTTERY
H. & G.
BURSLEM

  mark includes lion and crown

Holmes, Plant & Maydew
earthenware, 1876–85

H.P. & M.
printed

Hope & Carter
earthenware, 1862–80

H. & C.
printed

Hughes, Thomas
earthenware, 1860–94

THOMAS HUGHES
IRONSTONE CHINA
impressed

Hughes & Son Ltd., Thomas,
general ceramics,
1895–1957

THOS. HUGHES &
SON
ENGLAND

Hulme & Sons, Henry
earthenware, 1906–32
(mark previously used
by Wood & Hulme)

W. & H.
B

Hulme, William
earthenware, 1891–1941

printed
1891–1936

printed or impressed,
1936–41

ALPHA WARE
H
ENGLAND

Jackson, Job & John
earthenware, 1831–5

J. & J. JACKSON
JACKSON'S
WARRANTED
impressed or printed

Johnson, Ltd., Samuel   S.J.
earthenware, 1887–1931
   'Ltd.' 1912–   S.J.B.
   'BRITANNIA POTTERY',   S.J. LTD.
   1916–31   printed

Jones, George   GEORGE JONES
earthenware, *c.* 1854

Keeling & Co. Ltd.   K. & CO.
earthenware, 1886–1936

                         K. & CO. B.

   'England' usually added
   from 1891
   'Losol Ware', *c.* 1912–   all
                                        printed

Kennedy, William Sadler   W. S. KENNEDY
earthenware, 1843–54   impressed or printed

Kennedy & Macintyre   W. S. KENNEDY
earthenware, 1854–60   & J. MACINTYRE
                     impressed or printed

Kensington Pottery Ltd.
c. 1937–
(also at Hanley 1922–37)
now Price & Kensington Potteries Ltd.

Kent (Porcelains) Ltd., William
earthenware 1944–62

King & Barrett, Ltd.
general pottery, 1898–40

K. & B.
impressed or printed

Lakin & Poole
pottery and figures, *c.* 1791–5

LAKIN & POOLE

L. & P.
BURSLEM
impressed

Leighton Pottery Ltd.
earthenware, 1940–54

'ROYAL LEIGHTON WARE'

Machin & Potts
general ceramics
1833–7
colour-print patent 1835

MACHIN & POTTS

MACHIN & POTTS
PATENT

Machin & Thomas
earthenware, *c.* 1831–2

M. & T.
printed

Macintyre & Co. Ltd.,
James, earthenware, *c.*
1860–1928, '& Co.' from
   1867– (continued with
industrial wares only)

MACINTYRE
J. MACINTYRE
J.M. & CO.
printed or impressed

Maddock & Seddon
earthenware, *c.* 1839–42

M. & S.

Maddock, John
earthenware, 1842–55
   (not to be confused with
'M' for Minton)

M
printed

Maddock & Sons (Ltd.)
general pottery, 1855–
specialist hotel-ware
'Ltd.' added 1896–

various fully named
marks, and
'ROYAL VITREOUS'
'ROYAL IVORY'
'IVORY WARE'
'EMBASSY'

Malkin, Frederick
earthenware, 1891–1905

printed, *c.* 1900–5

Malkin, Samuel
slip-wares, early 18th century

S.M.
moulded in
relief

Mayer, Thomas, John
& Joseph, general
ceramics, 1843–55

T. J. & J. MAYER
printed

Mellor, Taylor & Co.
earthenware, *c.* 1880–1904

'ROYAL IRONSTONE CHINA'

printed or impressed
with name of firm

'SEMI PORCELAIN'

Mellor, Venables & Co.
general ceramics, 1834–51

MELLOR, VENABLES
& CO.

M.V. & CO.
printed or impressed

112

Midwinter Ltd., W. R. earthenwares, 1910–
    added numbers indicate
    month and year
(*now Wedgwood Group*)
	various fully-named marks with:
	'PORCELON'
	'STYLECRAFT'

Moorcroft Ltd., W. earthenware, 1913–	MOORCROFT BURSLEM
signature of William Moorcroft (*d.* 1945)	*WMMoorcroft*
mark of Walter Moorcroft (son)	*W.M*
Morgan, Wood & Co. earthenware, 1860–70	M.W. & CO. printed (at times with bee)
Mountford, A. J. earthenware, 1897–1901	 BURSLEM printed
New Wharf Pottery Co. earthenware, 1878–94	N.W.P.C.O. B printed
Newport Pottery Co. Ltd. earthenware, 1920– (now Wedgwood group)	various fully named marks
c. 1938–66	'Clarice Cliff'

Parrott & Co. Ltd.
earthenware, 1921
(manufacture ceased *c.* 1962)

Phillips & Son, Thomas
earthenware, *c.* 1845-6

T. PHILLIPS & SON
BURSLEM
printed or impressed

Pinder, Thomas
earthenware, 1849-51

PINDER BURSLEM
printed or impressed

Pinder, Bourne & Hope
earthenware, 1851-62

P.B. & H.
printed

Pinder, Bourne & Co.
earthenware, 1862-82
(taken over by Doultons
in 1878, but name unchanged
until 1882)

P.B. & CO.

Plant Bros. Crown Pottery
porcelain, 1889-1906
(at Longton from 1898)

Plant, Enoch
earthenware, 1898-1905
 (such crowns are a
  common form of mark)

printed or impressed

Poole, J. E.
earthenware, *c.* 1796-
early 19th century

POOLE
impressed

Price Bros.
earthenware, 1896–1903

Price Bros. (Burslem) Ltd.   printed
earthenware, 1903–61   'star-mark', as above
                              until 1910

   trade-names:
   'PALM ATHLO'
   'ATHLO WARE'
   'MATTONA WARE'

Price & Kensington   PRICE
Potteries Ltd.   KENSINGTON
earthenware, 1962–   printed within wreath

Radford Handcraft   G. RADFORD
Pottery, earthenware,   BURSLEM
1933–48   printed signature

Riley, John & Richard   J. & R. RILEY
general ceramics, 1802–28

   marks painted,   RILEY'S
   printed or impressed   SEMI-CHINA

Robinson, Joseph   J.R.
earthenware, 1876–98   B
                        printed or impressed

Roddy & Co., E.   STAFFORDSHIRE
earthenware, 1925–8   RODDY
                               WARE

Sadler & Sons, Ltd.,
James, earthenware,
1899–
  impressed or printed
  from 1937–

ENGLAND
J.S.S.B.
impressed

SADLER
BURSLEM
ENGLAND

Simpson, Ralph
slip-wares, 1651–*c.* 1724
  name slip-trailed on front
  of large chargers

RALPH SIMPSON
slip-trailed

Simpson, John
slip wares, first half of
18th century

JOHN SIMPSON
I.S.
slip-trailed

Smith & Co., Ambrose
earthenware, *c.* 1784–6

A.S. & CO.
impressed or printed

Smith & Ford
earthenware, 1895–8
  printed (*see also*
  Samuel Ford)

S & F

Stanyer, A.
earthenware, *c.* 1916–41

A.S.
B
ENG.

A.S.
ENG.
B
impressed

Steel, Daniel,
1790–1824
earthenwares and
'Wedgwood-type' stonewares

STEEL
impressed

Stubbs, Joseph
earthenwares, *c.* 1822–35

JOSEPH STUBBS
LONGPORT
impressed or printed

Stubbs & Kent
earthenware, *c.* 1828–30
   mark impressed or
   printed

Sudlow & Sons, Ltd., R.
earthenware, 1893–
(Part of Howard Pottery
Co. Shelton from 1965)

full-name marks
impressed or printed
from *c.* 1920–

Till & Sons, Thomas
earthenware, *c.* 1850–1928

   1861–

   'Globe-mark' from 1880
   'Tillson' ware, *c.* 1922–8

Tundley, Rhodes &
Proctor, earthenware,
1873–83, then:
Rhodes & Proctor,
1883–5, earthenware

T.R. & P.
printed

R. & P.
printed

Venables & Baines
earthenware, *c.* 1851–3

VENABLES &
BAINES

Venables & Co.
earthenware, *c.* 1853–5

J. VENABLES
& CO.
printed or impressed

117

Vernon & Son, James earthenware, 1860–80	J.V.
1875–	J.V. & Son
	J.V. & S. J.V. junr.

Wade & Son, Ltd., George, earthenware 1922–, 1936–

WADE Figures

1947–

Wade & Co. earthenware, 1887–1927	WADES
	W. & CO.
	B

Wade, Heath & Co., Ltd., earthenware, 1927–

WADES (with lion)

c. 1934–

WADEHEATH
ORCADIA
WARE

c. 1934–

WADEHEATH
(with lion)

Trade-names: 'Flaxman Ware', 'ROYAL VICTORIA'

Walley, John earthenware, 1850–67

J. WALLEY
J. WALLEY'S
WARE
printed or impressed

118

Walton, John
earthenware groups and
figures, *c.* 1818–35

impressed on raised
scroll

Wedgwood & Sons, Ltd.
Josiah, general ceramics, 1759–
   very rare incised initials or   'J.W.'
   signature, *c.* 1760
   rare, *c.* 1759–69   wedgwood WEDGWOOD
   c. 1759   WEDGWOOD

Wedgwood & Bentley   WEDGWOOD
partnership, 1769–80   & BENTLEY
concerned only with
the manufacture of   WEDGWOOD
ornamental neo-classical   & BENTLEY
wares   ETRURIA

   impressed on cameos, etc.   W. & B.
   impressed or raised mark

   c. 1780–98   Wedgwood

   rare impressed mark   WEDGWOOD & SONS
   c. 1790
   printed on bone-china   WEDGWOOD
   c. 1812–22   red, blue or gold

rare printed mark on stone china, *c.* 1827–61	WEDGWOOD'S STONE CHINA
impressed mark *c.* 1840–5	WEDGWOOD ETRURIA
impressed on 'pearlware' *c.* 1840–68	PEARL
as above, post–1868	P

From 1860 the Wedgwood factory in addition to their usual name-mark, adopted a system of date-marking consisting of three letters side by side: the first indicates the month, the second a potter's mark and the third the year of manufacture. As from 1907 the first letter, which had hitherto denoted the month of manufacture, was replaced by a number indicating the cycle of year marks in use; previously there was no indication whether the piece was made in the first second, or third cycle.

This system was further changed in 1930 when the cycle number was replaced by the chronological number of the month, e.g.: January = 1, February = 2, etc., and the initial which had previously indicated the year was now replaced by the last two years of the actual date of manufacture.

Examples:	Month	Potter	Year	
	Y	O	R	May, 1863
	L	O	E	July, 1902
	Cycle	Potter	Year	
	3	O	N	1911
	4	O	A	1924

Month	Potter	Year	
3	O	32	March, 1932
11	O	48	November, 1948

Monthly marks indicated by the first letter from
1860–1864:

January J	April A	July V	October O
February F	May Y	August W	November N
March M	June T	September S	December D

1865–1907:

January J	April A	July L	October O
February F	May M	August W	November N
March R	June T	September S	December D

First cycle of year marks:

O	1860	R	1863	U	1866	X	1869
P	1861	S	1864	V	1867	Y	1870
Q	1862	T	1865	W	1868	Z	1871

Second cycle of year marks:

A	1872	H	1879	O	1886	V	1893
B	1873	I	1880	P	1887	W	1894
C	1874	J	1881	Q	1888	X	1895
D	1875	K	1882	R	1889	Y	1896
E	1876	L	1883	S	1890	Z	1897
F	1877	M	1884	T	1891		
G	1878	N	1885	U	1892		

Note: 'ENGLAND' added to mark from 1891

Third cycle of year marks:

A 1898	H 1905	O 1912	V 1919
B 1899	I 1906	P 1913	W 1920
C 1900	J 1907	Q 1914	X 1921
D 1901	K 1908	R 1915	Y 1922
E 1902	L 1909	S 1916	Z 1923
F 1903	M 1910	T 1917	
G 1904	N 1911	U 1918	

Fourth cycle of year marks:

A 1924	C 1926	E 1928
B 1925	D 1927	F 1929

the last two years of the date then appear in full.

'Portland Vase' mark printed
on bone-china from *c.* 1878
occasionally seen impressed
on earthenware, *c.* 1891–1900
Note: 'ENGLAND' added
    after 1891 'MADE IN
ENGLAND' from about 1910
'*Bone China*' added *c.* 1920

WEDGWOOD
BONE CHINA

MADE IN ENGLAND

printed on creamwares
from *c.* 1940

OF ETRURIA
WEDGWOOD
MADE IN
ENGLAND
BARLASTON

Lessore, Emile, decorator
c. 1858–76

E Lessore

Thomson, E. G.,   E. G. Thomson
decorator, *c.* 1870

Barnard, Harry, decorator
c. 1900

marks on red stonewares,
probably Wedgwood
second-half of
18th century   impressed

Whittingham, Ford & Co.,   W.F. & CO.
1868–73,   printed
earthenware

Whittingham, Ford & Riley,   W.F. & R.
earthenware, 1876–82   printed

Wilkinson, Arthur J.,   many fully-named
1885–*c.* 1970, earthenwares   marks including:
'ROYAL SEMI-PORCELAIN', *c.* 1891–
'ROYAL IRONSTONE CHINA', *c.* 1896–
'IRONSTONE CHINA', *c.* 1910
'Clarice Cliff', *c.* 1930
'Honeyglaze', *c.* 1947
(merged with W. R. Midwinter Ltd., 1964)

Withinshaw, W. E.,   W.E.W.
1873–8, general ceramics   W. E. WITHINSHAW
printed or impressed

Wood, Enoch   WOOD   E. WOOD
c. 1784–*c.* 1790 general   W (***)
ceramics   E.W.   W.

Enoch Wood's marks
can be seen impressed,
moulded or incised

ENOCH WOOD
SCULPSIT

E. WOOD
SCULPSIT

ENOCH WOOD

Wood & Caldwell
1790–1818, earthenware
especially figures, etc.

WOOD & CALDWELL
impressed

Wood & Sons, Enoch
1818–1846, earthenware
blue-printed wares made
for U.S.A. include the
American eagle in mark

ENOCH WOOD
& SONS
BURSLEM
STAFFORDSHIRE

E. WOOD & SONS
E. & E. WOOD
BURSLEM

E.W. & S.
E. & E. WOOD
E. & E.W.
all printed

Wood, H. J.
1884–, earthenware
many various fully-named marks including:
'Bursley-Ware' *c.* 1930–
'E. Radford' *c.* 1935–
'CHINESE ROSE' *c.* 1960–, etc.

Wood, Isaiah
1710–15, earthenware

ISA WOOD
1712
incised

Wood, John Wedge 1841–4 (also at Tunstall 1845–60)	w.w. impressed J. WEDGWOOD printed

Wood, Ralph (Snr.)   R. WOOD   Ra. WOOD
(1715–72), son of same   Ra. WOOD
name (1748–95)   BURSLEM
grandson (1781–1801)   Ralph Wood
    impressed or incised marks
    c. 1770–1801

    rebus of trees (rare)
    c. 1770–90

Wood & Son
1865–, earthenware, etc.
  '& Sons', from 1907
  'Ltd.' added *c.* 1910
	various fully-named
	marks from *c.* 1890–

Wood & Co., Thomas 1885–96, earthenwares	T.W. & CO. printed or impressed

Wood & Sons, Thomas *c.* 1896–7, earthenware	T.W. & S. printed

Wood & Co., W.   w.w. & CO.
1873–1932, earthenware   printed or impressed
  mark of initials printed in 'Staffordshire
  knot', 1880–1915, with crown, 1915–32

Wood & Baggaley	w. & b.
1870–80, earthenware	printed
Wood & Barker, Ltd.	w. & b. Ltd.
1897–1903, earthenware	printed
Wood & Bowers	w. & b.
1839, earthenware	(can be confused
	with Wood & Baggaley)
Wood & Clarke	w. & c.
c. 1871–2, earthenware	printed with 'lion
	rampant'
Wood & Hulme	w. & h.
1882–1905, earthenware	b
	printed or impressed
Wooldridge & Walley	w. & w.
1898–1901, earthenware	b
	printed

COBRIDGE (Staffordshire)

J. & G.A.

Alcock, John & George	J. & G. ALCOCK
1839–46, earthenware and	COBRIDGE
'INDIAN IRONSTONE'	impressed or printed
Alcock, Junior, John &	J. & S. ALCOCK JR.
Samuel, *c.* 1848–50	printed or impressed
earthenware	

Alcock, John 1853–61, earthenware	JOHN ALCOCK COBRIDGE printed

Alcock & Co., Henry
1861–1910, earthenware
  fully-named mark from
  1880, 'Ltd.' from 1900
	H.A. & CO.
	printed

Alcock Pottery, The Henry 1910–35, earthenware	fully named 'coat of arms' mark printed

Alcock & Co., Samuel
c. 1828–53, general ceramics
  (Also at Burslem
  c. 1830–59)
  printed, painted or
  impressed, sometimes
  with Royal Arms or
  bee-hive
	SAMUEL ALCOCK & CO.
	COBRIDGE
	printed or impressed
	S.A. & CO.
	S. ALCOCK & CO.

Bates & Bennett 1868–95, earthenware	B. & B. printed or impressed
Birks Brothers & Seddon 1877–86, earthenware	IMPERIAL IRONSTONE CHINA BIRKS BROS. & SEDDON printed below Royal Arms
Blackhurst & Co. Ltd., John 1951–9, earthenware	J. BLACKHURST ENGLAND

Brownfield, William
1850–91, earthenware (also
porcelain after 1871) much
'parian ware'

W.B.

printed, impressed
or moulded

impressed, often with
crown, from 1860–   BROWNFIELD
'S' or '& Son', added 1871
'& Sons', added 1876
printed 'double-globe' mark, 1871–91

Brownfields Guild Pottery   B.G.P. CO.
Society Ltd., 1891–1900,   impressed
general ceramics
(Brownfield's Pottery Ltd.,
c. 1898–1900)

printed monogram

printed within circular
strap device   BROWNFIELDS

Cartledge, John   JOHN CARTLEDGE
c. 1800, earthenware   rare incised mark
figures

Clews, James & Ralph   CLEWS WARRANTED
1818–34, pottery and porcelain STAFFORDSHIRE
                           impressed under
                              crown

impressed mark on
blue-printed wares

C.C. & CO.

Cockson & Chetwynd
1867–75, earthenware

COCKSON &
CHETWYND
printed

Cockson & Seddon
1875–7, earthenware

IMPERIAL IRONSTONE
CHINA
COCKSON & SEDDON
printed under Royal
Arms

Crystal Porcelain Pottery
Co. Ltd., 1882–6,
pottery and porcelain
　(dove sometimes
　included in mark)

C.P.P. CO.
printed or impressed

Daniel, John
c. 1770–*c.* 86, earthenware

JOHN DANIEL
incised

Dillon, Francis
1834–43, earthenware

DILLON
impressed

F.D.
printed with various
back-stamps

Furnival & Co., Jacob
c. 1845–70, earthenware

J.F. & CO.
printed

Furnival & Sons, Thomas
1871–90, earthenware
　various 'T. F. & Sons'
　monograms

Furnivals (Ltd.)
1890–1968, earthenware
'Ltd.' added *c.* 1895

FURNIVALS
ENGLAND

c. 1905–13
(Taken over by Barratt's
of Staffordshire in 1967,
closed 1968)

1913 date included in
marks from that year

FURNIVALS
(1913)
ENGLAND

Globe Pottery Co. Ltd.
1914–, earthenware (now
Royal Doulton Group)

fully-named
printed 'globe' marks

Godwin, Benjamin E.
1834–41, earthenware

B.G.
printed with back-
stamp

Godwin, John & Robert
1834–66, earthenware

J. & R.G.
printed

Harding & Cockson 1834–60, earthenware	COBRIDGE H. & C. printed
Hughes & Co., Elijah 1853–67, earthenware	E. HUGHES & CO. impressed
Hulme, William 1948–54, earthenware printed mark	
Jones, Elijah 1831–9, earthenware	fully named impressed mark or E.J. printed
Jones & Walley 1841–3, earthenware	fully named impressed or moulded mark or printed J. & W.
Meakin, Henry 1873–6, earthenware	IRONSTONE CHINA H. MEAKIN printed with Royal Arms

North Staffordshire Pottery Co. Ltd.
1940–52, earthenware

    trade-mark registered
    in 1944

Portland Pottery Ltd.
1946–53, earthenware
 ('P.P.C.' monogram,
  Portland Pottery, Cobridge)

Regal Pottery Co. Ltd.
1925–31, earthenware

Richardson, Albert G.   REGAL WARE
c. 1920–21   A.G.R.
                         printed

Richardsons (Cobridge) Ltd.,   REGAL WARE
1921–25   R(C) LTD.
                              printed

Robinson, Wood &   R.W. & B.
Brownfield, 1838–41,
earthenware, printed

Sant & Vodrey   S. & V.
1887–93, earthenware   COBRIDGE
                    printed or impressed

Shaw, Ralph   Made by Ralph Shaw
c. 1740–, earthenware   October 31, Cobridge
                              gate

Simpsons (Potters) Ltd.   fully-named marks
1944–, earthenware
 including various trade-names:
  'Ambassador Ware', 'Solian Ware', 'Loh
  Yueh Mei Kuei', 'Vogue', 'Chinastyle',
  'Marlborough Old English Ironstone',
  'Chanticleer'

132

Stevenson, Andrew
c. 1816–30, earthenware

STEVENSON
A. STEVENSON

impressed 'ship'
mark could also refer to
following potter

Stevenson, Ralph
c. 1810–32, earthenware

R. STEVENSON

marks impressed

R.S.

Stevenson & Son, Ralph
c. 1832–35, earthenware
marks printed

R.S. & S.

R. STEVENSON
& SON

Stevenson, Alcock &
Williams, earthenware *c.* 1825,
marks printed

STEVENSON
ALCOCK &
WILLIAMS

Stevenson & Williams
c. 1825, earthenware

R.S.W.

marks printed

STEVENSON & WILLIAMS

Viking Pottery Co.
1950–63, general ceramics

Walley, Edward
1845–56, general ceramics
marks impressed or printed

E. WALLEY

W.

Warburton, John *c.* 1802–25, earthenwares and stonewares	WARBURTON impressed
Warburton, Peter *c.* 1802–12, general ceramics *c.* 1810–12	WARBURTON'S PATENT printed or written under crown
Warburton, Peter & Francis 1795–1802, earthenware marks impressed	P. & F.W. P. & F. WARBURTON
Wood, Son & Co. 1869–79, earthenware	WOOD, SON & CO. printed under Royal Arms
Wood & Brownfield *c.* 1838–50, earthenware	W. & B. impressed or printed
Wood & Hawthorne 1882–7, earthenware	WOOD & HAWTHORNE printed under Royal Arms

FENTON (Staffordshire)

Bailey Potteries, Ltd. 1935–40, earthenware	BEWLEY POTTERY MADE IN ENGLAND printed
Baker & Co., W. 1839–1932, earthenware	W. BAKER & CO. printed or impressed

printed or impressed   BAKER & CO.
'Ltd.' added 1893

Barkers & Kent   B. & K.
1889–1941, earthenware   B. & K.L.
'Ltd.' added 1898   printed or impressed

Beardmore & Co., Frank   F.B. & CO.
1903–14, earthenware   F
    impressed on printed mark

    printed mark

Bourne, Charles   C.B.
1817–30, porcelain   (pattern no.)

Bowker, Arthur   STAFFORDSHIRE
1948–58, porcelain   FINE BONE CHINA
    OF
mark printed under crown   ARTHUR BOWKER

Brain & Co. Ltd.   HARJIAN
1903–67   ENGLAND
porcelain

    E.B. & CO.
1905–   F.
(now Coalport   impressed or
a division of   printed within
the Wedgwood   Staffordshire
Group at   knot
Foley Works)

(Coalport China Ltd., taken over by
E. Brain & Co. Ltd. in 1958)

British Art Pottery Co. (Fenton) Ltd.
1920–6, porcelain

mark printed or impressed

Broadhurst & Sons, James
c. 1862–, earthenware
printed in mark, 1862–70　　　　　J.B.

printed in mark, 1870–1922　　　J.B. & S.
'Ltd.' added 1922

Challinor & Co., E.　　　　E. CHALLINOR & CO.
1853–62, earthenware　　　　　　printed

Challinor, E. & C.　　　　　　E. & C.C.
1862–91, earthenware

E. & C. CHALLINOR
FENTON
printed

Challinor, C. & Co.　　　C. CHALLINOR & CO.
1892–6, earthenware　　　　　ENGLAND

Clulow & Co.　　　　　　CLULOW & CO.
c. 1802, earthenware　　　　　FENTON

Crown Staffordshire Porcelain Co. Ltd.
1889–, porcelain
(renamed Crown Staffordshire China Co. Ltd. in
1948)

printed 1889–1912
(Wedgwood China Div.
from 1973)
 printed marks of from
 1906, this firm makes
 bone-china reproductions
 of Chelsea 'raised-
 anchor' birds

'STAFFORDSHIRE'
with a crown within
wreath

Edge, Barker & Co.
1835–6, earthenware

E.B. & CO.
printed

Edge, Barker & Barker
1836–40, earthenware

E.B. & B.
printed

Edwards, John
1847–1900, general ceramics
 '& Co.' added *c.* 1873–9
 named marks including
 'PORCELAINE DE TERRE' or
 'WARRANTED IRONSTONE CHINA'
 from *c.* 1880–1900

J.E.

J.E. & CO.
PORCELAINE
IRONSTONE

Elkin, Knight & Co.
1822–6, earthenware
 marks impressed or
 printed

E.K. & CO.

ELKIN KNIGHT
& CO.

Elkin, Knight & Bridgwood
c. 1827–40, earthenware
and porcelain

E.K.B.
printed

Forester & Sons, Thomas   T.F. & S.
1883–1959, earthenware

'Ltd.' added, 1891–
'Phoenix China', 1912–

Forester & Hulme   F. & H.
1887–93, earthenware   printed under bee

Hulme & Christie   H. & C.
1893–1902, earthenware   F
   mark printed with a dove

Garner, Robert   R.G.
late 18th century, earthenware   moulded

Gimson & Co., Wallis   WALLIS GIMSON &
1884–90, earthenware   CO.
    printed under beehive

Ginder & Co., Samuel   S. Ginder & Co.
1811–43, earthenware   printed

Greatbatch, William   GREATBATCH
c. 1760– *c*, 1780, modeller   printed
potter and engraver of
transfer-prints

Green, Thomas   T. GREEN
1847–59, general   FENTON POTTERIES
ceramics   printed

Green, Thomas

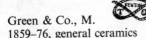

Green & Co., M.　　　M. GREEN & CO.
1859–76, general ceramics　　printed

Green, T. A. & S.　　　T.A. & S.G.
1876–89, china　　initials printed in
　　　　'Staffordshire knot'

From 1889 this firm became known as
'Crown Staffordshire Porcelain Co.'

Greenwood, S.　　　S. GREENWOOD
late 18th century　　rare impressed mark
black basaltes

Hines Bros.　　　H.B.
1886–1907, earthenware　　impressed

　　　　HINES BROS.
　　　　printed

Hoods, Ltd.　　　H. LTD.
c. 1919–, earthenware　　printed
(firm now closed)

Hughes & Co., E.　　　H
1889–1953, porcelain
　　impressed mark, 1889–98

　　impressed or printed　　H.F.
　　1898–1905

printed mark
c. 1908–12

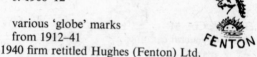

various 'globe' marks
from 1912–41
1940 firm retitled Hughes (Fenton) Ltd.

Hulme & Christie   H. & C.
1893–1902, earthenware   F
(Christie & Beardmore   printed with dove
1902–3)

Jones, A. G., Harley-   H.J.
1907–34, earthenware
and porcelain
  initials printed with   A.G.H.J.
  various trade-names:
  'FENTONIA WARE', 'PARAMOUNT',
  'WILTON WARE'

Kirkby & Co., William   W.K. & CO.
1879–85, general ceramics
  'K. & Co.', also used in   K. & CO.
  monogram form   printed or impressed

Knight, Elkin & Co.   K.E. & CO.
1826–46, earthenware
                             KNIGHT ELKIN
  printed initials with   & CO.
  variously designed
  backstamps   K. & E.

Knight, John King   J. K. KNIGHT
1846–53, earthenware   printed

Knight, Elkin & Bridgwood	K.E. & B.
c. 1829–40, earthenware	
marks printed	K.E.B.
Knight, Elkin & Knight	K.E. & K.
1841–4, earthenware	printed
Malkin, Ralph	R.M.
1863–81, earthenware	printed
Malkin & Sons, Ralph	R.M. & S.
1882–92, earthenware	printed
Moore & Co.	M. & CO.
1872–92, earthenware	impressed or printed
Moore, Leason & Co.	M.L. & CO.
1892–6, earthenware	printed in shield
	under crown
	or initials alone
	impressed or printed
Morley, Fox & Co. Ltd.	M.F. & CO.
1906–44, earthenware	printed

c. 1906–

'HOMELEIGHWARE', 1929–

Morley & Co. Ltd., William
1944–57, earthenware

Pratt & Co. (Ltd.), F. & R. *c.* 1818–, earthenware	F. & R.P.
	PRATT
'Co.' added 1840	F. & R.P. CO.
c. 1847–60	F. & R. PRATT & CO.
	FENTON
this firm is known	MANUFACTURER'S
to have made a great	TO H.R.H. PRINCE ALBERT
number of the popular	
printed pot-lids and	
similarly printed jugs,	
etc. *c.* 1850	FENTON

the firm was taken over in *c.* 1925
by Cauldon Potteries Ltd., who continue
original name together with their own

Pratt & Co., John 1872–8, earthenware	J.P. & CO. (L.) printed
Pratt, Hassall & Gerrard 1822–34, general ceramics	P.H.G P.H. & G. printed
Pratt & Simpson 1878–83, earthenware	P. & S. printed
Radford (Ltd.), Samuel 1879–1957, porcelain 'R.S.' monogram from about 1880, 'England' added 1891	

various 'S.R.' monograms
used during this century

Rainbow Pottery Co.   RAINBOW POTTERY
1931–41, earthenware   FENTON
                           MADE IN ENGLAND
                      printed or impressed

Reeves, James   J.R.   J.R.
   1870–1948, earthenware   F
   printed or impressed   J. REEVES

Rubian Art Pottery Ltd.   L.S. & G.
1906–33, earthenware
   impressed or printed   RUBAY ART WARE
   c. 1926–33

Sterling Pottery Ltd.
1947–53, earthenware

   other marks include:
   'RIDGWAY'   printed

Stubbs Bros.
1899–1904, bone-china
   printed

Victoria Porcelain (Fenton) Ltd.
1949–57, earthenware
   printed

Victoria & Trentham Potteries Ltd.
1957–60, general ceramics
   lion mark as above but includes new name

Wathen & Lichfield 1862–4, earthenware	W. & L. FENTON

Wathen, James, B. 1864–9, earthenware	J.B.W. J.B.W. F printed

Wileman, James & Charles 1864–9, general ceramics 'J. Wileman & Co.'	J. & C.W. J.F. & C.W. C.J.W. J.W. & CO.

Wileman, James F. 1869–92	J.F.W. J. F. WILEMAN

Wileman & Co.
1892–1925
   'SHELLEY' mark used
   from *c.* 1911

Wilson & Sons, J.
1898–1926, bone-china

printed

FOLEY (Staffordshire)
  Hawley & Co.   HAWLEY
  1842–87, earthenware   HAWLEY & CO.
                                      impressed

  Mayer, John   J.M.
  1833–41, earthenware   F
                                      printed

HANLEY (Staffordshire)
  Adams & Co., John   J. ADAMS & CO.
  1864–73, earthenwares and   ADAMS & CO.
  stonewares, etc.   impressed

  Adams & Bromley   A. & B.   A. & B.
  1873–86, earthenware   SHELTON
  stonewares, etc.   ADAMS & BROMLEY
                            printed or impressed

  Alcock, Lindley & Bloore (Ltd.)
  1919, earthenware
  (now Allied English Potteries)
    printed or impressed

  Art Pottery Co.   ART POTTERY CO.
  1900–11, earthenware   ENGLAND
    printed mark   (with crown)

  Ashworth & Bros. (Ltd.)
  1862–1970, earthenware   ASHWORTH
    1862–80   impressed
  (now Mason's Ironstone
  China Co. Ltd.)   A. BROS.
  Wedgwood Group from 1973
                    145

Ashworth & Bros.   G.L.A. & BROS.
    printed *c.* 1862–90
    with designs including
    pattern names
    From 1862 Ashworths used mark similar
    to that of Mason's 'Patent Ironstone'
(Mason's Ironstone China
Ltd. from 1968)
    'England' added 1891

    printed mark from
    about 1880

    'LUSTROSA' trade-name
    1932–

    printed on ironstone
    c. 1957–

Baddeley, Thomas   T. BADDELEY
1800–34, engraver of   HANLEY
plates for transfer-prints   printed

Baddeley, William   EASTWOOD
1802–22, 'Wedgwood-   impressed
type' ware

Bakewell Bros. Ltd.   BAKEWELL BROS.
1927-43, earthenware   LTD.
    printed

146

Bates, Brown-Westhead & Moore 1859–61, general ceramics	B.B.W. & M. printed or impressed
Baxter, John Denton 1823–7, earthenware	I.D.B. J.D.B. printed
Bednall & Heath 1879–99, earthenware	B. & H. printed
Bennett & Co., J. 1896–1900, earthenware	J.B. & CO. printed or impressed
Bennett (Hanley) Ltd., William 1882–1937 earthenwares	W.B. H printed or impressed
Bevington, James & Thomas 1865–78, porcelains	J. & T.B. impressed
Bevington & Co., John 1869–71, earthenware printed in backstamp	J.B. & CO. H

Bevington, John
1872–92, porcelains

This mark was   underglaze-blue
obviously adopted to
imitate that of Meissen on pieces made in
'Dresden' style

Bevington, Thomas
1877–91, general ceramics

printed

Birch & Whitehead
c. 1796, 'Wedgwood type'
wares

B. & W.
impressed

Bishop & Stonier
1891–1939, general
ceramics

B. & S.
printed or impressed

printed marks
1891–
'England' added
on fully named
marks from *c.* 1899–

1936–9

BISHOP
ENGLAND

Blue John Pottery Ltd.
1939, earthenware

various 'Blue John'
printed marks

Booth, G. R.	PUBLISHED BY
1829–44, earthenware	G. R. BOOTH & CO.
'& Co.' added *c.* 1839	HANLEY
impressed mark	STAFFORDSHIRE

Booth & Colcloughs Ltd.   various marks
1948–54, general ceramics   including
(see Ridgway Potteries Ltd.)   name
  also trade-names:
  'Blue Mist', 'Malvern Chinaware'
  and 'Royal Swan'

Bourne, Samuel   S. BOURNE
early 18th century   impressed
pottery figures

Bournemouth Pottery Co.   BOURNEMOUTH
(Bournemouth, 1945–52)   POTTERY
Hanley 1952–, earthenware   ENGLAND

Boyle, Zachariah   BOYLE
1823–50, general
ceramics
  '& S.' added from   Z.B.   Z.B. & S.
  1828

Brown-Westhead, Moore & Co.   B.W.M.
1862–1904
general ceramics   B.W.M. & CO.

                  printed or impressed

impressed

T. C. BROWN
WESTHEAD-MOORE
& CO.

printed or impressed
1891–

later marks include
initials & 'CAULDON'

Bullers Ltd.
c. 1937–55, earthenware

BULLERS MADE
IN ENGLAND
painted

Bullock & Co., A.
1895–1915, earthenware

A.B. & CO. H.
A.B. & CO.
printed or impressed

Burgess, Thomas
1903–17, earthenware
(mark of Harrop & Burgess
was continued)

printed or impressed

Burton, Samuel & John
1832–45, earthenware

S. & J.B.
impressed on
applied tablet

Cauldon Ltd.
1905–20, general ceramics

CAULDON
ENGLAND
printed under crown

marks previously used by Ridgway
and Brown—Westhead, Moore & Co., used
with addition of 'CAULDON'

150

Cauldon Potteries, Ltd.　ROYAL CAULDON
1920–62, general ceramics　ENGLAND
　　　　　　　　　　　EST. 1774

    similar printed marks used from 1930–62,
    when factory was taken over by
Pountney & Co. Ltd. of Bristol (now
Cauldon Bristol Potteries Ltd., Redruth, Cornwall)

Ceramic Art Co. Ltd.　THE CERAMIC ART
1892–1903, decorators　CO. LTD. HANLEY
　　　　　　　　　　　STAFFORDSHIRE
　　　　　　　　　　　ENGLAND
　　　　　　　　　　　printed

Clementson, Joseph　　　J.C.
c. 1839–64, earthenware　J. CLEMENTSON
　　　　　　　　　　　printed

Clementson Bros.　CLEMENTSON BROS.
1865–1916, earthenware　with Royal Arms
and stoneware
    printed 1867–80
    various fully named printed marks with
    phoenix from 1870–
    'Ltd.' added 1910

　　　　　　　　　　　CLEMENTSON BROS.
    printed, 1913–16　　　ENGLAND
　　　　　　　　　　　under crown

Clementson, Young & Jameson　C.Y. & J.
1844, earthenware

Clementson & Young　CLEMENTSON &
1845–7, earthenware　　YOUNG
　　　　　　　　　　　impressed or printed

Coalbrook Potteries 1937–, decorative wares printed–	COALBROOK MADE IN ENGLAND
Coopers Art Pottery Co. *c.* 1912–58, earthenware	ART POTTERY CO. ENGLAND with crown

Cotton, Ltd., Elijah
1880–, earthenware
   Trade-names: 'NELSON WARE', *c.* 1913–;
   'LORD NELSON WARE', 1956–
	various fully-
	named marks

Creyke & Sons, G. M.
1920–48, earthenware
   initials also used in
   monogram form
   Trade-name 'BROADWAY'
   c. 1935–
	G.M.C.
	printed or impressed

Davenport, Banks & Co.
1860–73, earthenware
 	
   impressed or printed
   marks
	D.B. & CO.
	
	DAVENPORT
	BANKS & CO.
	ETRURIA

Davenport, Beck & Co. 1873–80, earthenware	D.B. & CO.
Davis, J. Heath 1881–91, earthenware	J. H. DAVIS HANLEY

Diamond Pottery Co. Ltd.   D.P. CO.
1908–35, earthenware   D.P. CO. LTD.
                                     printed

Dimmock (Junr.) & Co., Thomas   D.
1828–59, earthenware

    impressed or printed
    'double D' monogram

Dimmock & Co., J.   J.D. & CO.
1862–1904, earthenware

firm taken over by

W. D. Cliff in *c.* 1878–
    'Cliff' used in varying   CLIFF
    forms *c.* 1878–1904   ENGLAND

    written on ribbon   ALBION WORKS
    under 'lion rampant'   printed

Dudson, James   DUDSON
1838–88, earthenware   impressed
(this firm made many
'Spaniels' and 'Rockingham-type' dogs)

Dudson, J. T.   J. DUDSON
1888–98, earthenwares
and stonewares   J. DUDSON
    'England' added 1891   ENGLAND
                                   impressed

Dudson Bros., Ltd.
1898–, earthenwares and
stonewares

    printed mark, 1936–45

DUDSON ENGLAND

Dudson, Wilcox & Till, Ltd.
1902–26, earthenware
    printed or impressed,
    figure of Britannia also
    used within double-ring
    with full name of firm

Dura Porcelain Co. Ltd.
1919–21, porcelain

    printed mark

Ellis, Unwin & Mountford
1860–61, earthenware

E.U. & M.
printed

Fancies Fayre Pottery
c. 1946, earthenware
    Trade-name 'KNICK
      KNACKS'
(now Bairstow & Co.)

STAFFORDSHIRE
F.F.
ENGLAND
printed or impressed

Fenton & Sons, Alfred
1887–1901, general
ceramics

A.F. & S.
impressed or printed
(also written within
circular crowned strap)

154

Fletcher, Thomas
c. 1786–1810, printer and
decorator

T. FLETCHER
SHELTON

Ford, Charles
1874–1904, porcelain

impressed
or printed

   'Swan' mark, impressed
   or printed, *c.* 1900–4

Ford, T. & C.
1854–71, earthenware
   impressed or printed
   marks

T. & C.F.

Ford, Thomas
1871–4, porcelain

   numerals indicate
   month and year, e.g.
   JULY, 1872

impressed or printed

Ford & Pointon Ltd.
1917–36, porcelain
(absorbed by Cauldon
c. 1921)

Furnival, Jacob & Thomas
c. 1843, earthenware

J. & T.F.
printed under
Royal Arms

Furnival & Co., Thomas
c. 1844–6, earthenware

T.F. & CO.
printed

Futura Art Pottery Ltd.
1947–56, earthenware

FUTURA
ART POTTERY LTD.
printed

Gelson Bros.
1867–76, earthenware

GELSON BROS.
HANLEY
printed

Glass, John
c. 1784–1838, earthenware
and stoneware

GLASS HANLEY
J. GLASS HANLEY
impressed

Glass, Joseph
c. 1700, slipwares

JOSEPH GLASS

Goldscheider (Staffordshire) Pottery Ltd.
1946–59, figures in
pottery and porcelain

Goldscheider
printed

Gray & Co. Ltd., A. E.
1912–61, earthenware
(known as 'Portmeirion
Potteries Ltd.' from 1962)
moved to Stoke in 1934

printed mark
1934–61

various printed marks
depicting ships with
factory name

Grimwade Bros.
1886–1900, earthenware

G. Bros.
on star within
circle

Grimwades Ltd.
1900–, earthenware
printed mark, *c.* 1900–

STOKE POTTERY

many various fully named marks including
name or trade-name:
'WINTON' *c.* 1906, 'RUBIAN ART' *c.* 1906–,
'VITRO HOTEL WARE' *c.* 1930, 'ROYAL
WINTON IVORY' *c.* 1930, 'ATLAS' *c.* 1934–9

Hackwood & Co.
1807–27, earthenware and
stoneware

H. & CO.
HACKWOOD & CO.
impressed

Hackwood, William
1827–43, earthenware
impressed or printed

W.H.
HACKWOOD
printed or impressed

Hackwood & Keeling
1835–6, earthenware

H. & K.
printed

Hall, Samuel
c. 1840–56, earthenware

HALL
impressed

Hall & Read
1883–8, earthenware
'H. & R.' also probably
used

HALL & READ
HANLEY
printed

Hammersley, J. & R.
1877–1917, general ceramics

J.R.H.
printed

Hanley Porcelain Co.
1892–99, porcelain

printed

Hanley China Co.
1899–1901, porcelain
   printed

H
C C°.
in knot

Harrop & Burgess
1894–1903, earthenware

printed

Heath, J.
c. 1770–1800, earthenware

I.H.

HEATH
impressed

Heath, Joshua
c. 1740, earthenware

JOSHUA HEATH
incised

Hollins, T. J. & R.
c. 1818–22, earthenware

T.J. & R. HOLLINS
impressed

Johnson Bros. (Hanley) Ltd.
1883–, earthenware
   impressed or printed
   name with various
   coat-of-arms, crowns,
   etc.
(now part of Wedgwood Group)

JOHNSON BROS.
ENGLAND

Johnson Bros
England.

Jones & Son
c. 1826–8, earthenware

JONES & SON
printed

Keeling, Joseph
c. 1802–8, earthenware and
stoneware

JOSEPH KEELING
impressed

Keeling & Co., Samuel
1840–50, earthenware

S.K. & CO.

S. KEELING & CO.
printed

Keeling, Toft & Co.
1805–26, stonewares
in Wedgwood style

KEELING & TOFT

KEELING, TOFT & CO.
impressed

Kensington Fine Art Pottery Co.
1892–9, earthenware

printed or impressed

Lancaster & Sons
1900–44, earthenware
  '& Sons' & 'Ltd.' added
    c. 1906
    c. 1920–

L. & SONS LTD.
HANLEY. ENG.

'ROYALL & LANSAN' 1930–
'BRITISH CROWN WARE', *c.* 1935–
'CROWN DRESDEN WARE', *c.* 1935–

c. 1934–44

LANCASTERS LTD.
HANLEY. ENGLAND

Lancaster & Sandland Ltd.
1944–1968, earthenware

BRITISH
CROWN WARE

many various printed
marks including name
'SANDLAND'

CROWN DRESDEN WARE

SANDLAND
STAFFORDSHIRE
ENGLAND

Langdale Pottery Co. Ltd.
1947–58, earthenware
printed

Langdale
MADE IN ENGLAND

Lear, Samuel
1877–86, general ceramics

LEAR
impressed

Livesley, Powell & Co.
1851–66, earthenware
and stoneware

LIVESLEY POWELL
& CO.
L.P. & CO.
impressed or printed

Powell & Bishop
1867–1878, general
ceramics

P. & B.
POWELL & BISHOP
printed or impressed

Powell, Bishop & Stonier
1878–91, general
ceramics

P.B. & S.
printed or impressed

'Chinaman' mark first
registered 1880, but
continued by Bishop
& Stonier

Bishop & Stonier
1891–1939, general ceramics
full name printed in
various designs, 1899–1936
'Bishop' only used 1936–9

B. & S.

BISHOP & STONIER

Lloyd, J. & R.
c. 1834–52, 'Staffordshire
figures'

LLOYD SHELTON
impressed

Lockett, Baguley &
Cooper, 1855–60, porcelain

LOCKETT BAGULEY
& COOPER

Lockitt, William H.
1901–19, earthenware
'DURA-WARE' 1913–19

W.H.L.
H
printed in crescent

Mann & Co.
1858–60, general ceramics

MANN & CO.
HANLEY
printed

Manzoni, Carlo
c. 1895–8, studio pottery

incised mark including
date

Mayer, Elijah
c. 1790–1804, various
Wedgwood-type wares

E. MAYER
impressed

Mayer & Son, Elijah
1805–34
Wedgwood-type wares

E. MAYER & SON
impressed or printed

Mayer & Co., Joseph
c. 1822–33, earthenware

JOSEPH MAYER & CO.
HANLEY

MAYER & CO.

Meakin, Charles
1883–9, earthenware

CHARLES MEAKIN
HANLEY
under Royal Arms

Meakin (Ltd.), J. & G.
1851–, earthenwares
(now part of Wedgwood
Group)
1890–

J. & G. MEAKIN
impressed or printed

'ENGLAND' added from
1891
'Sun-face' marks from
1912–
'PASTEL VITRESOL'
'STUDIO WARE' and 'SOUTH
SEAS' recent trade-names

printed

Meigh, Job
c. 1805–34, earthenware
'Son' added *c.* 1812

MEIGH
impressed
OLD HALL
impressed or printed
J.M. & S.

Meigh, Charles
1835–49, earthenware and
stonewares

CHARLES MEIGH
impressed
G.M.
printed with device
and pattern name

printed or impressed marks of various
bodies and styles of decoration include:
'Indian Stone China', 'French China',
'Improved Stone China', 'Enamel Porcelain'

Meigh, Son & Pankhurst,
Charles, 1850–51, earthenware

C.M.S. & P.
printed

Meigh & Son, Charles
1851–61, earthenware

C.M. & S.

many of the marks
used by this firm
include the Royal
Arms

M. & S.

C. MEIGH & SON

MEIGH'S
CHINA

printed or impressed

OPAQUE
PORCELAIN

Old Hall Earthenware Co Ltd.
1861–86

O.H.E.C.

printed

O.H.E.C.(L.)

printed or impressed

mark registered in 1884 and
continued by Old Hall
Porcelain Works Ltd.
printed

Old Hall Porcelain Works (as above)
Ltd., 1886–1902, general
ceramics

Mills, Henry   H. MILLS
c. 1892, earthenware   printed

Moore & Co.   M. & CO.
1898–1903, earthenware   printed with name
                                             of pattern

Morley & Co., Francis   F.M.
1845–58, earthenware

late form of Masons'   F.M. & CO.
Ironstone mark used
from 1845   F. MORLEY & CO.
                                        printed with many
                                        various backstamps

Morley & Ashworth   M. & A.
1859–62, earthenware   MORLEY &
   impressed or printed   ASHWORTH
   with pattern name   HANLEY

164

Neale & Co., James *c.* 1776–*c.* 86, all manner of wares in Wedgwood style	N NEALE I. NEALE I. NEALE. HANLEY
'& Co.' added *c.* 1778	NEALE & CO. impressed
Neale & Bailey *c.* 1790–1814, earthenware	NEALE & BAILEY printed or impressed
Neale, Harrison & Co. 1875–85, general ceramics	N.H. & CO. printed
Neale & Palmer *c.* 1769–76, earthenwares in Wedgwood style	NEALE & PALMER impressed
Neale & Wilson *c.* 1784–95, earthenware and Wedgwood-type wares	NEALE & WILSON NEALE & CO. impressed

New Hall Porcelain Works
1781–1835, hard-paste
porcelain 1781–*c.* 1812
bone-china, *c.* 1812–35

printed on bone-china

New Hall Pottery Co. Ltd.
1899–1956, earthenware

  printed, *c.* 1930–51

New Pearl Pottery Co. Ltd.
1936–41, earthenware,
'Royal Bourbon Ware'

PEARL POTTERY CO.
printed

Palmer, Humphrey
c. 1760–78, earthenware
and Wedgwood-type
stonewares

PALMER

impressed

Pankhurst & Co., J. W.
1850–82, earthenware
   '& Co.' added *c.* 1852

J.W.P.

J. W. PANKHURST

Pearl Pottery Co. Ltd.
1894–1936, earthenware
   1894–1912

PP

printed or impressed

   printed in various
   forms, 1912–36

P.P. CO. LTD.

Physick & Cooper
1899–1900, earthenware

P. & C.
over crown

Art Pottery Co.
1900–11, earthenware

ART POTTERY CO.
over crown

Coopers Art Pottery Co.
c. 1912–58, earthenware

printed as above

Podmore China Co.
1921–41, porcelain

'P.C. CO.' monogram
under crown

Pointon & Co. Ltd.
1883–1916, porcelain

POINTONS
STOKE-ON-TRENT
printed with coat-
of-arms

Poole, Richard
1790–5, earthenware

R. POOLE
impressed

Ratcliffe, William
c. 1831–40, earthenware

R
HACKWOOD
printed or impressed

printed in underglaze blue

Ridgway, Job
c. 1802–8, earthenware

R   J.R.
printed
(J.R. also used by
John Ridgway)

Ridgway & Sons, Job
c. 1808–14, earthenware

RIDGWAY & SONS
impressed or printed

Ridgway, John & William
1814–*c.* 1830

J.W.R.   J. & W.R.
J. & W. RIDGWAY
printed or impressed

Ridgway & Co., John c. 1830–55, general ceramics	JOHN RIDGWAY J.R.
	JHN RIDGWAY
printed or impressed marks usually including name of pattern	I. RIDGWAY '& CO.' added *c.* 1841
Ridgway, Bates & Co., J. 1856–58, general ceramics	J.R.B. & CO. printed
Bates, Brown-Westhead & Moore, 1859–61, general ceramics	B.B.W. & M. printed or impressed
Brown-Westhead, Moore & Co. 1862–1904, general ceramics	*see p.* 149
Cauldon Ltd. 1905–20, general ceramics	*see p.* 150
Cauldon Potteries Ltd. 1920–62, general ceramics	*see p.* 151
Ridgway & Robey c. 1837–9, figures marks very rare	RIDGWAY & ROBEY HANLEY STAFFORDSHIRE POTTERIES
Ridgway, Morley, Wear & Co., 1836–42 earthenware	R.M.W. & CO. RIDGWAY, MORLEY WEAR & CO. printed

Ridgway & Morley	R. & M.
1842–44, earthenware	RIDGWAY & MORLEY
	printed
Ridgway & Abington	E. RIDGWAY & ABINGTON
c. 1835–60, earthenware	HANLEY
	impressed
Ridgway, Son & Co.,	W.R.S. & CO.
William, *c.* 1838–48	W. RIDGWAY, SON
	& CO. HANLEY
	printed
Ridgway, Sparks & Ridgway	R.S.R.
1873–79, earthenware	also printed in
	'Staffordshire knot'

Ridgways
1879–20
   mark of 1880–

   'RIDGWAYS' and 'ENGLAND' in various
   marks from *c.* 1905–20
   RIDGWAYS (BEDFORD WORKS) LTD.
   1920–52, earthenware
   'RIDGWAYS' and/or 'BEDFORD' in variety
   of marks used from 1920–52
This firm became 'Ridgway & Adderley Ltd.'
in 1952, Ridgway, Adderley, Booths &
Colcloughs Ltd.' from 1955 and in same year
'Ridgway Potteries Ltd.'
(part of Allied English Potteries, Ltd.
from 1952, now Royal Doulton Group)

name of American firm, John R. Roth & Co. seen on some Ridgway exports, *c.* 1930–56	JONROTH J.H.R. & CO. monogram printed
Rigby & Stevenson 1894–1954, earthenware	R. & S. printed
Rivers, William *c.* 1818–22, earthenware	RIVERS impressed
Robinson & Wood 1832–6, earthenware	R. & W. printed
Salt, Ralph *c.* 1820–46, earthenware	'SALT' impressed on scroll
Sandlands & Colley, Ltd. 1907–1910, general ceramics	full name & 's.c.' monogram printed under crown
Scrivener & Co., R. G. 1870–83, general ceramics	R.G.S.
printed or impressed	R.G.S. & CO.

Sherwin & Cotton
1877–30, tiles
impressed

Shorthose & Co.
c. 1817–1822

SHORTHOSE & CO.
written
impressed or printed

Shorthose & Heath
c. 1795–1815, earthenware

SHORTHOSE &
HEATH
impressed or printed

Shorthose, John
1807–23, earthenware

S

　impressed marks

SHORTHOSE

Sneyd & Hill
c. 1845, earthenware
　printed

SNEYD & HILL
HANLEY
STAFFORDSHIRE
POTTERIES

Sneyd, Thomas
1846–7, earthenware

T. SNEYD
HANLEY
impressed

Stevenson, William
c. 1802, earthenware
　rare impressed mark

W. STEVENSON
HANLEY

Swinnertons Ltd.
1906–71, earthenware
(Allied English Potteries)
Ltd.), mark printed
　c. 1906–17, later marks all include
　full-name of firm

Sylvan Pottery Ltd.
1946–, earthenware

　'B' included in mark
　prior to 1948

SWINNERTONS
HANLEY

Studio Szeiler, Ltd.
c. 1951–, earthenware

printed or impressed

Taylor, George   G. TAYLOR
c. 1784–1811, earthenware   GEO. TAYLOR

impressed or incised

Taylor, Tunnicliffe & Co.   T.T.
1868–, general ceramics   T.T. & CO.
(now electrical &   printed
industrial wares only)

Thomas & Co., Uriah
1888–1905, earthenware

printed or impressed

Toft, James (*b.* 1673)   James Toft
Ralph (*b.* 1638),   Ralph Toft
Thomas (*d.* 1689), slipware   Thomas Toft

Unwin, Mountford &   U.M. & T.
Taylor, *c.* 1864, earthenware   printed

Unwin, Holmes &   U.H. & W.
Worthington, *c.* 1865–8   printed
earthenware

Upper Hanley Pottery Co.   U.H.P. CO.
c. 1895–1902, then at   ENGLAND
Cobridge until 1910
earthenware   impressed or printed
   'Ltd.' from 1900

172

Wardle & Co.
1871–1910, earthenware
Wardle Art Pottery Co. Ltd.
1910–1935, earthenware

WARDLE
impressed

printed, *c.* 1885–90

printed, *c.* 1890–1935

Wardle & Ash
1859–62, earthenware

W. & A.
impressed

Weatherby & Sons, Ltd.
1891–, earthenware
  c. 1925–

J.H.W. & SONS

FALCON WARE

  c. 1936–, (trade-name)

WEATHERBY WARE
printed

Wellington Pottery Co.
1899–1901, earthenware

printed or impressed

Westminster Pottery Ltd.
1948–56, earthenware

  1952–, (trade-name)

CASTLECLIFFE WARE

173

Whittaker & Co.　　　　　　w. & co.
1886–92, earthenware　　　printed

Whittaker, Heath & Co.　　w.h. & co.
1892–8, earthenware　　　printed

Wilson, Robert　　　　　　WILSON
1795–1801, earthenware

　impressed marks

Wilson, David　　　　　　WILSON
c. 1802–18, general ceramics　impressed

Winkle & Wood
1885–90, earthenware

　　　　　　　　　　　printed

Worthington & Harrop　　w. & h.
1856–73, earthenware　　　printed

Wulstan Pottery Co. Ltd.
c. 1940–58, earthenware

　printed

Yates, John　　　　　　　J.Y.
c. 1784–1835, earthenware

　　　　printed or impressed

LANE DELPH (Staffordshire)
Edge, William & Samuel
1841–8, earthenware

W. & S.E.
printed

Harrison, George
c. 1790–5, earthenware

G. Harrison
impressed

Mason, William
c. 1811–24, earthenware

W. MASON
printed

Mason, Miles
c. 1792–1816, porcelain
  marks impressed *c.* 1800–16

M. MASON
    MILES MASON

printed mark on
chinoiserie patterns

Mason, G. M. & C. J.
1813–29, earthenware
(ironstone)

G.M. & C.J. MASON

G. & C.J.M.

impressed marks
c. 1813–25

MASON'S PATENT
IRONSTONE CHINA

patented in 1813

PATENT IRONSTONE
CHINA

standard mark of
c. 1820, continued by
  Ashworth (*c.* 1862)
'Mason's Ironstone China
Ltd.' from 1968–
(a Division of Josiah
Wedgwood & Sons Ltd., 1974)

printed mark with
pattern number *c.* 1825–

Mason & Co., Charles
James, 1829–45,
earthenware, (ironstone)
printed

FENTON
STONE WORKS
C.J.M. & CO.
GRANITE CHINA

printed

C.J. MASON & CO.
LANE DELPH

c. 1840–

'MASON'S CAMBRIAN ARGIL',
'MASON'S BANDANA WARE'
impressed or printed
c. 1825–40

Mason, Charles James
c. 1845–8, earthenware
(ironstone), also at
Longton, 1851–4

printed
F.M.

Morley & Co., Francis
1845–58, earthenware
(Hanley)

F.M. & CO.
F. MORLEY & CO.

Morley & Ashworth
1859–62, earthenware
(Hanley)

M. & A.
impressed or printed

Myatt, late 18th- early 19th centuries, earthenware	MYATT impressed
Pratt, William *c.* 1780–99, earthenware	PRATT

LANE END (Staffordshire)

Abbott, Andrew *c.* 1781–3, earthenware	ABBOTT POTTER impressed
Abbott & Mist 1787–1810, earthenware	ABBOTT & MIST impressed or painted
Aynsley, John 1780–1809, engraver of prints for earthenwares	'*J. Aynsley Lane End*' printed
Barker, John, Richard & William, *c.* 1800 earthenware	BARKER impressed
Batkin, Walker & Broadhurst, 1840–5, earthenware	B.W. & B. printed
Booth & Sons 1830–5, earthenware	BOOTH & SONS impressed
Bott & Co. *c.* 1810–11, earthenware	BOTT & CO. impressed

Carey, Thomas & John
c. 1823–42, earthenware

CAREYS
impressed or
printed with anchor

Chesworth & Robinson
1825–40, earthenware

C. & R.
printed

Chetham & Woolley
1796–1810, earthenware

CHETHAM &
WOOLLEY
LANE END
incised

Cyples, Joseph
c. 1784–1840
    (initials of various
    potters in this family
    rarely used)

CYPLES

I. CYPLES
impressed

Deakin & Son
1833–41, earthenware
    printed mark

Everard, Glover &
Colclough, *c*. 1847–
general ceramics

E.G. & C.
printed

Floyd, Benjamin
c. 1843, earthenware

B.F.
printed

Goodwin, Bridgwood &
Orton, 1827–9
earthenware

G.B.O.
G.B. & O.

Goodwin, Bridgwood & Harris   G.B.H.
1829–31, earthenware

Goodwins & Harris   GOODWINS &
c. 1831–8, earthenware   HARRIS
                                     printed

Griffiths, Beardmore &   G.B. & B.
Birks, 1830, earthenware   printed

Harley, Thomas   HARLEY
1802–8, earthenware   T. HARLEY
                                     impressed

printed or written

                                     T. HARLEY
                                     LANE END

Harvey, Bailey & Co.   H.B. & CO.
1833–5, earthenware   printed

Heathcote & Co., Charles   C. HEATHCOTE & CO.
1818–24, earthenware   printed

Hilditch & Son
1822–30, general ceramics

  printed in various
  surrounds

Hulme & Sons, John   HULME & SONS
c. 1828–30, earthenware   printed

Lockett, J. & G.
c. 1802–5, earthenware

J. & G. LOCKETT
impressed

Lockett, John
1821–58, earthenware

J. LOCKETT
impressed

Lockett & Co., J.
c. 1812–89, earthenware
(also at Longton 1882–
1960, and 1960– Burslem)

J. LOCKETT & CO.
impressed
or
printed

Lockett & Hulme
1822–6, earthenware

L. & H.
L.E.
printed

Mayer & Newbold
c. 1817–33, general ceramics

M. & N.

marks painted or
printed

MAY^R & NEWB^D

Plant, Benjamin
c. 1780–1820, earthenware
marks incised

Plant, Thomas
1825–50, earthenware

T P
painted

Ray, George, modeller
early 19th century

G. RAY
Lane End

Turner, John (also entered under Longton) *c.* 1762–1806, earthenware and porcelain	TURNER I. TURNER
early impressed marks	
printed or impressed from 1784 after Turner was potter to the Prince of Wales	 **TURNER**
impressed, *c.* 1780–6 1803–6	TURNER & CO.
painted on earthenwares 1800–5	*Turner's Patent*
Turner & Abbott *c.* 1783–7 (Abbott probably only agent) earthenwares and stoneware in Wedgwood style	TURNER & ABBOTT impressed

LONGPORT (Staffordshire)

Bodley & Son, E. F. 1881–98, earthenware	E.F.B. & SON
trade-mark, 1883–98	

Bourne, Edward
1790–1811, earthenware

E. BOURNE
impressed

Corn, W. & E.
1864–1904, earthenware
(also at Burslem *c.* 1864–
1904, nearly all marks
  are late and include 'ENGLAND' (post-1891)

W. & E.C.

W.E.C.

Davenport & Co., W.
c. 1793–1887, general
ceramics; 1798–1815

Davenport

c. 1815–60
  'Davenport' or 'DAVENPORT'
  is impressed with or
  without anchor

DAVENPORT

marks on 'Stone-China'
c. 1815–30

19th century mark to
about 1860, including
last two numerals of
year
  anchor mark alone *c.* 1820–40

many printed wares of 1820–60 bear
name of pattern and 'DAVENPORT'

182

printed on porcelain   DAVENPORT
c. 1815–   LONGPORT
three numerals denote month and last
two numerals of year made
'Manufacturers of China to His Majesty
and the Royal Family' on porcelain
c. 1830–37

                    DAVENPORT
impressed *c.* 1850–70   PATENT

printed in underglaze-blue
c. 1850–70
(sometimes in enamel
colours prior to 1830)

This mark was used   DAVENPORT
from *c.* 1830–45 in puce   LONGPORT
and from *c.* 1870–87   STAFFORDSHIRE
in red   printed under crown

printed on earthenware   DAVENPORTS LTD.
c. 1881–7

Liddle, Elliott & Son   L.E. & S.
1862–71, general   impressed or printed
ceramics

Mayer & Elliott
1858–61, earthenware
   number of month and   M & E
   last two numerals of year   printed

impressed, e.g. $\frac{6}{59}$ = June, 1859

Phillips, Edward & George 1822–34, earthenware	PHILLIPS LONGPORT
printed marks	E. & G.P.
Phillips, George 1834–48, earthenware name with or without knot, sometimes 'Longport' also	PHILLIPS
Rogers, John & George *c.* 1784–1814, earthenware	ROGERS J.R.
impressed marks	L.
Rogers & Son, John *c.* 1814–36, earthenware	as above and J.R.S. ROGERS & SON
Smith, Ltd., W. T. H. 1898–1905, earthenware	W.T.H. SMITH & CO. LONGPORT printed with 'globe'
Wood & Son (Longport) Ltd., 1928–, earthenware 'ROYAL BRADWELL ART WARE' trade-name	ARTHUR WOOD full name printed in variety of marks
Wood, Arthur 1904–28, earthenware mark impressed or printed	A.W. L ENGLAND

LONGTON HALL (Staffordshire)
  c. 1749–60, porcelain
    rare marks painted in
    underglaze blue

LONGTON (Staffordshire)

Adams & Co. Harvey
1870–85, general ceramics

H.A. & CO.
over crown
printed

Adams & Cooper
1850–77, porcelain

A. & C.
printed

Adderleys Ltd.
1906–, general ceramics

  printed mark 1906–26
  many other marks all
  including full name of firm

Adderley, J. Fellows
1901–5, porcelain

  printed marks

J.F.A.

Adderley, William Alsager
1876–1905

  and 'sailing-ship' trade-
  mark as above

W.A.A.

W.A.A. & CO.

185

Adderley Floral China Works
1945– bone-china
decorative wares
　printed mark
(Royal Doulton Group
from 1973)

Aldridge & Co.
1919–49, earthenware

ALDRIDGE & CO.
LONGTON
impressed

Allerton & Sons, Charles
1859–1942, general
ceramics
　printed or impressed
　marks, *c.* 1890–1942
　Many other fully named
　marks also used

C.A. & SONS

CHAS. ALLERTON &
SONS
ENGLAND

Alton China Co. Ltd.
1950–7, bone-china

ALTON
BONE CHINA
printed

Amison, Charles
1889–1962, porcelain
　impressed initials, 1889–

C.A.
L.

　printed mark of 1906–30
　'& Co.' added 1916
　'& Co. Ltd.', 1930

　further late marks include
　'Stanley' and 'Staffordshire
　Floral Bone China'

Anchor Porcelain Co. Ltd.   A.P. CO.
1901–18, porcelain
  impressed marks   A.P. CO. L.

impressed or printed
'anchor-mark', 1901–15
'ROYAL WESTMINSTER CHINA' printed
with 'A.P. CO. L.', 1915–18

Aristocrat Florals & Fancies
1958–, bone-china decorative
wares (Wedgwood Group
from 1973)

Asbury & Co.   ASBURY
1875–1925, general ceramics   LONGTON
  printed marks

                A. & CO.

Avon Art Pottery
1930–69, earthenware
  recent mark, printed
(seemingly merged with
Elektra Porcelain Co., 1962)

Aynsley & Co., H.   H.A. & CO.
1873–, earthenware   L.
  'Ltd.' added 1932
  late marks include
  name in full

Aynsley & Sons, John   AYNSLEY
1864–, porcelain   impressed
    various later marks include full name and
    'ENGLAND' added from 1891
(now Aynsley China Ltd.–Waterford Glass Co.
Ltd.)

Baddeley, William   EASTWOOD
1802–22, earthenware   impressed
(Wedgwood-type)

Baggerley & Ball   B. & B.
1822–36, earthenware   L.
    printed in blue
    within oval frame

Bailey & Sons, William
1912–14, earthenware
    printed mark

Bailey & Batkin   BAILEY & BATKIN
1814–*c*. 27, earthenware
including lustreware
    marks impressed or moulded   B. & B.

Bailey & Harvey   BAILEY & HARVEY
1834–5, earthenware   impressed
including lustre

Balfour China Co. Ltd.   BALFOUR
1947–52, bone-china   ROYAL CROWN
(then known as: POTTERY
Trentham Bone China   printed with crown
Ltd.)

Barker Bros. Ltd.   B.B.
1876–, general ceramics   impressed
   large variety of other printed marks
   including such trade names as:
   MEIR CHINA, MEIR WARE, TUDOR WARE
   and ROYAL TUDOR WARE
(Alfred Clough Ltd.)

Barlow & Son Ltd., T. W.   B. B. & S.
1882–1940, earthenware   rare impressed
                                                       marks
   marks used from about 1928 include
   'CORONATION WARE'

Barlow, Thomas   B.
1849–1882, general ceramics   impressed

Barlows (Longton) Ltd.   B. Ltd.
1920–52, earthenware   impressed
   later marks include 'MELBAR WARE'

Baxter, Rowley & Tams   B.R. & T.
1882–5, porcelain   impressed

Beardmore & Edwards   B. & E.
1856–8, earthenware   printed

Bentley & Co. Ltd., G. L.   G.L.B. & CO.
1898–1912, porcelain   LONGTON
   'Ltd.' added from 1904

Beswick & Son　　　　　　　　　B. & S.
1916–30, porcelain　　　printed or impressed
　'ALDWYCH CHINA', trade-name also used by
　Bridgett & Bates, former prop's.

Beswick Ltd., John　　　　　　BESWICK
1936–, earthenware　　　　　ENGLAND
(Royal Doulton Group 1973)　printed

Blackhurst & Hulme　　　　　　B. & H.
1890–1932, porcelain
　early mark of printed
　initials, later full　　　　THE BELGRAVE
　mark used from *c.* 1914　　　CHINA
　　　　　　　　　　　　　　B. & H.
　　　　　　　　　　　　　　L
　　　　　　　　　　　　ENGLAND

Blair & Co.
1880–1930, porcelain
　'Ltd.' added *c.* 1912
　(LONGTON) added *c.* 1923
　early impressed 'B'
　up until about 1900
　'BLAIRS CHINA, ENGLAND'
　impressed or printed
　c. 1900–
　printed mark of *c.* 1900–

Blyth Porcelain Co. Ltd.　　B.P. CO. LTD.
c. 1905–35, porcelain　　　printed in
　'DIAMOND CHINA'　　　varying forms
　also used from *c.* 1913

Boulton & Co.   B. & CO. B. & CO.
1892–1902, porcelain   L
           printed or impressed

Bradbury, Anderson & Bettanny B.A. & B.
1844–52, general ceramics   printed

Bradley, F. D.   BRADLEY
1876–96, porcelain   impressed

Bradleys (Longton) Ltd.   BRADLEYS
1922–41, porcelain   LONGTON
  mark printed with crown   MADE IN
               ENGLAND

Bridgett & Bates   B. & B.
1882–1915, porcelain   impressed or printed
  'ALDWYCH CHINA' trade-name from *c.* 1912

Bridgett, Bates & Beech
1875–82
  printed or impressed mark

Bridgwood & Son Ltd.,   BRIDGWOOD & SON
Sampson, 1805–, earthenware
(porcelain until *c.* 1887)

               S. BRIDGWOOD &
  impressed or printed marks   SON
  from *c.* 1850–
              S.B. & S.

other various printed marks include
full name of firm or initials

'Parisian Granite' mark
c. 1870–, printed

Britannia China Company
1895–1906, porcelain

B.C. CO.
impressed

other fully-named marks
also used
1904–6

printed or impressed

British Anchor Pottery Co. Ltd.
1884–, earthenware
(from 1971, Hostess Tableware Ltd.)
    printed or impressed
    1884–*c.* 1913

other various marks include full
names and such trade names as:
REGENCY, MONTMARTRE, RICHMOND,
HOSTESS and TRIANON

British Pottery Ltd.
c. 1930–, agents only

B.P. LTD.
printed

Brough & Blackhurst
1872–95, earthenware

BROUGH &
BLACKHURST
printed or impressed

192

Burgess Bros.
1922–39, earthenware
  'Burgess Ware' also
  used

"BURCRAFT"
BURGESS BROS.
MADE IN ENGLAND
printed

Capper & Wood
1895–1904, earthenware

C. & W.
printed or impressed

Cara China Co.
1945–, porcelain

CARA CHINA
printed

Cartlidge & Co., F.
1889–1904, porcelain
  '& Co.' added *c.* 1892

F.C.
F.C. & CO.
printed or impressed

Cartwright & Edwards, Ltd.
c. 1857–
(Alfred Clough Ltd.)
  printed mark of 1912–
  'Ltd.' added *c.* 1926–
  trade names of 'Norville'
  & 'Baronian' ware used
  with 'C. & E.' from *c.* 1930–

C. & E.
printed or impressed

Chapman & Sons, David
1889–1906, porcelain
  'Atlas' mark of 1889–1906

Chapmans Longton Ltd.
1916–*c.* '67 porcelain
  printed 1916–30
(now Paragon China Ltd.)

STANDARD CHINA
crown
ENGLAND

193

various other marks including trade-names of:
'ROYAL STANDARD' and 'ROYAL
MAYFAIR', (from 1973 part of Royal Doulton
Group)

Chetham 1810–34, earthenware '& Son' added 1818	CHETHAM impressed
Chetham, Jonathan Lowe 1841–62, earthenware	J.L.C. printed
Chetham, J. R. & F. 1846–69, earthenware	J.R. & F.C. printed
Chetham & Robinson 1822–37, earthenware	C. & R. printed
Chew, John 1903–4, porcelain	J.C. L impressed

Clare China Co. Ltd.
1951–, decorators
  printed mark, possibly
  taken over by Taylor &
  Kent
	BONE CHINA
	CLARE
	MADE IN ENGLAND
	with crown

Clough's Royal Art
Pottery, 1961–69,
earthenware
  mark also used by
  Alfred Clough Ltd.
  (Royal Art Pottery), 1951–61
	'ROYAL ART POTTERY'
	ENGLAND
	with crown
	printed

Transferred to Alfred Clough, Ltd., Longton
under name of Barker Bros. Ltd. in 1968

194

Coggins & Hill
1892–8, porcelain

C. & H.
printed or impressed

Colclough & Co.
1887–1928, general ceramics
  printed marks

R.S. monogram

'ROYAL STANLEY WARE'

Colclough, H. J.
1897–1937, general ceramics
  various marks including 'H.J.C.' and/or
  'VALE CHINA'

H.J.C.
L

Colclough China Ltd.
1937–48, porcelain

  late printed marks

Colclough
GENUINE
BONE CHINA
MADE IN ENGLAND

Collingwood Bros. Ltd.
1887–1957, porcelain

COLLINGWOOD
early impressed mark

  initials used with crown
  c. 1887–1912
  later marks fully named

C.B.
L

Collingwood & Greatbatch
1870–1887, porcelain

  printed or impressed
  (crown also used
  alone)

C. & G.

Cone Ltd., Thomas   T.C.   T.C.
1892–*c.* 1967   L   LONGTON
earthenware   printed or impressed
   mark of 1892–1912
(moved to Meir in 1964)
     printed 1912–35   T.C. monogram
     'Alma Ware' 1935–
     'ROYAL ALMA' 1946–68

Conway Pottery Co. Ltd.   CONWAY
1930–, earthenware   POTTERY
   mark printed from 1945–   ENGLAND

Cooke & Hulse   COOKE & HULSE
1835–55, porcelain   printed

Cooper & Dethick   C. & D.
1876–88, earthenware   printed

Co-operative Wholesale Society Ltd.
1922, porcelain and   MADE IN
from 1946 also earthenware   BONE
   printed mark on porcelain   WINDSOR
   from *c.* 1946, also   CHINA
   'Clarence Bone-China'   ENGLAND

   'Crown Clarence'   STAFFORDSHIRE
   earthenware from 1946–   CROWN MADE
   also 'Balmoral'   CLARENCE IN
(from 1971–, Jon Anton Ltd.)   ENGLAND

J. H. Cope & Co. Ltd.   C. & CO.
1887–1947, porcelain   impressed or printed

printed with 'back-stamps'   J.H.C. & CO.
from *c.* 1900
'WELLINGTON CHINA' with crown *c.* 1906–
'WELLINGTON CHINA' and profile of Duke
c. 1924–1947

Cotton & Barlow   C. & B.
1850–5, earthenware   printed

Cyples & Barker   CYPLES & BARKER
1846–7, earthenware   impressed

Day, George   STAFFORDSHIRE
1882–9, earthenware
  printed mark

Day & Pratt   DAY & PRATT
1887–8, porcelain   printed or impressed

Decoro Pottery Co.   TUSCAN
1933–49, earthenware   DECORO
  various fully-named   POTTERY
  printed marks

Denton China (Longton) Ltd.   DENTON
1945–, porcelain   CHINA
(Aynsley China Ltd.)

Dewes & Copestake   D. & C.
1894–1915, earthenware   L
  various printed marks
  including initials

Diane Pottery Co.
1960–, now closed,
porcelain
   various printed marks
   with full name

DIANE
POTTERY
LONGTON
STAFFORDSHIRE

Dinky Art Pottery Co. Ltd.
1931–47, earthenware
   printed mark

MADE IN
DINKY WARE
ENGLAND

Dixon & Co., R. F.
1916–29, ceramic retailers
and importers

various marks
include 'D.C.'
for Dixon & Co.

Dresden Floral Porcelain Co. Ltd.
1945–56, porcelain
   printed mark

Dresden Porcelain Co.
1896–1904, porcelain

D.P. CO.

D.P. CO.
L

printed or impressed

printed mark 1896–1903

Edwards & Brown
1882–1933, porcelain

E. & B.
L

   impressed or printed mark 1882–1933
   'E. & B.L.' with 'DUCHESS CHINA', 1910–33

Elektra Porcelain Co Ltd.
1924–71, earthenware
   printed mark of 1924–
(now Allied English Potteries)
   similar mark 'VULCAN WARE' *c.* 1940–

Elkin, Samuel
1856–64, earthenware
                    S.E.
                 printed

Elkin & Newbon
c. 1844–5, earthenware
                 E. & N.

Fell & Co., J. T.
1923–57, earthenware
             EMBOSA WARE

            MADE BY CYPLES
   printed or impressed   OLD POTTERY
                 1793

Finney & Sons Ltd., A. T.
1947, porcelain
   trade-name in a variety
   of styles
               DUCHESS
           BONE CHINA
             printed

Flacket, Toft & Robinson
1857–8, earthenware
            F.T. & R.
            printed

Floral China Co. Ltd.
1940–51, porcelain
   printed mark

Forester & Co., Thomas
1888–, earthenware
   printed mark

199

Forester & Sons, Thomas
1883–1959, general ceramics
  'Ltd.' added 1891
  printed, 1891–1912
  later marks include
  'PHOENIX CHINA'

T.F. & S.

Gallimore, Robert
1831–40, earthenware

R.G.
impressed

Gallimore & Co. Ltd.,
1906–34, earthenware
  mark impressed or printed

Gladstone China (Longton)
Ltd., 1939–1952,
porcelain
  printed mark until
  1961 after firm became:
Gladstone China
1952–, porcelain

GLADSTONE
BONE   CHINA

MADE IN ENGLAND
various marks with
'Gladstone Bone China'

Green & Clay
1888–91, earthenware
  printed or impressed

Grove & Stark
1871–85, earthenware
  printed or impressed
  'G.S.' impressed
  monogram also used

G. & S.
printed

GROVE & STARK
LONGTON

Hallam & Day
1880–85, earthenware

H. & D.
printed, often with
Royal Arms

Hammersley & Co.
1887–1932, porcelain
(Hammersley & Co., Longton) Ltd.
from 1932–present
   crown mark used without
   initials, 1887–1912
   many various fully-named marks from 1912–
(now Carborundum Group)

H. & C.   H. & CO.

Hammersley & Asbury
1872–5, earthenware

H. & A.
printed, sometimes
with 'Prince of Wales'
feathers

Hampson & Broadhurst
1847–53, earthenware

H. & B.
printed

Harvey, C. & W. K.
1835–53, general ceramics
   name also printed with
   Royal Arms and 'REAL
   IRONSTONE CHINA'

C. & W.K.H.

HARVEY
printed

Hawley, Webberley & Co.
1895–1902, earthenware
   printed mark

Hewitt & Leadbeater
1907–19, porcelain
then Hewitt Bros. until
c. 1926   printed

Hibbert & Boughey
1889, general ceramics

H. & B.
printed with crown

Hill & Co.
1898–1920, porcelain

H. & CO.
impressed or printed

Holdcroft, Joseph
1865–1940, general ceramics
(Holdcrofts Ltd., *c.* 1906–,
later Cartwright & Edwards Ltd.)
    mark of 'H.J.' monogram on globe from
    1890–1939

printed or
impressed
1865–1906

Holland & Green
1853–82, earthenware

H. & G.
LATE HARVEY
printed or impressed

Holmes & Son
1898–1903, earthenware
    other marks include
    full name

H. & S.
LONGTON
impressed or printed

Hudden, John Thomas
1859–1885, earthenware

J.T.H.
J.T. HUDDEN
printed

Hudson, William
1889–1941, porcelain
    printed mark 1892–1912
    other later marks
    include 'SUTHERLAND
    CHINA'

W.H.
printed

Hudson & Middleton, Ltd.
1941–, porcelain
   various late marks
   include 'SUTHERLAND'
   and 'H.M.' with lion

Hulse & Adderley
1869–75, general
ceramics
   printed mark as
   used later by
   W. A. Adderley & Co.

H. & A.

Hulse, Nixon & Adderley   H.N. & A.
1853–68, earthenware   printed

Jackson & Gosling   J. & G.   J. & G.
1866–1968, porcelain   L
   'Ltd.' added *c.* 1930   impressed or printed
   variety of marks including trade-name of
   'Grosvenor China'

Jones (Longton) Ltd., A. E.
1905–46, earthenware
   printed or impressed
   c. 1908–36   ENGLAND
   other 'Palissy' mark continued by
Palissy Pottery, Ltd., now a subsidiary of
Royal Worcester, Ltd.

Jones & Co., Frederick　　　F. JONES LONGTON
1865–86, earthenware　　　impressed or printed

Jones & Sons, A. B.　　　A.B.J. & S.
1900–, porcelain　　　A.B.J. & SONS
(A. B. Jones from 1876)　　A.B. JONES & SONS
　large variety of marks including
　initials, full name and/or trade-name of
　'GRAFTON' or 'ROYAL GRAFTON'
(acquired in 1966 by Crown House Glass Ltd.)

Jones, Shepherd & Co.　　　J.S. & CO.
1867–8, earthenware　　　printed

Jones, Josiah Ellis　　　J.E.J.
1868–72, earthenware　　　or full name
　　　　　　　　　　　printed

Kent, James　　　　　JAMES KENT
1897–, general ceramics　　ENGLAND
　'Ltd.' added 1913　　with Royal Arms &
　printed mark of　　'ROYAL SEMI CHINA'
　1897–1915
　various shield or 'globe' marks with full name
　or J.K.L. or J.K., from 1897–present, when
　'Old Foley' is used

Lawrence (Longton) Ltd., Thomas
1892–1964, earthenware
　printed or impressed
　marks include name
　'Falcon Ware'

204

Leadbeater, Edwin
1920–24, porcelain
  printed or impressed mark

Ledgar, Thomas P.
1900–5, general ceramics
  impressed or printed mark

T.P.L.

Lockett & Sons, John
1828–35, earthenware

J. LOCKETT & SONS
impressed

Longton New Art Pottery Co.
Ltd., 1932–66, earthenware
  various printed marks

KELSBORO'
WARE

Longton Porcelain Co. Ltd.
1892–1908, porcelains

L.P. CO.
monogram

Longton Pottery Co. Ltd.
1946–55, earthenware

L.P. CO. LTD.
printed

Lowe, William
1874–1930, porcelain

        printed or impressed
also full name or initials with trade-names
'ROYAL SYDNEY WARE', 'COURT CHINA'

Lowe, Ratcliffe & Co.
1882–92, earthenware
  printed or impressed

Mackee, Andrew
1892–1906, general ceramics

A.M.
L.
impressed or printed

Malkin, Walker & Hulse
1858–64, earthenware

M.W. & H.
printed

Martin, Shaw & Cope
c. 1815–24, general ceramics

MARTIN SHAW
& COPE
IMPROVED CHINA
printed

Mason, Holt & Co.
1857–84, porcelain

M.H. & CO.
printed or impressed

Massey, Wildblood & Co.
1887–9, porcelain

M.W. & CO.
printed

Matthews & Clark
c. 1902–6, general ceramics
  printed mark in frame

M. & C.
L.

Mayer & Sherratt
1906–41, porcelain

M. & S.
L.
under crown
also other printed marks including trade-name
of 'MELBA CHINA'

McNeal & Co. Ltd.
1894–1906, earthenware
  printed

Middleton & Co., J. H.
1889–1941, porcelain
　various printed marks
　with trade-name of
　'DELPHINE'

Moore Bros.
1872–1905, porcelain

MOORE
printed or impressed

　'Bros.' added 1872–1905　　MOORE BROS.

　printed from *c.* 1880　　MOORE (with globe)

　printed mark, 1902–5
Bernard Moore
continued at Stoke
until 1915

Morris, Thomas
1892–1941, porcelain

　early printed mark, from
　c. 1912 trade-name of
　'CROWN CHELSEA CHINA' used

New Chelsea Porcelain Co. Ltd.
　from 1913 many marks used
　including anchor and
　'Chelsea', 'New Chelsea'
　or 'Royal Chelsea'

New Chelsea China Co. Ltd.
1951–61, porcelain

New Park Potteries Ltd.
1935–57, earthenware
   initials or factory-
   name printed in
   varying frames

N.P.P. LTD.
NEW PARK
POTTERIES
LONGTON
NEW PARK

Osborne China Co. Ltd.
1909–40, porcelain

'Osborne China'
with torch

Palissy Pottery Ltd.
1946–, earthenware
(subsidiary of Royal
Worcester Ltd.)
   variety of printed marks include,
   'Palissy Pottery' or 'Palissy Ware', etc.

Paragon China Ltd.
1920–, porcelain
   large variety of marks
   include 'Royal Arms'
   and 'Paragon'
(now an Allied English
Potteries Ltd. company)

Pattison, J.
c. 1818–30, earthenware

JOHN PATTISON
incised

Plant, Benjamin
c. 1780–1820, earthenware

BPlant
LaneEnd.
incised

Plant & Co., R. H.
1881–98, porcelain

'R.H.P. & CO.'
in knot under a
winged crown

Plant, Ltd., R. H. & S. L.
c. 1898–1970, porcelain
numerals under
mark indicate last
two numerals of year
made. From 1973:

'TUSCAN CHINA'
trade-name in
many various
forms
'WEDGWOOD–ROYAL
TUSCAN DIVISION'

Plant & Sons, R.
1895–1901, earthenware

P. & S.
L
printed

Poole, Thomas
1880–1952, general ceramics

impressed or printed
crown, 1880–1912
(common mark)
early form of 'ROYAL
STAFFORD CHINA' used
from 1912–

Poole & Unwin
1871–6, earthenware

P. & U.
printed or impressed

Proctor & Co., J. H.
1857–84, earthenware

WARRANTED
P
printed or impressed
under crown

Procter, John
1843–6, earthenware

J.P.
L
printed or impressed

Procter & Co. Ltd., G.
1891–1940, porcelain
  with or without 'L'
  for Longton
  'GLADSTONE CHINA'
  from 1924–40

G.P. & CO.
L
printed

trade-name

Ratcliffe & Co.
1891–1914, earthenware

printed

Redfern & Drakeford Ltd.
1892–1933, porcelain
  printed or impressed
  mark, 'BALMORAL
  CHINA' added in
  1909–33

Regency China Ltd.
1953–, porcelain

Reid & Co.
1913–46, porcelain

   'PARK PLACE CHINA'
   c. 1913–24

   'ROSLYN CHINA'
   c. 1924–46
   (see ROSLYN CHINA)   all printed

Riddle & Bryan   RIDDLE & BRYAN
c. 1835–40, earthenware   Longton
      printed

Robinson, W. H.   W.H. ROBINSON
1901–4, porcelain   LONGTON
   printed mark in   BALTIMORE CHINA
   circle under crown

Robinson & Son   R. & S.
1881–1903, porcelain   L.

   'Foley' is a name   FOLEY CHINA
   used by several potters

Roper & Meredith   R. & M.
1913–24, earthenware   LONGTON

Roslyn China
1946–63, porcelain
   printed mark also
   used by Reid & Co.

Rowley & Newton Ltd. R. & N.
1896–1901, general ceramics printed or impressed
  'R. & N.' often with lion 'rampant'

Royal Albion China Co. ROYAL ALBION CHINA
1921–48, porcelain L
  printed marks ENGLAND
  with crown

Royal Stafford China variety of marks
1952–, porcelain with
  printed marks 'ROYAL STAFFORD'

Salisbury Crown China Co.
(Salisbury China Co. from
1949)
c. 1927–61, porcelain

  printed mark of *c.* 1952

Salt & Nixon, Ltd. S. & N.
1901–34, porcelain L
  various marks with initials
  & 'SALON CHINA' printed

Shaw & Sons (Longton) Ltd., John
1931–63, general ceramics

  printed mark of *c.* 1949
  various other marks,
  include 'Burlington'

212

Shaw & Copestake
1901–, earthenware
   various printed or impressed
   marks with trade-name of 'SYLVAC'

Shelley Potteries, Ltd.
1925–67, porcelain
(now Royal Albert Ltd.)
   various printed marks
   with 'SHELLEY' (Royal Doulton Group)

Shepherd & Co., Alfred   A. SHEPHERD & CO.
1864–70, earthenware   printed

Shore & Co., J.   J.S. & CO.
1887–1905, porcelain   printed

Shore, Coggins & Holt   S.C.H.
1905–10, general ceramics   L
   initials printed under   *ENGLAND*
   crown

Shore & Coggins
1911–*c.* 67, porcelain
   mark of *c.* 1930, other
   marks include trade-name
   'Bell China' (now Royal Doulton Group)

Smith, Sampson   S.S.
c. 1846–1963, general   impressed
ceramics

'S.S.' monogram used in a variety of
marks during this century and 'WETLEY
CHINA' or 'OLD ROYAL CHINA'

Stanley & Lambert
c. 1850–4, earthenware

S. & L.
printed

Stanley Pottery Ltd.
1928–31, general ceramics

same printed marks as
used by Colclough & Co.

Star China Co.
1900–19, porcelain

S.C. CO.
printed with crown
or star with
'THE PARAGON CHINA'

Stevenson, Spencer & Co. Ltd.
1948–60, porcelain
  fully named marks
  with 'WILLOW' or
  'ROYAL STUART'

Sutherland & Sons, Danial
1865–75, general
ceramics

S. & S.
impressed or
printed

Swift & Elkin
1840–3, earthenware

S. & E.
printed

Tams, John   J.T.
c. 1875–, earthenware   (or as monogram)
   printed marks

                      J. Tams

   '& Son' added 1903–12   J.T. & S.
   'LTD.' from 1912, with trade-marks:
   'NANKIN WARE', 'ELEPHANT BRAND',
   'TAMS REGENT' and 'CHININE'

Tams & Lowe   T. & L.
1865–74, earthenware   printed

Taylor & Kent   T. & K.
1867–, porcelain   L
             printed or impressed
   variety of named or initialled marks
   with 'KENT' or 'ELIZABETHAN'

Thorley China Ltd.   THORLEY CHINA
1940–70, decorative   LTD.
porcelain   printed under crown
(last six years in Fenton)

Tomkinson & Billington   T. & B.
1868–70, earthenware   printed

Townsend, George   G. TOWNSEND
c. 1850–64, earthenware   printed ·

Trentham Bone China Ltd.
1952–7, porcelain
   printed

Turner, John
c. 1762–1806, Wedgwood-
type earthenwares and
stonewares

    TURNER
    impressed

  printed or impressed
  from 1784

  impressed *c.* 1780–6,
    1803–6

    TURNER & CO.

  painted mark on
  'ironstone' type ware
  1800–5

Turner & Abbott
c. 1783–7, Wedgwood-
type wares

  TURNER & ABBOTT
  impressed

Universal Pottery (Longton) Ltd.
1949–62, general ceramics
  various printed marks
  with 'Universal Ware'

Unwin, Joseph
1877–1926, earthenware
figures, etc.

  UNWIN
  moulded in
  relief

Wagstaff & Brunt
1880–1927, general
ceramics

  W. & B.
  LONGTON
  printed

Wain & Sons, Ltd., H. A.
1946–, earthenware

Waine & Co., Charles
1891–1920, porcelain
   printed, 1891–1913
   'Ltd.' from 1913

C.W.
or as monogram

Walker & Carter
1866–72, earthenware
(at Stoke 1872–89)

W. & C.
printed

Walton, J. H.
1912–21, porcelain

printed or impressed

J. H. W.
LONGTON

Warrilow, George
1887–1940, porcelain
   '& S.' or '& Sons'
   and 'Ltd.' added
   from 1928

G.W.

G.W. & S.

G.W. & S. LTD.

Rosina China Co. Ltd.
1941–
   various marks with
   trade-names 'Rosina'
   or 'Queen's' China

ROSINA
CHINA
ENGLAND

Wayte & Ridge
c. 1864, general
ceramics & figures

W. & R.
L
printed

217

Wedgwood & Co. Ltd., H.F.   H.F.W. & CO. LTD.
c. 1954–9, general   ISLINGTON
ceramics   printed

Wild Bros.   J.S.W.
1904–27, porcelain   or in monogram
                    W. Bros.

Wild & Co., Thomas C.   T.W. & CO.
1896–1904
   printed or impressed   T.C.W. with crown

Wild, Thomas C.
1905–17, porcelain
   printed mark, 1905–7

Wild & Sons (Ltd.), Thomas C.
1917–*c.* 72, porcelain
   various printed marks
   with trade-name
   'Royal Albert', now Royal Doulton Group

Wild & Adams   W. & A.
1909–27, earthenware   printed or impressed
   'Ltd.' from 1923
   various marks with 'ROYAL CROWN'

Wildblood, Richard Vernon
1887–8, porcelain

   printed

Wildblood & Heath
1889–99, porcelain
  printed

Wildblood, Heath & Sons
1899–1927, porcelain

  'Ltd.' added from 1915

Williamson & Sons, H. M.
c. 1879–1941, porcelain

  various marks of 'W. & Sons',
  'H.M.W.' or 'Heathcote
  China'
  printed mark of *c.* 1908–

Winterton Pottery (Longton)   'WINTERTON'
Ltd., 1927–54, earthenware   printed over crown

  'Bluestone Ware'

Wood & Co., J. B.
1897–1926, earthenware

  late printed or impressed
  mark

Woolley, Richard   WOOLLEY
1809–14, earthenware   impressed

Yale & Barker	Y. & B.
1841–53, earthenware	printed

MIDDLEPORT (Staffordshire)	FIVE TOWNS CHINA
Five Towns China Co. Ltd.	CO. LTD.
1957–67, porcelain	ENGLAND
name with various	
printed marks	

SHELTON (Staffordshire)	ASTBURY
Astbury, mid-18th	incised or impressed
century, earthenware	

Astbury, Richard Meir	R.M.A.
1790–, earthenware	impressed

Baddeley, John & Edward	B
1784–1806, earthenware	I.E.B.
impressed initials	
	I.E.B.
then:	W
Hicks & Meigh	HICKS & MEIGH
1806–22, earthenware	impressed or
and 'Ironstone'	printed
then:	
Hicks, Meigh & Johnson	H.M.J.
1822–35, earthenware	
and 'Ironstone'	
	H.M. & J.
	printed with
	Royal Arms
then:	

Ridgway, Morley, Wear & Co., 1836–42, earthenware	R.M.W. & CO.
	RIDGWAY, MORLEY WEAR & CO. printed
then: Ridgway & Morley 1842–44	R. & M.
various printed marks (backstamps) with names of pattern	RIDGWAY & MORLEY
Baddeley, Ralph & John 1750–95, earthenware marks impressed	BADDELEY
	R. & J. BADDELEY
Bairstow & Co., P. E. 1954–. earthenware and porcelain	Fancies Fayre England
Bentley, Wear & Bourne 1815–23, decorators printed mark (Bentley & Wear 1823–33)	BENTLEY, WEAR & BOURNE
Birch, Edmund John 1796–1814, Wedgwood-type wares	BIRCH
	E.I.B. impressed
Birch & Whitehead 1796, Wedgwood-type	B. & W. impressed

Cockson & Harding 1856–62, earthenware marks printed or impressed	C. & H.
	C. & H. LATE HACKWOOD
Cutts, James *c.* 1834–70, engraver and designer	J. CUTTS signature on prints
Dakin, Thomas early 18th century earthenware	THOMAS DAKIN sliptrailed
Hackwood & Son, Wm. 1846–9, earthenware	W.H. HACKWOOD printed
Harding, W. J. 1862–72, earthenware	W. & J.H. printed
Hicks & Meigh 1806–22, earthenware 'Stone-China' & Royal Arms also used	HICKS & MEIGH impressed or painted
Hicks, Meigh & Johnson 1822–35, earthenware 'Stone-China' and Royal Arms also used	H.M.J. H.M. & J. printed
Hollins, Samuel *c.* 1784–1813	S. HOLLINS

'Wedgwood-type' ware   HOLLINS
impressed

Hollins, T. & J.   T. & J. HOLLINS
c. 1795–1820, earthenware   impressed

Howard Pottery Co.
1925–, earthenware
   printed mark of 1925–

Keeling, Charles   C.K.
1822–5, earthenware   printed

Meir John   JOHN MEIR
late 17th – early 18th-   sliptrailed
centuries, slipware

Meir, Richard   RICHARD MEIR
late 17th – early 18th-   sliptrailed
centuries, slipware

Phillips, Edward   EDWARD PHILLIPS
1855–62, earthenware   SHELTON
   printed mark   STAFFORDSHIRE

Read & Clementson   R. & C.
1833–5, earthenware   printed

Read, Clementson &   R.C. & A.
Anderson   printed
c. 1836, earthenware

Ridgway, John & William
1814–1830, general
ceramics

J.W.R.
J. & W.R.
J. & W. RIDGWAY
printed or impressed

Ridgway, William
c. 1830–54, earthenware
(also at Hanley from
c. 1838–48)
   '& Co.' added *c.* 1834
   'QUARTZ CHINA' used
   from *c.* 1830–50

W. RIDGWAY

W.R.
printed or impressed

W.R. & CO.

Tittensor, Charles
c. 1815–23, earthenware
including figures

TITTENSOR
impressed or
printed

Twemlow, John
1795–7, earthenware
and stoneware

J.T.

rare initials

Washington Pottery Ltd.
1946–, earthenware
(now Washington Pottery
(Staffordshire) Ltd.)

Worthington & Green
1844–64, earthenware
and Parianware

WORTHINGTON
&
GREEN
impressed

STOKE (Staffordshire)
Alton Towers Handcraft
Pottery (Staffs.) Ltd.
1953–, earthenware

printed or impressed

Arkinstall & Sons (Ltd.)   A. & S.
1904–24, bone-china   printed, 1904–12

   trade marks on   ARCADIAN
   souvenir wares 1904–
   24   ARCADIAN CHINA
(under various other
firms from 1908)   printed marks

Atlas China Co. Ltd.   'ATLAS CHINA' with
1906–10, china   figure supporting
(name revived by   globe
Grimwades Ltd. 1930–6)   printed

Bennett & Co., George   G.B. & CO.
1894–1902, earthenware   impressed or printed

Bilton (1912) Ltd.
1900–, earthenware
   current mark, printed
(now Biltons Tableware Ltd.)

Birks & Co., L. A.   BIRKS
1896–1900, general   impressed
ceramics

              B. & CO.

Birks, Rawlins & Co. (Ltd.)
1900–33, bone-china
   other marks include
   trade-names of:
SAVOY CHINA
CARLTON CHINA

printed

Booth & Son, Ephraim   E.B. & S.
c. 1795, earthenware   impressed

Booth, Hugh   H. BOOTH
1784–9, earthenware   impressed
including creamware

Carlton Ware Ltd.
1958–, earthenware
(Arthur Wood & Son Group)

modern printed mark

Ceramic Art Co. (1905)   C.A. & CO. LTD.
Ltd., 1905–19, earthenware   printed or impressed

Close & Co.   CLOSE & CO. LATE
1855–64, earthenware   W. ADAMS & SONS
                 STOKE-UPON-TRENT
                 printed or impressed

Copeland & Garrett
Copeland, W. T., etc.
(*see under* Spode)

226

Coronation Pottery Co.
1903–54, earthenware

   'Ltd.' from 1947

CORONATION POTTERY
COMPANY LTD.
B
MADE IN ENGLAND
printed or impressed

Crown China Crafts Ltd.
1946–58, general ceramics
   printed mark

HAND MADE; HAND PAINTED
IN ENGLAND
CROWN CHINA CRAFTS LTD.

Daniel, H. & R.
1820–41, pottery and
porcelain
   fully named printed
   marks also used

H. & R. Daniel

H. Daniels & Sons

written marks

Empire Porcelain Co.
1896–1967, earthenware
   printed mark, 1896–1912
(1958–67, Qualcast Group)

RADPING WORKS
Staffordshire
England
STOKE ON TRENT
ENGLAND.
P

EMPIRE
ENGLAND   *Shelton Ivory*

late printed or impressed marks

Era Art Pottery Co.
1930–47, earthenware

   printed mark, 1936–

Featherstone Potteries
1949–50, earthenware
marks impressed or
printed

F.P.

F.N.P.

Fielding & Co., S.
1879–, earthenwares
(part of Crown Devon
Group)

FIELDING
impressed

S.F. & CO.
(over crown and
lion)
printed

'Crown Devon' trade-
mark from *c.* 1930

date-mark:
10th March 1954

FIELDING
10 M 54

Floyd & Sons, R.
1907–30, earthenware

printed or impressed

Folch, Stephen
1820–30, earthenware

FOLCH'S GENUINE
STONE CHINA
impressed

Goss, W. H.
1858–1944, pottery and
porcelain

W.H.G.

W.H. GOSS

printed mark from
c. 1862

Greta Pottery
1938–41, earthenware

G
P
printed or painted

Hamilton, Robert
1811–26, earthenware

HAMILTON
STOKE
impressed or printed

Hancock & Co., F.
1899–1900, earthenware
  printed mark

Hancock, B. & S.
1876–81, earthenware

B. & S.H.
printed

Hancock & Sons, Sampson
1858–1937, earthenware
(at Tunstall prior
to 1870)

S.H.

S. HANCOCK
printed

  printed 1891–1935

S.H. & S.

S.H. & SONS

  printed 1900–12
From 1935–37:–
S. Hancock & Sons
(Potters) Ltd.

Hancock & Whittingham
1873–9, earthenware

H. & W.
printed

Heath, Job
early 18th century
earthenware

JOB HEATH
sliptrailed

Jones, George
1861–1951, general ceramics

'& Sons', added on
crescent from 1873

in relief, impressed
or printed

Keys & Mountford
1850–7, 'Parian' ware

K. & M.

S. KEYS
& MOUNTFORD
impressed

Kirkham, William
1862–92, earthenware

W. KIRKHAM
impressed

Kirkhams Ltd.
1946–61, earthenware
(now Portmeiron
Potteries Ltd.)

Mayer, Thomas
1836–8, earthenware
(last three years at
Longport)

T. MAYER
T. MAYER, STOKE
printed

Meigh, W. & R.
1894–9, earthenware
   printed mark

Minton
1793–, general ceramics
(Royal Doulton Group from 1973)
Sèvres type mark used
on porcelain *c.* 1800–30,
sometimes with   in blue enamel
pattern number

printed mark with
'M', 1822–1836

printed 1822–36

'M. & B.' for Minton &
Boyle partnership
1836–41, printed

'M. & Co.' Minton &
Co., 1841–73

'M. & H.', Minton &
Hollins partnership
1845–68

231

1862–71, 's' added
in 1873

MINTON
impressed

printed 1860–*c*. 69

impressed for 'BEST
BODY' mid-19th century

B.B.

'Globe-mark', 1863–72
'S' added to Minton
in 1871

impressed mark with
year 1875, used from
1868–80

18
MINTON
75

printed mark from 1873,
'England' added from
1891, and 'Made in
England' about 1910

impressed or moulded
c. 1890–1910

MINTONS
ENGLAND

'Globe-mark', *c.* 1912–50

standard factory-mark
adopted in 1951

'Ermine' mark used
from *c.* 1850 to identify
wares that had been
dipped in a soft-glaze
on which painting was
to be applied

relief mark of *c.* 1847–8
on 'Summerly's Art
Manufacturers' made
by Minton

Solon, Marc Louis, 1870–1904
decorator

signature on 'Henri Deux'   TOFT
reproductions
Mussill, W. (*d.* 1906)   W. Mussill
decorator in 1870s

233

YEARLY MARKS OF MINTONS LTD., 1842–1942:

✳	△	▢	✕	⬭
1842	1843	1844	1845	1846
⌒	—	⨝	♧	∴
1847	1848	1849	1850	1851
∨	♞	∿	✳	♀
1852	1853	1854	1855	1856
◇	♈	⚭	♉	⅄
1857	1858	1859	1860	1861
✢	⬦	Z	〰	✕
1862	1863	1864	1865	1866
⋈	Ƨ	⊡	ⓜ	NC
1867	1868	1869	1870	1871
⊗	⁜	↓	Ɛ	⏃
1872	1873	1874	1875	1876
⬯	◬	◬	⚠	⊞
1877	1878	1879	1880	1881
⊗	◓	⊠	⋈	B
1882	1883	1884	1885	1886
♔	∞	S	T	⛨
1887	1888	1889	1890	1891

1892	1893	1894	1895	1896
1897	1898	1899	1900	1901
1902	1903	1904	1905	1906
1907	1908	1909	1910	1911
1912	1913	1914	1915	1916
1917	1918	1919	1920	1921
1922	1923	1924	1925	1926
1927	1928	1929	1930	1931
1932	1933	1934	1935	1936
1937	1938	1939	1940	1941
		1942		

At the commencement of 1943 the system of yearly date-marks that had operated from 1842 was discontinued, being replaced by figures denoting the year of production, preceded by a number allocated to the actual maker of the article, Number one was given to the factory's leading plate-maker, and plates he produces today have stamped in the clay 1–76, the last two digits representing the year.

Moore, Bernard 1905–15, art pottery and porcelain, with *flambé* glazes	**BM** painted
painted or printed	**BERNARD BMOORE**
Mountford, G. T. 1888–98, earthenware	G.T.M. STOKE printed
Mountford, John 1857–9, 'Parian' ware	J. MOUNTFORD STOKE incised signature

Myott, Son & Co. Ltd. 1898–, earthenware (now subsidiary of Interpace Corporation) (later Cobridge and Hanley)

late marks fully named

1898–1902

c. 1900–

Ollivant Potteries Ltd.
1948–54, earthenware

O.P.

O.P.L.

printed marks, usually
together with pattern

OLLIVANT

Plant & Co., J.
1893–1900, earthenware
printed mark

STOKE POTTERY

Portmeirion Potteries Ltd.
1962–, earthenware

PORTMEIRION
POTTERY
STOKE-ON-TRENT

printed mark

MADE IN ENGLAND

Ridgway Potteries Ltd.
1955, earthenware
(an Allied English
Potteries Ltd., company)

contemporary marks (1972)

Robinson & Leadbeater
1864–1924, 'Parian' ware
and bone-china
'Ltd.' added to marks
from *c.* 1905

R & L

impressed

Ruscoe, William
c. 1920– (to Exeter in
1944)
　full year-date added
　to initials from *c.* 1925

incised or painted

Shorter & Son, Ltd.
(member of Crown Devon
Group), 1905–
earthenware

late printed mark

Smith, James
1898–1924, general ceramics

JAMES SMITH

printed or impressed

printed

Spode, Josiah (*b.* 1733–
d. 1797) 1770–
earthenware
(Copeland & Garrett
from 1833)

Spode　SPODE
impressed or
　in blue

　　c. 1784–1805

SPODE　S
impressed

painted marks with pattern numbers, *c.* 1790–1820	SPODE 1989 2417 Spode
c. 1805–	SPODE printed
mark on stone-china, in black *c.* 1805–15, in blue *c.* 1815–30	 **Stone China** printed
painted	'Spode Stone China'
impressed 1810–15	**SPODES** **NEW STONE**
printed *c.* 1805–33	N.S. **Spode's** **Imperial**
printed in puce enamel on felspar porcelain *c.* 1815–27	Spode
painted, impressed or printed *c.* 1797 to 1816	SPODE, SON & COPELAND

Copeland & Garrett
1833–47, general ceramics

C. & G.
painted or printed

printed in blue, with
name of pattern, *c.* 1833–
47

printed *c.* 1833–47

COPELAND & GARRETT
NEW
JAPAN STONE

Copeland & Sons, Ltd.,
W. T., 1847–
impressed or printed
c. 1847–67

COPELAND, LATE
SPODE

printed on Parian figures
c. 1847–55

COPELAND'S
PORCELAIN
STATUARY

printed, 1850–67

printed, *c.* 1847–51

printed, 1851–85

impressed on earthenware
1850–67

printed on porcelain
c. 1891–

SPODE
COPELANDS CHINA
ENGLAND

printed in various
colours on 'New Stone'
of this century

present-day mark

Spode
ENGLAND

Alcock, S., decorator
c. 1890–

S. Alcock

Hürten, C. F., designer
1859–1897

C.F.H.

Steele & Wood
1875–1892, tiles

printed or impressed

Tittensor, Jacob
1780–95, earthenware

Jacob Tittensor
signature

Turner, Hassall & Peake T.H.P.
1865–9, general ceramics

printed or impressed

Turner & Wood TURNER & WOOD
1880–8, general ceramics STOKE
impressed

Wiltshaw & Robinson Ltd.
1890–1957, general
ceramics
  printed mark, 1894–
  various marks include
  trade-mark 'CARLTON
  WARE'

Winkle & Co., F. F.W. & CO.
1890–1931, earthenware ENGLAND

  printed or impressed F. WINKLE & CO.
  marks, 1890–1910
  'Ltd.' added in 1911

  printed, 1890–1925

  misleading mark used
  by Winkle & Co., 1908–25
  (the wares of the
  18th century potter,
  Thomas Whieldon, were
  not marked)

242

Wolfe, Thomas 1784–1800, earthenware and later, *c.* 1811–18	WOLFE impressed
Wolfe & Hamilton *c.* 1800–11, earthenware	WOLFE & HAMILTON STOKE impressed or painted

TUNSTALL (Staffordshire)
Adams & Sons (Potters)
Ltd., William,

impressed, 1769–1800 (on creamware)	ADAMS & CO.
impressed, 1787–1864	ADAMS
on blue-printed wares 1804–40	
impressed on earthenware 1810–25	
impressed mark *c.* 1815	W. ADAMS & CO.
W. Adams & Sons 1819–64, printed	W.A. & S.

impressed on parian-ware, 1845–64	ADAMS
printed, mid-19th century	W. ADAMS
printed as 'back-stamp' with name of pattern, 1893–1917. 'ENGLAND' added in 1891	W.A. & CO.

printed from 1879–

printed from 1896–
with varying names
of ceramic bodies
used, e.g. TITIAN
WARE, IMPERIAL
STONE WARE, etc.

impressed on Wedgwood-type jasperwares 1896 with confusing establishment date	ADAMS ESTBD 1657 TUNSTALL ENGLAND

printed mark, 1914–40

late impressed or
printed mark

Calyx Ware

late printed mark
c. 1950–

W. Adams & Sons
England
under crown

Adams, Benjamin
c. 1800–20, earthenware
and stoneware

B. ADAMS

impressed

Adams, W. & T.
1866–92, earthenware
  printed mark

W. & T. ADAMS
TUNSTALL
under coat-of-arms

Beech & Hancock
1857–76, earthenware

B. & H.
printed

Blackhurst, Jabez
1872–83, earthenware

JABEZ BLACKHURST
printed

Booth & Son, Thomas
1872–6, earthenware

T.B. & S.
printed

Booth, Thomas, G.
1876–83, earthenware
  name of pattern on strap

Booth, T. G. & F.
1883–91, earthenware

T.G. & F.B.
printed

Booth (Limited)
1891–1948, earthenware
  printed, 1891–1906

painted or printed on
earthenware reproductions
of Worcester porcelain, 1905–

variety of marks used with 'Silicon China'
from about 1906. 'England' sometimes included

late mark of 1930–48

Boulton, Machin & Tennant
1889–99, earthenware

mark printed or impressed

Bourne, Nixon & Co.
1828–30, earthenware
  mark impressed

BOURNE NIXON
& CO.

printed initials included
in backstamp

B.N. & CO.

Bowers & Co., G. F.
1842–68, pottery &
  porcelain
  other printed or
  impressed marks
  include full name

G.F. B.B.T.
printed

Breeze & Son, John
1805–12, pottery & porcelain
(other potters of this
name were operating from
late 18th century to *c.* 1826)

BREEZE
incised or
painted

British Pottery Ltd.
1920–26, earthenware

mark printed

Brougham & Mayer
1853–5, earthenware

BROUGHAM &
MAYER
printed

Brownhills Pottery Co.
1872–96, earthenware

B.P. CO.
printed or impressed

printed marks of
c. 1880–96

Butterfield, W. & J.
1854–61, earthenware

W. & J.B.
printed

Challinor, Edward
1842–67, earthenware

E.C.

E. CHALLINOR
printed

Christie & Beardmore   C.B.
1902–3, earthenware

C.B.
F.

printed initials with
various backstamps

Clews & Co. Ltd., George
1906–61, earthenware
  printed 'globe' mark from
  1906, other marks all
  include full name

Clive, J. H.
1802–11, earthenware

CLIVE
impressed

Clive, Stephen   S.C.
1875–80, earthenware

S.C. & CO.
printed

Colley & Co. Ltd., A.
1909–14, earthenware
  mark printed or impressed

Cumberlidge & Humphreys
1886–9; 1893–5
earthenware
  marks printed or impressed

C. & M.

C. & M.
TUNSTALL

Dean & Sons, Ltd., T.
1879–1947, earthenware
  printed 1896–1947

1937–47

248

Eardley & Hammersley
1862–6, earthenware

E. & H.
printed

Edge & Grocott
c. 1830, earthenware
figures

EDGE & GROCOTT

Elsmore & Forster
1853–71, general ceramics

ELSMORE & FORSTER
printed with
variety of backstamps

Elsmore & Son, T.
1872–87, earthenware

ELSMORE & SON
ENGLAND

Emberton, William
1851–69, earthenware

W.E.
printed

Emberton, T. I. & J.
1869–82, earthenware

T.I. & J.E.
printed

Ford, Challinor & Co.
1865–80, earthenware

F.C.   F.C. & CO.
initials used with
various printed
marks

Gater & Co., Thomas
1885–94 (at Burslem)
earthenware

G.H. & CO.
later printed initials

Gater, Hall & Co.
1895–1943, earthenware
printed mark of 1914–

printed mark from 1914–
(firm moved to Burslem
in 1907). Taken over
by:
Barratt's of Staffordshire
1943–. Some former
marks continued:

other marks include
full name of Barratt's.
'Delphatic' from 1957
(Barratt's now member of the manufacturing
division of G.U.S. Ltd.)

Gem Pottery Ltd.
1961–, earthenware
printed mark

printed

Goodfellow, Thomas
1828–59, earthenware

T. GOODFELLOW
printed

Grenville Pottery Ltd.
1946–, earthenware

Grindley & Co. Ltd., W. H.
1880–, earthenware
printed mark to 1914
('England' included from 1891)

printed from 1914–25
'Ltd.' included from 1925
other marks include full
name of firm

modern printed mark

(W. H. Grindley & Co.
now a subsidiary of
Alfred Clough Ltd.)

Grindley Hotel Ware Co. Ltd.
1908–, earthenware
  mark printed from *c.* 1946–

GRINDLEY HOTEL WARE
ENGLAND
VITRIFIED

Hall, Ralph
1822–49, earthenware
  printed in backstamp
  1822–41   R. HALL
  c. 1836   R. HALL & SON

  1841–49   R. HALL & CO.

                                       R.H. & CO.

Heath & Co., Joseph   J. HEATH
1828–41, earthenware   printed

Heath, Joseph   J. HEATH & CO.
1845–53, earthenware   printed
  Note: the letter 'J' is   J.H. & CO.
  often printed as 'I'   printed

251

Holland, John
1852–4, earthenware

J. HOLLAND
printed

Hollingshead & Kirkham
1870–1956, earthenware
  1870–1900

H. & K. H. & K.
TUNSTALL
printed or impressed

mark of 1890 after
take-over of Wedgwood
& Co.

H. & K.
LATE WEDGWOOD
impressed

printed mark, 1900–24

later marks all include
name or initials of
firm

TRADE MARK
HOLLINSHEAD & KIRKHAM
TUNSTALL
ENGLAND

Ingleby & Co., Thomas
c. 1834–5, earthenware

T.I. & CO.
printed

Keele Street Pottery Co.
1915–, earthenware
  other later printed marks include full name

K.S.P.

Keeling, Anthony & Enoch
c. 1795–1811, general ceramics

A. & E. KEELING

A.E. KEELING

Kirkland & Co. (Etruria)
1892–, earthenware
  printed on various
  backstamps

K. & CO.

K. & CO.
E

252

other various printed marks include full name
of Kirkland & Co. or K. & Co./E.

'Kirklands (Etruria Ltd.)'
from *c*. 1938, printed
'Kirklands (Staffordshire)
Ltd.' from *c*. 1947

Knapper & Blackhurst
1867–71, earthenware

KNAPPER AND
BLACKHURST
impressed or printed

(1883–8 at Burslem)
initials also probably used

K. & B.

Lingard Webster & Co. Ltd.
1900–, earthenware

impressed or printed from
c. 1946–

Maudesley & Co., J.
1862–4, earthenware
(J.M. & CO. was also
used by other firms)

STONE WARE
J.M. & CO.

Mayer & Maudesley
1837–8, earthenware

M. & M.
printed

Meakin Ltd., Alfred
1875–, earthenware

ALFRED MEAKIN
impressed or printed

'Ltd.' added in 1897
and omitted from *c.* 1930
early mark *c.* 1875–97

Firm re-named 'Alfred
Meakin (Tunstall) Ltd.'
in *c.* 1913

ALFRED MEAKIN
LTD.

printed mark from *c.* 1891
when the word 'ENGLAND'
was added

later marks include 'M. IRONSTONE'
'BLEU DE ROI', 'GLO-WHITE' and
'TRADITIONAL IRONSTONE, LEEDS'

Meir, John
c. 1812–36, earthenware

J.M.   I.M.
printed

Meir & Son, John
1837–97, earthenware
    initials used in various
    printed or impressed
    marks
    Date codes sometimes
    used e.g. $\frac{9}{75}$: Sept. 1875

J.M. & S.
          I.M. & S.
J.M. & SON

J. MEIR & SON

MEIR & SON

Pitcairns Ltd.
1895–1901, earthenware
    printed mark

Podmore, Walker & Co. P.W. & CO.
1834–59, earthenware printed in various
backstamps

Podmore, Walker & P.W. & W.
Wedgwood, *c.* 1856–9
 various printed marks WEDGWOOD
 included the confusing,
 name of 'Wedgwood' WEDGWOOD & CO.
 Enoch Wedgwood being
 a partner. Name of firm changed to
Wedgwood & Co. in *c.* 1860

Rathbone, Smith & Co. R.S. & CO.
1883–97, earthenware printed
then:
Smith & Binnall
1897–1900, earthenware
 printed
then:
Soho Pottery, Ltd.
1901–6, earthenware
(1906–44 at Cobridge)

 other later marks include full name of
 firm and various trade-names, e.g.
 'SOLIAN WARE', 'AMBASSADOR WARE',
 'QUEENS GREEN', 'CHANTICLEER' and
 'HOMESTEAD', etc.
then:
Simpsons (Potters) Ltd.
1944–, earthenware
(at Cobridge)

Simpsons (Potters) Ltd. of Cobridge continue
to use many of the Soho Pottery Ltd.
trade-names plus 'MARLBOROUGH',
'Ironstone' and 'CHINASTYLE'
e.g.

Rathbone & Co., T.　　T.R. & CO.
1898–1923, earthenware　　TUNSTALL

　　late printed mark:

Richardson, Albert G.　　A.G.R. & Co. Ltd.
1915–34, earthenware　　printed
(moved to Cobridge
in *c.* 1934)
　　various printed marks including trade-
　　name of 'Crown Ducal'

Salt Bros.　　SALT BROS.
1897–1904, earthenware　　TUNSTALL
(then 'taken-over' by　　ENGLAND
T. Till & Sons of　　printed or impressed
Burslem)

Selman, J. & W.   SELMAN
c. 1864–65, earthenware   impressed
figures

Shaw, Anthony   ANTHONY SHAW
1851–1900, earthenware

     A. SHAW   A. SHAW
   '& Son' added to   BURSLEM
   mark in *c.* 1882–*c.* 98

     SHAWS   SHAW
   '& Son' replaced by   BURSLEM
   '& Co.' from *c.* 1898
Shaws taken over by A. J. Wilkinson Ltd.
in *c.* 1900

Simpson, William   WILLIAM SIMPSON
late 17th- early 18th-   in slip-trailing
century, slip-trailed earthenware
(this name is also recorded at other
pottery towns in Staffs.)

Smith, Theophilus   T. SMITH
1790–*c.* 97, earthenware   impressed

Smith & Binnall   (*see* Rathbone,
1897–1900, earthenware   Smith & Co.,
              Tunstall)

Soho Pottery Ltd.   (*see* Rathbone,
1901–6, earthenware   Smith & Co.,
              Tunstall)

Summerbank Pottery Ltd.
1952–, earthenware
(now Summerbank Pottery
(1970) Ltd.)

SUMMERBANK
printed

COOPERCRAFT
MADE IN
ENGLAND

Tunnicliff, Michael
1828–41, earthenware toys
and figures

TUNNICLIFF
TUNSTALL

Turner, Goddard & Co.
1867–74, earthenware
'ROYAL PATENT
IRONSTONE'

TURNER, GODDARD
& CO.
printed

Turner & Tomkinson
1860–72, earthenware

TURNER &
TOMKINSON

printed in various marks

T. & T.

Turner & Sons, G. W.
1873–95, earthenware

TURNERS

various forms of
initials used in a
variety of backstamps
sometimes in the form
of a Royal Arms
'England' added in
1891

G.W.T. & SONS

G.W.T.S.

G.W.T. & S.

G.T. & S.

Walker, Thomas
1845–51, earthenware
  various printed
  backstamps include
  name

T. WALKER

THOS. WALKER

Wedgwood & Co.
(Enoch Wedgwood
(Tunstall) Ltd. from 1965)
  printed mark from *c.* 1862

WEDGWOOD & CO.
impressed

'Ltd.' added from 1900

variety of printed marks used with the
following trade-names: 'IMPERIAL
PORCELAIN', 'WACOLWARE', 'WACOL
IMPERIAL', 'EVERWARE', 'ROYAL
TUNSTALL' and 'VITRILAIN'. From 1965
renamed Enoch Wedgwood (Tunstall) Ltd.
also producing former patterns of
Furnivals, 'Quail', 'Old Chelsea' and
'Denmark'

Staffs. (Tunstall)	**England**	*Staffs. (Tunstall)*
Wood & Challinor 1828–43, earthenware		W. & C. printed
Wood, Challinor & Co. *c.* 1860–64, earthenware		W.C. & CO. printed
Wood & Pigott 1869–71, earthenware		W. & P. printed
Wooliscroft, George 1851–3: 1860–4 earthenware		G. WOOLISCROFT or G. WOOLLISCROFT

FRESHWATER (I.o.W.)
  Island Pottery Studio
  Lester, Joe
  earthenware, 1956–
    'Freshwater' sometimes   printed or impressed
    added to mark

WHIPPINGHAM (I.o.W.)
  Isle of Wight Pottery
  Saunders, S. E., *c.* 1930–40
  earthenware
    (same monogram used at
      Carisbrooke Pottery Works, Newport, 1929–32)

CHANNEL ISLANDS

GUERNSEY (Channel Islands)
  The Guernsey Pottery Ltd.
  red ware, studio pottery
  1961–

JERSEY (Channel Islands)   JERSEY POTTERY
  Jersey Pottery Ltd., 1946–   C.I.
  earthenware   painted

            1946–   1951
  impressed or printed marks
                261

ISLE OF MAN

Isle of Man Potteries, Ltd.
earthenware, 1963–

Isle of Man
Pottery
Handmade

NORTHERN IRELAND

PORTADOWN (Co. Armagh)
Wade (Ireland) Ltd., 1947–
porcelain, industrial
and artware
(subsidiary of Wade
Potteries, Ltd.)

printed

SCOTLAND

AIRTH (Central Region)
Dunmore Pottery Co.,
1903–11, earthenware,
c. 1860–1903
(Dunmore Pottery)

PETER GARDNER
DUNMORE POTTERY
DUNMORE
impressed

BO'NESS (Central Region)
McNay & Sons, Charles W.
earthenware, 1887–1958
'Dalmeny' trade-name

stick-on labels

Marshall & Co. Ltd., John   JOHN MARSHALL &
earthenware, 1854–99   CO.
    'Ltd.' added in 1897   printed

COATBRIDGE (Strathclyde)
   Crest Ceramics (Scotland)
   earthenware souvenirs,
   etc.

DUNOON (Strathclyde)
   West Highland Pottery Co. Ltd.
   earthenware, 1961–
     trade-names: 'Flow' ware,
     'Argyll', 'Cowal'
     printed

EDINBURGH (Lothian)   JOHN MILLAR
   Millar, John, 1840–82   printed
   retailer only

GLASGOW (Strathclyde)   B.M. & CO.
   Bayley, Murray & Co.   SARACEN POTTERY
   earthenware, 1875–   printed or impressed
   1900 (Saracen
   Pottery Co. from *c.* 1884)

   Britannia Pottery Co. Ltd.
   earthenware, 1920–35
    'HIAWATHA' trade-name
    from *c.* 1925   printed

Campbellfield Pottery Co. Ltd.   C.P. CO.
earthenware, 1850–1905
  'Ltd.' added *c.* 1884

printed or impressed   CAMPBELLFIELD
marks

                              C.P. CO. LTD.

printed mark of *c.* 1884–
c. 1905
or,
'SPRINGBURN' with thistle

Cochran & Fleming   C. & F.   C. & F.
earthenware, 1896–   G
1920   ROYAL
                      IRONSTONE CHINA

printed

PORCELAIN OPAQUE   COCHRAN & FLEMING
GLASGOW. BRITAIN   GLASGOW BRITAIN
FLEMING   printed

Cochran & Co., R.   R.C. & CO.
general ceramics   impressed
1846–1896

Geddes & Son, John
earthenware and porcelain
c. 1806–27
　'& Son' added in 1824

JOHN GEDDES
Verreville
Pottery
printed

Govancroft Potteries Ltd.
pottery, 1913–
　trade-names: 'Croft',
　'Hamilton', 'Lunar'
　1913–49

　printed 1949–

CROWN　　　　　　　GOVAN
printed or impressed

Grosvenor & Son, F.
pottery, *c.* 1869–1926

　printed mark from 1879

Kennedy & Sons Ltd., Henry
stoneware, 1866–1929

Lockhart & Arthur
earthenware, 1855–64
　marks impressed or
　printed

L. & A.

LOCKHART &
ARTHUR

Lockhart & Co., David
earthenware, 1865–98

D.L. & CO.
printed

Lockhart & Sons Ltd., David
earthenware, 1898–1953
   printed in backstamps

D.L. & SONS

Murray & Co. Ltd., W. F.
pottery, 1870–98
   mark impressed or
   printed

Nautilus Porcelain Co.
   porcelain, 1896–1913
   printed mark

North British Pottery
earthenware, 1869–75

J.M. CO.

   printed marks   J.M. & CO.   I.M. & CO.

Port Dundas Pottery Co. Ltd.
stoneware, *c.* 1850–1932

PORT DUNDAS
GLASGOW POTTERY

   impressed or printed

Possil Pottery Co.
general ceramics,
1898–1901

printed

'Star Pottery'
stoneware and 'majolica'
1880–1907

impressed or printed

Thomson & Sons, John   J.T.
c. 1816– late 19th century   ANNFIELD
  '& Sons' added *c.* 1866

               J.T. & SONS
               GLASGOW

Williamson, John   WELLINGTON
pottery, 1844–94   POTTERY

  marks impressed or
  printed   WILLIAMSON
               WELLINGTON
               POTTERY

GREENOCK (Strathclyde)   CLYDE
  Clyde Pottery Co. Ltd.
  earthenware, *c.* 1815–
  1903   G.C.P. CO.
    'Ltd.' used *c.* 1857–63

               GREENOCK
        impressed or printed

Greenock Pottery   GREENOCK
earthenware, *c.* 1820–   POTTERY
60

  mark impressed or
  printed

Shirley & Co., Thomas T.S. & COY.
earthenware, *c.* 1840–57

T.S. & C.

impressed

INVERDRUIE (Highland Region)
Castlewynd Studios, Ltd.
earthenware and stoneware
 trade-names, 'Castlewynd'
 'Aviemore'
Started Edinburgh 1950
moved to Gifford 1954
(Castlewynd Studios
(Highland China) 1974
at Fort William)

printed

KIRKCALDY (Lothian) R.H. & S.
Heron & Son, Robert
earthenware, *c.* 1850–
1929
 Date of 1820 in mark
 is that of an earlier
 pottery taken over by Heron

printed

Methven & Sons, David D.M. & S.
19th century–*c.* 1930
earthenware

METHVEN

D. METHVEN & SONS

NORTH BERWICK Tantallon
(Lothian)   Ceramics
 Tantallon Ceramics NORTH BERWICK
 earthenware, 1962–

268

PAISLEY (Strathclyde)
Brown & Co., Robert   BROWN PAISLEY
earthenware, 1876–1933

                 printed or impressed

PORTOBELLO (nr. Edinburgh, Lothian)
Buchan & Co. Ltd., A. W.
stoneware, 1867
    trade-name: 'Thistle'
    printed mark from 1949–

Gray & Sons, Ltd., W. A.   W. A. GRAY
pottery, *c.* 1857–1931   printed
    '& Sons' from 1870, 'Ltd.'
    from 1926

Milne Cornwall & Co.   MILNE CORNWALL
stoneware, *c.* 1830–40   & CO.
                   impressed

Rathbone & Co., Thomas   T.R. & CO.
earthenware, *c.* 1810–45

    marks printed or   T. RATHBONE
    impressed   P

Scott Brothers   SCOTT BROTHERS
earthenware, *c.* 1786–96
         SCOTT BROS.   SCOTT
    marks impressed   P.B.

PRESTONPANS (Lothian)   FOWLER THOMPSON
Fowler, Thompson & Co.   & CO.
earthenware, *c.* 1820–40   printed or impressed

Gordon's Pottery
earthenware, 18th century–
1832
    GORDON
    impressed

  initials in printed
  backstamps
    G.G.

Watson's Pottery
earthenware, *c.* 1750–
1840
    WATSON
    impressed

    WATSON & CO.
mark of *c.* 1800–40
    printed

WALES

CARDIFF AND SWANSEA
(Glamorgan)
  Primavesi & Son, F.
  retailers of earthenware
    c. 1850–1915 ('& Son'
    added *c.* 1860)

F. PRIMAVESI & SON
CARDIFF
Full name in a
variety of marks

CARDIGAN (Dyfed)
  Cardigan Potteries
  earthenware, *c.* 1875–90
  printed mark

CARDIGAN
POTTERIES
WOODWARD & CO.
CARDIGAN

CREIGIAU (nr. Cardiff)
  Creigiau Pottery, 1947–
  Southcliffe, R. G. & Co. Ltd.
  earthenware in copper
  lustre traditional style

'Creigiau'

LLANDUDNO (Gwynedd)   CAMBRIAN
  Cambrian Ceramic Co. Ltd.   STUDIO
  (formerly Cambrian Pottery   WARE
  Co. Ltd.), earthenware   impressed or printed
  1958–

LLANELLY (Dyfed)   G. & D.L.
  Guest & Dewsbury
  earthenware, 1877–1927   G.D.
    printed initials in   L
    backstamps

  South Wales Pottery   CHAMBERS
  earthenware, *c.* 1839–58   LLANELLY
  Chambers & Co.
  c. 1839–54   S.W.P.
  Coombs & Holland
  c. 1854–58   printed or impressed

NANTGARW (Glamorgan)
  Nantgarw China Works   **NANT-GARW**
  porcelain, 1813–14; 1817–22   **C.W.**
  Billingsley, William &   impressed
  Walker, Samuel   (painted and stencilled
    'C.W.' stands for 'China   marks used, but
    Works' (transferred to   also found on later
    Swansea in 1814 until   copies)
    1817)

SWANSEA (Glamorgan)
  Swansea Pottery, Cambrian Pottery
  c. 1783–1870, earthenwares

c. 1783–, mark impressed   SWANSEA

                       CAMBRIAN POTTERY

impressed or printed   CAMBRIA
marks, c. 1783–1810

                    CAMBRIAN.

impressed or printed   DILLWYN & CO.
marks, c. 1811–17   SWANSEA

                      D. & CO.

impressed from c. 1817–24   BEVINGTON & CO.

printed from c. 1847–50

impressed, c. 1847–50   CYMRO
                     STONE CHINA

impressed, c. 1824–50   DILLWYN

Evans, David & Glasson
pottery, c. 1850–62
impressed or printed

Evans, D. J. & Co.   D.J. EVANS & CO.
pottery, c. 1862–70

                     EVANS & CO.

printed, *c.* 1862–70

Swansea porcelain   SWANSEA
impressed marks, 1814–22

printed or written in red   *SWANSEA*
enamel
impressed, sometimes   *Swansea*
with 'SWANSEA'   DILLWYN & CO.

rare impressed mark   BEVINGTON & CO.
of *c.* 1820

Baker, Bevans & Irwin   BAKER BEVANS
Glamorgan Pottery   & IRWIN
earthenware, 1813–38   printed or impressed

example of printed mark

The name of Pellatt & Green, retailers
of St. Paul's Church Yard, London, is
sometimes seen on Welsh wares of *c.* 1805–30

273

Calland & Co., John F. Landore Pottery earthenware, 1852–56	C. & CO. CALLAND SWANSEA
YNYSMEDW (nr. Swansea) Ynysmedw Pottery earthenware, *c.* 1850–70	Y.M.P. Y.P. impressed

IRELAND

BELLEEK (Co. Fermanagh)
   porcelain, 1863–
   McBirney, David &
   Armstrong, Robert

BELLEEK
CO. FERMANAGH

FERMANAGH
POTTERY
impressed

   impressed or printed
   mark of 1863–80

   early version of usual
   mark, 1863–91

   post-1891 version
   includes 'Ireland'
   and 'Co. Fermanagh'
   to comply with the
   McKinley Tariff Act

printed

274

CORK
 Carrigaline Pottery Ltd.
 earthenware, 1928–   CARRIG WARE
                            CARRIGALINE
  printed marks   POTTERY

DUBLIN
 Chambers, John, *c.* 1730–
 c. 1745
 tin-glazed earthenware
   inscription painted on
   plate

 Delamain, Captain Henry (*d.* 1757)
 1752–*c.* 1771

 Donovan & Son, John   DONOVAN
 decorator of English
 pottery and porcelain   *DONOVAN*
 c. 1770–1829   *DUBLIN*
                              painted

   'DONOVAN' impressed on
   wares made to order

 Vodrey's Pottery   VODREY DUBLIN
 earthenware, 1872–*c.* 85   POTTERY

                              impressed

LIMERICK
  Stritch, John, *c.* 1760
  tin-glazed earthenware

Made by John Stritch
Limerick, 4th June 1761

inscription on plate

ADDENDUM OF RECENT MANUFAC-
TURERS, OTHER CHANGES, ETC.

BOURNEMOUTH (Dorset)
  Purbeck Pottery Ltd.
  stoneware, Dec. 1965–

    printed marks

Purbeck
Pottery
England

BROADSTAIRS (Kent)
  Broadstairs Pottery Ltd.
  stoneware, 1966–
  printed mark

BRUTON (Somerset)
  Goddard Ltd., Elaine
  earthenware, 1939–

    mark printed label

CHESTERFIELD (Derbyshire)
  Price, Powell & Co. Ltd.   No registered
  earthenware, 1740–   trade mark
  (Ltd. from 1961)
  Now subsidiary of Pearsons of Chesterfield

CHURCH GRESLEY
(Derbyshire)
   Mason, Cash & Co. Ltd.
   Pool Potteries, 1901
   domestic earthenware
   (Ltd. Co. since 1941)

products
unmarked

DARTMOUTH (Devon)
   Britannia Designs, Ltd.
   earthenware, 1959
     mark an applied label
     used from 1971

ELKESLEY (Nottinghamshire)
   Aston, Christopher S.
   stoneware, 1968
   (moved to Elkesley
   from Bawtry in 1971)

applied label

FARNHAM (Surrey)
   Harris & Sons, A.
   earthenware, 1872
   (established in 1864
   at Elstead, Surrey)

No special mark
used

HINDHEAD (Surrey)
   Surrey Ceramic Co. Ltd.
   Kingswood Pottery
   earthenware and
   stoneware, 1956–

LIVERPOOL (Merseyside)
  Prince William Pottery Co.
  earthenware, 1953–

'PRINCE WILLIAM'

LONDON
  Macbride, Kitty
  (Brown & Muntzer)
  earthenware figures of
  mice. Trade-name:
  'The Happy Mice of
  Berkeley Square'
  1960–

Kitty MacBride
England

PAIGNTON (Devon)
  Barn Pottery, Ltd.
  earthenware, 1964

    Trade-name 'Barn' ware

REDRUTH (Cornwall)
  Foster's Pottery Co.
  earthenware, 1949–

    stamped mark

FOSTER'S
POTTERY
REDRUTH

STOKE D'ABERTON (Surrey)
  Everson, Ronald
  porcelain and bone-china
  1953
    mark in the form of
    a dated signature

Ronald Everson

279

HANLEY (Staffordshire)
   Mason's Ironstone China Ltd.
   earthenware, March 1968
   (from March 1974 name changed
   to: Mason's Ironstone, a Division
   of Josiah Wedgwood & Sons Ltd.)
      printed marks

LONGTON (Staffordshire)
   Anton Potteries, Ltd., Jon
   ironstone, 1974–
   (pottery established
   c. 1874, 'Crown Clarence'
   from *c.* 1953–1971
   Jon Anton Potteries
   1971–74)

      mark on bone-china

Blyth Pottery (Longton) Ltd.
earthenware (taken over by John Tams Ltd.
in April, 1973 and no longer trading on own
account)

LONGTON (Staffordshire)
  Hostess Tableware
  Thomas Poole &
  Gladstone China Ltd.
    'Royal Stafford' and
    'Hostess' bone china
    and 'Hostess' ironstone
    1971–

Hostess Tableware

FINE BONE CHINA
STAFFS, ENGLAND

& other full marks

Royal Albert Ltd.
(Royal Doulton Tableware
Ltd.) Ltd. added 1970
bone-china
  'Royal Albert' previously
  used by Thomas C.
  Wild & Sons Ltd.

ROYAL ALBERT
Bone China
ENGLAND

printed

Royal Grafton Bone China
(A. B. Jones & Sons, Ltd.
part of Crown Lynn Potteries
Group, N.Z. from 1971–)
bone-china from 1959–

Royal Tuscan
bone-china, *c.* 1962–
(Division of Wedgwood
Group from 1966)

STOKE (Staffordshire)
  Baifield Productions Ltd.
  (S. Fielding & Co. Ltd., Crown
  Devon Group), 1963–

Blakeney Art Pottery
earthenware, 1968–
  'Flow Blue Victoria'
  printed ware, Kent
  Staffordshire figures
  and floral art containers.
  M. J. Bailey & S. K. Bailey
  Note the lion and harp
  in coat-of-arms are in
  reverse positions to the
  authentic version

printed
backstamps in
blue

Similar Royal
Arms mark used,
with 'Romantic'
pattern

Blakeney Art Pottery (*cont.*)

printed backstamp
in brown 'M.J.B.'
(Michael J. Bailey)

IRONSTONE
STAFFORDSHIRE
ENGLAND

similar backstamp
used with:
FLO BLUE
T.M. STAFFORDSHIRE
ENGLAND

FLO BLUE
T.M. STAFFORDSHIRE
ENGLAND

Dorothy Ann Floral China
bone china floral
jewellery, 1946

STOKE ON TRENT
ENGLAND

TUNSTALL (Staffordshire)
　Wedgwood (Tunstall) Ltd., Enoch
　name changed from Wedgwood & Co. Ltd.
　in 1965 (see p. 259)

APPENDIX A

Patent Office Registration Mark

From 1842 until 1883 many manufacturers' wares are marked with the following 'diamond-mark', which is an indication that the design was registered with the British Patent Office; ceramics and glass are Classes IV and III, as indicated in the topmost section of the mark, and gave copyright protection for a period of three years (see Appendix B and Preface, page 11).

The date of the 'diamond mark' only indicates the time of registration, but a popular form of decoration was often produced for far longer than the three years. Printed marks usually refer to the applied pattern, whereas impressed or moulded applied versions are more likely to relate to the form of the ware.

When checking date to determine the name of the manufacturer it will sometimes be the case that the design was registered by retailers, wholesalers or even foreign manufacturers.

'Diamond-marks' impressed into bone-china can often be more accurately read when held before a strong artificial light.

Example of ceramic
design registered on
23rd May 1842

APPENDIX A

Index to letters for each year and month from 1842 *to* 1867:

Years

1842 X	1849 S	1856 L	1863 G
1843 H	1850 V	1857 K	1864 N
1844 C	1851 P	1858 B	1865 W
1845 A	1852 D	1859 M	1866 Q
1846 I	1853 Y	1860 Z	1867 T
1847 F	1854 J	1861 R	
1848 U	1855 E	1862 O	

Months

January	C	July	I	
February	G	August	R	⎱ For September 1857
March	W	September	D	⎰ query letter R used
April	H	October	B	from 1st–19th Sept.
May	E	November	K	⎱ For December 1860
June	M	December	A	⎰ query letter K used.

Index to letters for each year and month from 1868 *to* 1883:

Example of ceramic design, registered on 6th January 1868

Years

1868 X	1872 I	1876 V	1880 J
1869 H	1873 F	1877 P	1881 E
1870 C	1874 U	1878 D	1882 L
1871 A	1875 S	1879 Y	1883 K

Months

Jan. C	April H	July I	Oct. B
Feb. G	May E	Aug. R	Nov. K
Mar. W	June M	Sept. D	Dec. A

For Registration marks brought in with W for the year, see below:

From 1st to 6th March, 1878, the following Registration Mark was issued:

From 1884 this method of dating registrations ceased and the designs were numbered consecutively in the following manner: 'Rd. 12345' or 'Rd. No. 12345'. The following table gives a guide up until 1910 to the range of numbers used within a year:

Registered in January		Registered in January	
1	1884	90483	1888
19734	1885	116648	1889
40480	1886	141273	1890
64520	1887	163767	1891

185713	1892	368154	1901
205240	1893	385500	1902
224720	1894	402500	1903
246975	1895	420000	1904
268392	1896	447000	1905
291241	1897	471000	1906
311658	1898	494000	1907
331707	1899	519500	1908
351202	1900	550000	1909

Information concerning the work of the full members of the Craftsmen Potters Association (modern studio-potters) is well provided by an excellent directory, *Potters*, where the full particulars, including the mark and an illustration of the ware of 138 potters, are given. This directory may be obtained from the Craftsmen Potters Shop, William Blake House, Marshall Street, London, W.1., price 75p, plus postage.

The part of the Class IV Design Index in the Public Record Office that relates to pottery and porcelain is included in Appendix B, pages 288 to 392.

APPENDIX B

Index of Names and Dates of Manufacturers, Retailers, Wholesalers and others who registered designs from 1842 to 1883

(See Appendix A, page 284, and Preface, page 12)

Date	Parcel No.	Patent No.	Factory, Retailer Wholesaler, etc	Place
1842				
Sept 22	1	1694	James Dixon & Sons	Sheffield
Nov 2	1	2152	Joseph Wolstenholme	Sheffield
3	1	2163	idem	Sheffield
26	3	2503–4	Henry Hunt	London
Dec 2	3	2599–00	Joseph Clementson	Shelton
30	2	3346	James Edwards	Burslem
1843				
Jan 24	2	4296–7	John Ridgway & Co.	Shelton
Feb 3	4	4462	T. Woodfield	London
21	1	5266–70	Samuel Alcock & Co.	Burslem
Mar 21	5	5993–4	Josiah Wedgwood & Sons	Etruria
31	6	6266	Samuel Alcock & Co.	Burslem
May 2	4	6978	Josiah Wedgwood & Sons	Etruria
5	1	7037	W. S. Kennedy	Burslem
11	2	7074	idem	Burslem
13	4	7122	Jones & Walley	Cobridge
June 14	5	7503–5	Samuel Alcock & Co.	Burslem
Aug 30	8	9678–80	James Edwards	Burslem
Oct 6	2	10370	idem	Burslem
Nov 10	3	11292	Minton & Co.	Stoke
28	5	11690	Thos. Dimmock & Co.	Shelton
Dec 14	10	12331	G. F. Bowers & Co.	Tunstall

APPENDIX B

Date	Parcel No.	Patent No.	Factory, Retailer Wholesaler, etc	Place
1844				
Feb 15	9	16264–5	Samuel Alcock & Co.	Burslem
20	4	16374–5	idem	Burslem
Mar 1	6	16687	Hamilton & Moore	Longton
5	3	16831	Mellor, Venables & Co.	Burslem
7	4	16871	J. & T. Lockett	Lane End
Apr 3	3	17566–72	Thos. Edwards	Burslem
11	4	17714	Hilditch & Hopwood	Lane End
May 7	4	18207	Thos. Dimmock & Co.	Shelton
June 29	3	19182	idem	Shelton
July 20	5	19977–9	John Ridgway & Co.	Shelton
30	2	20332–4	Herbert Minton & Co.	Stoke
Aug 15	3	20779	King, Knight & Elkin	Stoke
21	7	21069–73	Herbert Minton & Co.	Stoke
Sept 9	7	21450	Cyples, Barlow & Cyples	Lane End
19	4	21700–1	Jn. Ridgway & Co.	Shelton
21	2	21715	Henry Hunt	London
30	7	21960	Charles Meigh	Hanley
Oct 14	4	22158	Copeland & Garrett	Stoke
17	3	22192	Clementson, Young & Jameson	Shelton
30	4	22394–6	Herbert Minton & Co.	Stoke
Nov 6	4	22424	idem	Stoke
11	5	22490	James Edwards	Burslem
13	4	22499–500	John Ridgway & Co.	Shelton
22	4	22834	Thos. Dimmock & Co.	Shelton
26	3	22883	Ray & Wynne	Longton
Dec 2	3	22919–20	Copeland & Garrett	Stoke
7	4	23207–10	Thos. Edwards	Burslem
16	6	23593	Willm. Ridgway, Son & Co.	Hanley
24	2	23843	John Meir & Son	Tunstall
1845				
Jan 11	6	24846	George Phillips	Longport

289

Date	Parcel No.	Patent No.	Factory, Retailer Wholesaler, etc	Place
15	2	24996	Clementson, Young & Jameson	Shelton
21	6	25199	T. J. & J. Mayer	Longport
27	5	25273	John Rose & Co.	Coalport
Feb 26	5	26532–3	W. S. Kennedy	Burslem
27	3	26543	George Phillips	Longport
Mar 5	1	26608	Copeland & Garrett	Stoke
6	5	26617	Herbert Minton & Co.	Stoke
17	10	26939	idem	Stoke
20	1	26949	idem	Stoke
31	4	27034	Thos. Pearce	London
Apr 10	1	27202	idem	London
25	2	27350	Copeland & Garrett	Stoke
26	1	27352	George Pearce	London
26	3	27354	T. & R. Boote, Walley & Jones	Burslem, Cobridge and Hanley
30	2	27383	Jacob Furnival & Co.	Cobridge
May 8	2	27451	Herbert Minton & Co.	Stoke
10	3	27482	Walley & T. & R. Boote	Cobridge and Burslem
31	1	27800	Francis Morley	Shelton
June 19	1	28150	George Phillips	Longport
26	3	28296	Minton & Co.	Stoke
July 5	1	28668–71	George Phillips	Longport
5	2	28672	Enoch Wood	Burslem
26	1	29173	William Adams & Sons	Stoke
Aug 28	3	29993	Joseph Clementson	Shelton
Sept 4	3	30161–3	Copeland & Garrett	Stoke
11	2	30286	Thos. Phillips & Son	Burslem
19	1	30383	Minton & Co.	Stoke
Oct 6	1	30543–4	H. Minton & Co.	Stoke
21	1	30699	Copeland & Garrett	Stoke

Date	Parcel No.	Patent No.	Factory, Retailer Wholesaler, etc	Place
22	2	30701	Clementson & Young	Shelton
Nov 15	2	31128	Bayley & Ball	Longton
22	2	31329	Minton & Co.	Stoke
Dec 4	4	31670–3	John Ridgway	Shelton
27	2	32553	James Edwards	Burslem
29	2	32555	Joseph Clementson	Shelton
30	3	32601	Furnival & Clark	Hanley
1846				
Jan 7	2	32698	Joseph Clementson	Shelton
24	2	33319	Jacob Furnival & Co.	Cobridge
Feb 26	5	34031	T. J. & J. Mayer	Longport
Mar 2	4	34108	Minton & Co.	Stoke
11	2	34281–5	W. S. Kennedy	Burslem
Apr 7	1	34564–66	idem	Burslem
17	3	34684	Copeland & Garrett	Stoke
May 21	3	35030–1	H. Minton & Co.	Stoke
26	2	35116–7	idem	Stoke
June 6	1	35219	W. Chamberlain & Co.	Worcester
26	2	35777	H. Minton & Co.	Stoke
30	3	35795	John Goodwin	Longton
July 11	1	36047	J. K. Knight	Longton
16	1	36167	Ridgway, Son & Co.	Hanley
17	1	36263	John Ridgway & Co.	Shelton
21	1	36278	F. Morley & Co.	Shelton
Aug 1	2	36447–8	Josiah Wedgwood & Sons	Etruria
3	1	36450	idem	Etruria
3	2	36451–2	H. Minton & Co.	Stoke
Sept 3	2	37170	G. Phillips	Longport
3	3	37171–2	F. Morley & Co.	Shelton
14	4	37254	Copeland & Garrett	Stoke
26	2	37419–21	John Ridgway & Co.	Shelton
29	3	37586	T. J. & J. Mayer	Longport
Oct 26	1	37806	F. Morley & Co.	Shelton
26	5	37864	J. Edwards	Burslem

APPENDIX B

Date	Parcel No.	Patent No.	Factory, Retailer Wholesaler, etc	Place
Nov 3	1	37935	Ridgway & Abington	Hanley
5	2	37986	G. Phillips	Longport
12	3	38068	C. Meigh	Hanley
16	2	38113	H. Minton & Co.	Stoke
21	2	38291–2	Thos. Furnival & Co.	Hanley
Dec 3	4	38606	Ridgway & Abington	Hanley
4	2	38610	H. Minton & Co.	Stoke
10	3	38786	Joseph Clementson	Shelton
14	3	39480	James Edwards	Burslem
14	4	39481	Minton & Co.	Stoke
16	1	39519	John Goodwin	Longton
17	2	39544–5	Copeland & Garrett	Stoke
26	5	39614	Henry Hunt	London
29	2	39703	Edward Challinor	Tunstall
31	3	39746	Josiah Wedgwood & Sons	Etruria

1847

Date	Parcel No.	Patent No.	Factory, Retailer Wholesaler, etc	Place
Jan 9	4	40104–5	John Ridgway & Co.	Shelton
9	7	40110	Copeland & Garrett	Stoke
Feb 2	7	41213	T. & R. Boote	Burslem
8	5	41266–7	T. J. & J. Mayer	Longton
15	4	41459–60	Copeland & Garrett	Stoke
Mar 17	3	42044	John Wedge Wood	Tunstall
17	6	42047–8	John Ridgway & Co.	Shelton
22	2	42233	Bailey & Ball	Longton
23	7	42279	Herbert Minton & Co.	Stoke
30	1	42363	James Edwards	Burslem
Apr 3	6	42435	Samuel Alcock & Co.	Burslem
27	1	42804	idem	Burslem
May 12	4	43154	Copeland & Garrett	Stoke
14	1	43170–1	Herbert Minton & Co.	Stoke
June 11	4	43536	James Edwards	Burslem
11	6	43557	Joseph Alexander	Norwich
21	5	43728	John Rose & Co.	Coalport
25	2	43780	James Edwards	Burslem

Date	Parcel No.	Patent No.	Factory, Retailer Wholesaler, etc	Place
uly 5	5	43916–7	Mellor, Venables & Co.	Burslem
15	1	44014–5	idem	Burslem
16	5	44036–9	James Edwards	Burslem
27	3	44398	T. J. & J. Mayer	Longport
ug 3	3	44872	John Rose & Co.	Coalport
16	2	45088	James Edwards	Burslem
17	2	45091–2	W. T. Copeland	Stoke
19	3	45175	H. Minton & Co.	Stoke
26	2	45367	James Edwards	Burslem
ept 9	3	45730	William Taylor Copeland	Stoke
16	3	45822	idem	Stoke
25	5	45992	John Wedge Wood	Tunstall
ct 1	4	46130	Thos. Peake	Tunstall
2	5	46192–4	John Ridgway & Co.	Shelton
4	3	46232	H. Minton & Co.	Stoke
8	4	46265	John Wedge Wood	Tunstall
13	1	46299	W. T. Copeland	Stoke
23	2	46516–8	H. Minton & Co.	Stoke
27	1	46529	John Ridgway & Co.	Shelton
Nov 11	4	46886	H. Minton & Co.	Stoke
23	4	47183	J. Wedgwood & Co.	Etruria
Dec 1	2	47417–20	John Rose & Co.	Coalport
10	3	47562–3	Minton & Co. & John Bell	Stoke
15	4	48130	Minton & Co.	Stoke
1848				
an 1	4	48540–2	Barker & Till	Burslem
6	4	48717	Geo. Grainger	Worcester
18	2	49040	W. T. Copeland	Stoke
eb 11	3	49780–1	H. Minton & Co.	Stoke
29	12	50473	Minton & Co.	Stoke
Mar 4	4	50549	Minton & Co.	Stoke
7	1	50635–6	Ridgway & Abington	Hanley
14	2	50798	W. T. Copeland	Stoke
15	2	50803	idem	Stoke

Date	Parcel No.	Patent No.	Factory, Retailer Wholesaler, etc	Place
20	7	50994	Wood & Brownfield	Cobridge
27	8	51185–91	J. & S. Alcock Jnr.	Cobridge
Apr 15	4	51542	John Ridgway & Co.	Shelton
17	6	51599	Frederick Harrison	London
22	3	51661	Josiah Wedgwood & Sons	Etruria
27	4	51763	idem	Etruria
28	5	51768	Giovanni Franchi	London
May 30	3	52162	Thos. Peake	Tunstall
June 20	4	52402	G. F. Bowers & Co.	Tunstall
30	2	52529	W. T. Copeland	Stoke
30	3	52530	Ridgway & Abington	Hanley
Aug 10	3	53782	Geo. Grainger	Worcester
16	8	53876	Thos. Pinder	Burslem
23	2	54018	John Wedge Wood	Tunstall
26	2	54067	John Meir & Son	Tunstall
Sept 15	3	54438	W. T. Copeland	Stoke
18	4	54487	Charles Meigh	Hanley
25	4	54578–9	Giovanni Franchi	London
30	7	54662	John Ridgway & Co.	Shelton
Oct 17	3	54901	T. & R. Boote	Burslem
Nov 4	2	55174	W. T. Copeland	Stoke
13	4	55337	idem	Stoke
21	5	55456–7	Minton & Co.	Stoke
27	2	55766	John Ridgway & Co.	Shelton
Dec 16	3	56631–3	James Edwards	Burslem
28	2	56845	John Ridgway	Shelton
1849				
Jan 3	2	56978	William Adams & Sons	Stoke
20	2	57506–8	W. Davenport & Co.	Longport
Feb 2	4	58069	Mellor, Venables & Co.	Burslem
16	5	58461	Minton & Co.	Stoke
16	11	58474	Ridgway & Abington	Hanley
26	2	58578	John Rose & Co.	Coalport
Mar 13	2	58874	Joseph Clementson	Shelton

Date	Parcel No.	Patent No.	Factory, Retailer Wholesaler, etc	Place
26	5	59232	Minton & Co.	Stoke
27	2	59245	Cope & Edwards	Longton
31	2	59286	John Ridgway & Co.	Shelton
pr 2	5	59308	Podmore, Walker & Co.	Tunstall
10	4	59400	W. T. Copeland	Stoke
16	6	59571	C. J. Mason	Longton
ay 24	1	60081	Mr. Wedge Wood	Tunstall
ne 7	3	60265	T. J. & J. Mayer	Longport
ly 16	2	61347	Ridgway & Abington	Hanley
ug 11	4	61865	W. T. Copeland	Stoke
15	2	61986	H. Minton & Co.	Stoke
17	2	62003	W. T. Copeland	Stoke
27	5	62316	Mellor, Venables & Co.	Burslem
ept 14	6	62498	F. & R. Pratt & Co.	Fenton
28	6	62690–4	J. Ridgway	Shelton
ct 10	2	62883	idem	Shelton
12	4	62914	Minton & Co.	Stoke
26	5	63267	J. Hollinshead	Shelton
ov 8	6	63490	John Cliff Quince	London
9	4	63523	W. T. Copeland	Stoke
17	2	63718	Minton & Co.	Stoke
22	2	64319	W. T. Copeland	Stoke
30	5	64627	John Rose & Co.	Coalport
ec 6	3	64739	W. T. Copeland	Stoke
15	4	64982	T. J. & J. Mayer	Longport
350				
an 3	1	65884	W. Davenport & Co.	Longport
14	4	66266–7	J. Ridgway	Shelton
26	6	66862	G. Grainger	Worcester
eb 13	1	67398	idem	Worcester
13	3	67413	J. & M. P. Bell & Co.	Glasgow
27	4	67783	G. Grainger	Worcester
lar 9	3	67987	W. T. Copeland	Stoke
30	9	68489	John Rose & Co.	Coalport

Date	Parcel No.	Patent No.	Factory, Retailer Wholesaler, etc	Place
Apr 4	4	68623	T. J. & J. Mayer	Longport
8	1	68720	J. Clementson	Shelton
13	7	68797	Minton & Co.	Stoke
18	11	68959	John Rose & Co.	Coalport
24	3	69142	William Pierce	London
25	3	69149	Minton & Co.	Stoke
June 4	1	69679	J. & M. P. Bell & Co.	Glasgow
5	3	69685	Barker & Son	Burslem
21	4	69884	E. Walley	Cobridge
July 2	2	70088	T. J. & J. Mayer	Longport
16	5	70364	C. & W. K. Harvey	Longton
Sept 9	5	71843	Thomas Till	Burslem
16	8	71952	J. & M. P. Bell & Co.	Glasgow
16	9	71953–4	J. Ridgway	Shelton
19	2	71989	W. T. Copeland	Stoke
21	1	72057	Mellor, Venables & Co.	Burslem
Oct 9	2	72395–6	Minton & Co.	Stoke
17	6	72544	W. T. Copeland	Stoke
Nov 4	4	73327	J. Wedgwood & Sons	Etruria
20	7	73693	F. Morley & Co.	Shelton
22	3	73719	John Rose & Co.	Coalport
Dec 5	3	74138	F. Morley & Co.	Shelton
19	5	74785	John Rose & Co.	Coalport
19	6	74786	T. J. & J. Mayer	Longport
20	6	75148	W. T. Copeland	Stoke
1851				
Jan 20	4	75883–4	James Green	London
Feb 10	9	76664	William Brownfield	Cobridge
Mar 17	13	77481–91	J. Ridgway & Co.	Shelton
31	4	77986	J. & M. P. Bell & Co.	Glasgow
Apr 9	2	78268	Thos. Till & Son	Burslem
11	4	78309–10	J. & M. P. Bell & Co.	Glasgow
11	6	78312	W. S. Kennedy	Burslem
14	7	78398–401	J. & M. P. Bell & Co.	Glasgow

APPENDIX B

Date	Parcel No.	Patent No.	Factory, Retailer Wholesaler, etc	Place
26	3	78634	E. Walley	Cobridge
May 30	4	79085	W. T. Copeland	Stoke
June 7	4	79164	J. Ridgway & Co.	Shelton
11	2	79183	W. T. Copeland	Stoke
11	3	79184	Ralph Scragg	Hanley
19	5	79300	W. T. Copeland	Stoke
July 10	3	79588	R. Britton & Co.	Leeds
14	3	79684	W. T. Copeland	Stoke
21	7	79750–3	T. & R. Boote	Burslem
24	2	79782	Thos. Till & Son	Burslem
26	3	79802	C. Collinson & Co.	Burslem
Aug 16	2	80184	Ridgway & Abington	Hanley
Sept 2	4	80365	T. J. & J. Mayer	Longport
19	3	80629–30	T. & R. Boote	Burslem
29	4	80815–16	James Edwards	Burslem
30	3	80826	idem	Burslem
Oct 1	1	80827	W. T. Copeland	Stoke
7	3	80887	Chamberlain & Co.	Worcester
10	4	80910–1	W. Brownfield	Cobridge
10	6	80913	T. & R. Boote	Burslem
14	4	80980	Thos. Till & Son	Burslem
16	4	80989	W. Brownfield	Cobridge
17	3	80997	George Bowden Sander	London
21	3	81057	Wm. Ridgway	Shelton
Nov 1	5	81225–6	Geo. B. Sander	London
10	4	81492	Ralph Scragg	Hanley
12	6	81510–12	Minton & Co.	Stoke
13	2	81518	Charles Meigh & Son	Hanley
14	4	81558	Geo. B. Sander	London
Dec 2	2	81815	T. J. & J. Mayer	Burslem
4	3	81843–4	Minton & Co.	Stoke
5	5	81864	John Ridgway & Co.	Shelton
8	8	81960	W. T. Copeland	Stoke
15	6	82052	Geo. B. Sander	London

APPENDIX B

Date	Parcel No.	Patent No.	Factory, Retailer Wholesaler, etc	Place
1852				
Jan 27	1	83342	W. & G. Harding	Burslem
Feb 17	1	83826	Venables & Baines	Burslem
Mar 4	2	84133–4	Wm. Brownfield	Cobridge
13	3	84239	Wm. Ridgway	Shelton
22	7	84385	Ralph Scragg	Hanley
24	3	84406	James Edwards	Burslem
24	4	84407	Minton & Co.	Stoke
25	1	84410	John Milner	Cobridge
26	3	84471	J. & M. P. Bell & Co.	Glasgow
Apr 1	1	84541	Thos. Till & Son	Burslem
8	4	84615	idem	Burslem
21	4	84837	George Ray	Longton
May 5	5	85001–2	J. M. Blashfield	London
6	5	85008	Geo. Bowden Sander	London
7	2	85010–3	J. M. Blashfield	London
14	5	85081	W. T. Copeland	Stoke
18	1	85102	Minton & Co.	Stoke
June 1	2	85224–5	J. M. Blashfield	London
5	5	85248	Minton & Co.	Stoke
14	4	85354	W. T. Copeland	Stoke
21	2	85404	J. & T. Lockett	Longton
July 5	3	85619	J. Pankhurst & Co.	Hanley
23	3	85803–4	Minton & Co.	Stoke
Aug 4	3	86070–1	W. T. Copeland	Stoke
13	5	86126	Thos. Till & Son	Burslem
25	4	86318	Chas. Meigh & Son	Hanley
25	5	86319	Geo. Bowden Sander	London
Sept 3	7	86473	Minton & Co.	Stoke
15	5	86649	Thos. Till & Son	Burslem
16	1	86657	Minton & Co.	Stoke
24	1	86815	idem	Stoke
27	3	86857	Warburton & Britton	Leeds
Oct 1	6	86931	W. T. Copeland	Stoke
7	5	87040	Ralph Scragg	Hanley

Date	Parcel No.	Patent No.	Factory, Retailer Wholesaler, etc	Place
23	4	87219	Davenports & Co.	Longport
25	2	87228	Wm. Brownfield	Cobridge
30	3	87464	Marple, Turner & Co.	Hanley
Nov 4	5	87541	John Holland	Tunstall
11	3	87633	Minton & Co.	Stoke
22	3	87883	J. Pankhurst & J. Dimmock	Hanley
25	4	88037	Keys & Mountford	Stoke
Dec 16	4	88350	John Rose & Co.	Coalport
27	1	88693	Warburton & Britton	Leeds

1853

Date	Parcel No.	Patent No.	Factory, Retailer Wholesaler, etc	Place
Jan 3	3	88808–9	W. T. Copeland	Stoke
12	6	88978	Thos. Goodfellow	Tunstall
14	3	88987	Davenports & Co.	Longport
18	2	89050	idem	Longport
Feb 4	9	89469	J. Pankhurst & J. Dimmock	Hanley
10	2	89626	Geo. Wooliscroft	Tunstall
11	6	89646	Thos. Worthington & J. Green	Shelton
12	3	89661–3	Minton & Co.	Stoke
17	4	89722–3	W. S. Kennedy & Co.	Burslem
26	5	89958	W. T. Copeland	Stoke
Mar 10	2	90253	J. & M. P. Bell & Co.	Glasgow
17	5	90360	J. W. Pankhurst & Co.	Hanley
19	2	90372	Minton & Co.	Stoke
Apr 4	6	90610	John Rose & Co.	Coalport
23	2	90876	Wm. Adams & Sons	Stoke
May 7	5	91121–4	John Alcock	Cobridge
June 7	3	91329	Geo. Wood & Co.	Shelton
14	2	91405–6	Livesley, Powell & Co.	Hanley
22	3	91469	Pankhurst & Dimmock	Hanley
24	3	91487	Geo. Wooliscroft	Tunstall
24	11	91512–3	Ridgway & Co.	Shelton

APPENDIX B

Date	Parcel No.	Patent No.	Factory, Retailer Wholesaler, etc	Place
July 18	4	91737	John Edwards	Longton
20	2	91749–50	J. H. Baddeley	Shelton
Aug 8	1	92001	Anthony Shaw	Tunstall
10	2	92018	Holland & Green	Longton
Sept 3	2	92340	T. & R. Boote	Burslem
6	3	92364	F. Morley & Co.	Shelton
21	2	92631–2	James Edwards	Burslem
Oct 5	2	92768–70	Venables, Mann & Co.	Burslem
10	3	92859	Barrow & Co.	Fenton
11	5	92864	Ralph Scragg	Hanley
12	3	92867	James Edwards	Burslem
12	4	92868–9	Livesley, Powell & Co.	Hanley
19	4	92952	Minton & Co.	Stoke
22	1	93008–9	T. J. & J. Mayer	Longport
Nov 24	2	93438–9	Thos. Till & Son	Burslem
26	2	93452	W. T. Copeland	Stoke
30	5	93483	Wm. Adams & Sons	Stoke
Dec 6	4	93536	J. Alcock	Cobridge
24	3	93706–7	Samuel Moore & Co.	Sunderlnd
24	4	93708	J. Alcock	Cobridge
1854				
Jan 10	4	94326	W. & G. Harding	Burslem
13	1	94343–4	Deaville & Baddeley	Hanley
14	3	94632	Samuel Moore & Co.	Sunderlnd
21	3	94727	J. & M. P. Bell & Co.	Glasgow
30	4	94815	Samuel Alcock & Co.	Burslem
Feb 23	3	95163	W. T. Copeland	Stoke
Mar 11	4	95275	Samuel Alcock & Co.	Burslem
20	1	95388	Thos. Till & Son	Burslem
22	2	95397	James Edwards & Son	Longport
24	3	95420	Minton & Co.	Stoke
27	3	95448	Geo. Baguley	Hanley
27	6	95451	J. Deaville	Hanley
31	1	95469	Holland & Green	Longton

APPENDIX B

Date		Parcel No.	Patent No.	Factory, Retailer Wholesaler, etc	Place
Apr	1	4	95510	Wm. Brownfield	Cobridge
	4	3	95523	Woollard & Hattersley	Cambdge
	5	3	95542	Ralph Scragg	Hanley
	6	3	95553	Samuel Alcock & Co.	Burslem
	10	3	95575	J. Deaville	Hanley
	10	4	95576	Samuel Alcock & Co.	Burslem
	11	5	95587–8	Pearson, Farrall & Meakin	Shelton
	15	1	95611	Geo. Baguley	Hanley
	21	3	95646	Warburton & Britton	Leeds
May	4	3	95733	John Ridgway & Co.	Shelton
	8	3	95751	Wm. Brownfield	Cobridge
June	3	2	96003	Thos. Till & Son	Burslem
	9	2	96039	Chas. Meigh & Son	Hanley
	21	5	96085–6	T. & R. Boote	Burslem
July	18	2	96296	idem	Burslem
	18	4	96298	Alcock & Co.	Burslem
Sept	5	3	96773	Samuel Alcock & Co.	Burslem
	12	2	96826	W. T. Copeland	Stoke
Oct	2	3	96980	Wm. Brownfield	Cobridge
	6	4	97141	Davenports & Co.	Longport
	9	4	97160	T. J. & J. Mayer	Longport
	31	2	97508	Geo. Ray	Longton
Nov	10	5	97659	John Ridgway & Co.	Shelton
Dec	27	3	98640	Samuel Alcock & Co.	Burslem
	27	4	98641	Pankhurst & Dimmock	Hanley
	29	1	98648	F. & R. Pratt & Co.	Fenton
1855					
Jan	4	2	98696	Worthington & Green	Shelton
	6	4	98786	Samuel Alcock & Co.	Burslem
	15	2	99042	Pinder, Bourne & Hope	Burslem
	15	4	99051	Brougham & Mayer	Tunstall
	19	3	99086	Pankhurst & Dimmock	Hanley
	30	1	99188	John Edwards	Longton

301

APPENDIX B

Date	Parcel No.	Patent No.	Factory, Retailer Wholesaler, etc	Place
Feb 3	4	99231	J. & M. P. Bell & Co.	Glasgow
5	7	99282	Coomb(e)s & Holland	Llanelly
7	2	99310	John Alcock	Cobridge
17	3	99394	Pratt & Co.	Fenton
26	3	99488	Lockett, Baguley & Cooper	Shelton
28	4	99528	J. Ridgway & Co.	Shelton
Mar 1	5	99538–40	Minton & Co.	Stoke
5	3	99579	Elsmore & Forster	Tunstall
13	4	99653	Warburton & Britton	Leeds
17	1	99679	Wm. Baker	Fenton
Apr 7	7	99814	W. T. Copeland	Stoke
17	4	99876	Stephen Hughes & Son	Burslem
26	1	99972–4	Wm. Brownfield	Cobridge
28	7	100008	Venables, Mann & Co.	Burslem
May 10	5	100094	Beech, Hancock & Co.	Burslem
14	3	100116	Minton & Co.	Stoke
June 7	4	100246–7	John Alcock	Cobridge
11	3	100299	Saml. Alcock & Co.	Burslem
July 4	5	100624	J. Thompson	Staffs.
24	1	100816	Chas. Meigh & Son	Hanley
Aug 6	1	101019	James Dudson	Shelton
8	5	101026	J. Edwards & Son	Longport
11	1	101082	Geo. Grainger & Co.	Worceste
20	3	101127	Thos. Ford	Shelton
27	2	101229–31	Barrow & Co.	Fenton
Sept 27	4	101623–4	Saml. Bevington & Son	Shelton
Oct 3	2	101681	Geo. Mayor & Co.	London
3	3	101682	Minton & Co.	Stoke
17	8	101932	John Williamson	Glasgow
25	3	102325	D. Chetwynd	Cobridge
29	6	102355	G. W. Reade	Burslem
Nov 1	3	102415	Josiah Wedgwood & Sons	Etruria
22	4	102744	J. & M. P. Bell & Co.	Glasgow
28	3	102785	Wm. Brownfield	Cobridge

APPENDIX B

Date	Parcel No.	Patent No.	Factory, Retailer Wholesaler, etc	Place
1856				
Jan 5	3	103103	J. Edwards	Longton
15	4	103404	James Pankhurst & Co.	Hanley
23	3	103506	J. Roberts	Kent (Upnor)
23	4	103507	Minton & Co.	Stoke
31	4	103616	Josiah Wedgwood & Sons	Etruria
Mar 11	1	104078	Davenports & Co.	Longport
12	3	104090	Pratt & Co.	Fenton
Apr 7	2	104313–16	A. Shaw	Tunstall
7	3	104317	J. & M. P. Bell & Co.	Glasgow
18	2	104392	Wm. Beech	Burslem
18	3	104393	Ralph Scragg	Hanley
18	6	104396	E. Walley	Cobridge
18	7	104397	Ridgway & Abington	Hanley
30	3	104602–3	Wm. Brownfield	Cobridge
May 8	2	104694	Minton & Co.	Stoke
22	1	104762	idem	Stoke
June 13	3	105059	Chas. Meigh & Son	Hanley
28	3	105223	Worthington & Green	Hanley
30	7	105258	J. Clementson	Shelton
July 28	3	105492	E. Challinor	Tunstall
30	5	105702	J. Edwards & Son	Longport
Aug 12	2	105871	F. & R. Pratt & Co.	Fenton
19	5	105926	idem	Fenton
22	4	105955–9	T. & R. Boote	Burslem
Sept 1	3	106161	W. T. Copeland	Stoke
Oct 2	3	106477	H. Baggaley	Hanley
16	2	106671–2	Minton & Co.	Stoke
22	3	106770	W. T. Copeland	Stoke
Nov 7	6	106950	F. & R. Pratt & Co.	Fenton
14	9	107038	Davenports & Co.	Longport
27	3	107708	idem	Longport
27	6	107714	Wm. Brownfield	Cobridge
29	1	107783–5	E. Walley	Cobridge

APPENDIX B

Date	Parcel No.	Patent No.	Factory, Retailer Wholesaler, etc	Place
Dec 11	4	107955	W. T. Copeland	Stoke
18	2	108052	Mayer & Elliott	Longport
23	4	108105	idem	Longport
1857				
Jan 15	5	108605	F. & R. Pratt & Co.	Fenton
26	7	108785	J. Edwards	Longport
Feb 4	5	108854–5	John Meir & Son	Tunstall
9	4	108930	Minton & Co.	Stoke
17	3	109063	idem	Stoke
23	9	109180	Podmore, Walker & Co.	Hanley
Mar 20	4	109427	John Alcock	Cobridge
Apr 16	1	109738	John Alcock	Cobridge
29	1	109810	W. T. Copeland	Stoke
June 5	3	110096–7	Wm. Brownfield	Cobridge
19	1	110160	W. T. Copeland	Stoke
19	2	110161	Wilkinson & Rickhuss	Hanley
25	1	110247	J. & M. P. Bell & Co.	Glasgow
July 30	2	110780	Ridgway, Bates & Co.	Shelton
Aug 4	5	110806	Taylor, Pears & Co.	Fenton
11	3	110862	Kerr & Binns	Worcester
Sept 7	2	111105	W. T. Copeland	Stoke
Oct 3	3	111495–6	Doulton & Watts	London
5	5	111515–6	idem	London
14	1	111585	Ridgway & Abington	Hanley
17	1	111642	Mayer Bros. & Elliott	Longport
17	2	111643–4	T. & R. Boote	Burslem
22	1	111677	Pratt & Co.	Fenton
Nov 3	3	111831–2	Maw & Co.	Broseley
28	2	112263	Kerr & Binns	Worcester
Dec 4	4	112350	Minton & Co.	Stoke
9	2	112354	Wm. Brownfield	Cobridge

APPENDIX B

Date	Parcel No.	Patent No.	Factory, Retailer Wholesaler, etc	Place
1858				
Jan 29	3	112875	Cockson & Harding	Hanley
29	4	112876	E. & W. Walley	Cobridge
Mar 25	2	113290	Kerr & Binns	Worcester
Apr 9	2	113387	idem	Worcester
17	4	113456	Ridgway & Abington	Hanley
22	5	113565	T. & R. Boote	Burslem
30	5	113631	Minton & Co.	Stoke
May 6	4	113668	J. Edwards	Longton
25	4	113864	A. Shaw	Burslem
31	1	113900	Holland & Green	Longton
31	4	113903	Wm. Adams	Tunstall
June 2	1	113905–6	Wm. Brownfield	Cobridge
23	6	114048	Samuel Alcock & Co.	Burslem
July 13	2	114214	Mayer & Elliott	Longport
29	4	114532	Samuel Alcock & Co.	Burslem
Aug 24	2	114763	Wm. Brownfield	Cobridge
Sept 3	2	115120	Sharpe Bros. & Co.	Swadlncte
6	5	115197	James Edwards	Longport
10	3	115217	John Edwards	Longton
10	6	115343	Bridgwood & Clarke	Burslem
Oct 5	2	115901	Minton & Co.	Stoke
5	3	115902	Wm. Brownfield	Cobridge
7	1	115953	Ridgway & Abington	Hanley
18	3	116176	Minton & Co.	Stoke
29	2	116468	B. Green	Fenton
Nov 3	8	116585	James Stiff	London
5	5	116607	Wm. Savage	Winchstr
11	2	116737	E. & W. Walley	Cobridge
Dec 8	11	117336–8	T. & R. Boote	Burslem
8	12	117339	J. Clementson	Hanley
17	6	117443	W. T. Copeland	Stoke
23	2	117516	J. Clementson	Hanley
23	9	117530	W. T. Copeland	Stoke
27	4	117559	J. Clementson	Hanley

305

Date	Parcel No.	Patent No.	Factory, Retailer Wholesaler, etc	Place
1859				
Jan 25	4	118119	W. T. Copeland	Stoke
Feb 2	3	118294	T. & R. Boote	Burslem
3	2	118303–4	Davenports & Co.	Longport
8	6	118415	Leveson Hill (Excrs. of)	Stoke
Mar 19	1	118827	Alsop, Downes, Spilsbury & Co.	London
21	7	118891	T. & R. Boote	Burslem
29	7	119137	idem	Burslem
May 7	1	119721–2	E. & W. Walley	Cobridge
10	2	119760	Samuel Alcock & Co.	Burslem
20	1	119968	Wm. Brownfield	Cobridge
26	1	120096	Lockett, Baguley & Cooper	Hanley
July 2	2	120560	W. T. Copeland	Stoke
Aug 6	7	121140	F. & R. Pratt & Co.	Fenton
27	6	121724	Samuel Alcock & Co.	Burslem
Sept 1	3	121833	James Edwards & Son	Longport
Oct 12	4	122959	Wm. Adams	Tunstall
14	4	123116	W. T. Copeland	Stoke
25	1	123389–91	Minton & Co.	Stoke
28	1	123604	Davenports & Co.	Longport
Nov 2	3	123738–40	Elsmore & Forster	Tunstall
5	4	123816	Wm. Brownfield	Cobridge
17	4	124140–3	Minton & Co.	Stoke
23	4	124274	idem	Stoke
Dec 10	5	124653	Josiah Wedgwood & Sons	Etruria
14	2	124716	E. & W. Walley	Cobridge
15	3	124725	Minton & Co.	Stoke
1860				
Jan 10	4	125365	W. T. Copeland	Stoke
23	7	125863	Mayer & Elliott	Longport
Feb 14	9	126446–7	W. T. Copeland	Stoke

APPENDIX B

Date	Parcel No.	Patent No.	Factory, Retailer Wholesaler, etc	Place
Mar 1	2	126950	Bates, Brown-Westhead & Moore	Hanley
27	1	127513	idem	Hanley
Apr 5	1	127766	Geo. Grainger & Co.	Worcester
12	4	127965	Minton & Co.	Stoke
May 2	2	128476	John Meir & Son	Tunstall
19	9	129129	Lockett, Baguley & Cooper	Hanley
30	10	129578	Edward Corn	Burslem
June 6	4	129680–2	Wm. Brownfield	Cobridge
22	2	130106	Minton & Co.	Stoke
28	2	130135	Minton & Co.	Stoke
Aug 21	2	131943	John Wedge Wood	Tunstall
Sept 24	3	133411	Minton & Co.	Stoke
29	7	133788	idem	Stoke
Oct 13	5	134204	B. Green	Fenton
18	4	134519–20	Bates, Brown–Westhead & Moore	Hanley
19	4	134555–7	J. Clementson	Shelton
19	5	134558–9	Holland & Green	Longton
29	3	134936	Minton & Co.	Stoke
29	9	134968	Wm. Brownfield	Cobridge
Nov 23	9	136032	T. & R. Boote	Burslem
Dec 3	3	136285–6	Bates, Brown–Westhead & Moore	Hanley
12	3	136643	Bates & Co.	Hanley
1861				
Jan 8	6	137217	T. & R. Boote	Burslem
21	7	137529	Wedgwood & Co.	Tunstall
Feb 15	3	138356	J. Furnival & Co.	Cobridge
27	5	138535	James Edwards & Son	Longport
Mar 7	7	138861–2	Turner & Tomkinson	Tunstall
19	3	139053	W. T. Copeland	Stoke
19	4	139054–5	W. H. Kerr & Co.	Worcester

APPENDIX B

Date	Parcel No.	Patent No.	Factory, Retailer Wholesaler, etc	Place
Apr 5	3	139360	Pinder, Bourne & Hope	Burslem
6	1	139369–72	Minton, Hollins & Co.	Stoke
12	3	139714–5	Davenports & Co.	Longport
18	5	139881	T. & R. Boote	Burslem
20	6	139945	F. & R. Pratt	Fenton
25	2	140200	James Dudson	Hanley
May 3	8	140367	W. T. Copeland	Stoke
6	3	140478	The Hill Pottery Co.	Burslem
6	5	140480–1	The Old Hall Earthenware Co.	Hanley
9	3	140578–9	Bates, Brown–Westhead & Moore	Hanley
13	7	140679	Minton & Co.	Stoke
14	2	140683	W. H. Kerr & Co.	Worcester
25	2	141055	idem	Worcester
31	3	141114	Cork, Edge & Malkin	Burslem
June 4	1	141214	Bates, Brown–Westhead & Moore	Hanley
7	5	141288	The Hill Pottery Co.	Burslem
11	2	141326–7	W. T. Copeland	Stoke
13	6	141369	Minton & Co.	Stoke
July 4	2	141715	Lockett & Cooper	Hanley
5	2	141727	Beech & Hancock	Tunstall
6	2	141732	Wm. Brownfield	Cobridge
18	4	141869–70	Josiah Wedgwood & Sons	Etruria
Aug 19	7	142755	T. & R. Boote	Burslem
22	7	142847	Wedgwood & Co.	Tunstall
23	2	142850	G. W. Reade	Cobridge
Sept 6	6	143313	Wm. Brownfield	Cobridge
12	6	143400	J. & J. Peake	Newcastle
17	2	143702	W. T. Copeland	Stoke
18	7	143769	Wm. Beech	Burslem
26	7	144179	John Cliff & Co.	London
Oct 10	5	144757	W. H. Kerr & Co.	Worcester
11	3	144767	Mountford & Scarratt	Fenton

Date		Parcel No.	Patent No.	Factory, Retailer Wholesaler, etc	Place
	15	3	144896	Leveson Hill (Excrs of)	Stoke
	18	3	145157	W. T. Copeland	Stoke
	24	5	145499	Hulse, Nixon & Adderley	Longton
	28	7	145686–7	Bates, Brown–Westhead & Moore	Hanley
Nov	15	3	146352–4	J. Clementson	Hanley
	29	5	146924	Josiah Wedgwood & Sons	Etruria
Dec	4	7	147309–10	Wm. Brownfield	Cobridge
	5	5	147322	Till, Bullock & Smith	Hanley
	20	7	147820	Lockett & Cooper	Hanley
	20	9	147823	Wedgwood & Co.	Tunstall
1862					
Jan	11	5	148517	Wm. Brownfield	Cobridge
	25	3	148870	idem	Cobridge
Feb	1	4	149090	Elliot Bros.	Longport
	10	6	149290	W. H. Kerr & Co.	Worcester
	10	8	149292	Minton & Co.	Stoke
	27	4	149673–4	James Dudson	Hanley
Mar	1	6	149716	T. & R. Boote	Burslem
	13	6	149938	W. T. Copeland	Stoke
	13	7	149939	Wm. Adams	Tunstall
	14	8	149955	J. Knight	Fenton
	14	9	149956	Wedgwood & Co.	Tunstall
	14	10	149957–8	Wm. Brownfield	Cobridge
	21	6	150100	Thompson Bros.	Burton-on-Trent
	22	9	150152	T. & R. Boote	Burslem
	27	1	150241	J. & M. P. Bell & Co.	Glasgow
	28	5	150301–3	idem	Glasgow
	29	3	150322	Minton & Co.	Stoke
Apr	1	5	150377	Josiah Wedgwood & Sons	Etruria
	4	2	150455	Minton & Co.	Stoke
	4	5	150458	J. & T. Furnival	Cobridge

APPENDIX B

Date	Parcel No.	Patent No.	Factory, Retailer Wholesaler, etc	Place
7	12	150515	Geo. Grainger & Co.	Worcester
9	3	150538	The Old Hall Earthenware Co. (Ltd.)	Hanley
17	5	151029–30	Thompson Bros.	Burton
24	2	151141	Turner & Tomkinson	Tunstall
May 1	7	151351	Eardley & Hammersley	Tunstall
3	3	151378	G. L. Ashworth Bros.	Hanley
5	5	151456	John Cliff	London
9	9	151568–9	Brown–Westhead, Moore & Co.	Hanley
14	3	151672–3	Geo. Jones & Co.	Stoke
27	3	151995	E. Challinor	Tunstall
29	5	152013	J. Furnival & Co.	Cobridge
June 24	5	152709	T. C. Brown–Westhead, Moore & Co.	Hanley
July 2	4	152859	Minton & Co.	Stoke
4	8	152963	J. Clementson	Hanley
12	4	153112	idem	Hanley
14	2	153127	Beech & Hancock	Tunstall
19	6	153366	J. Clementson	Hanley
31	3	153476	Jones & Ellis	Longton
31	4	153477	Minton & Co.	Stoke
Aug 16	5	153821	Richard Edwards	Longport
16	7	153823	J. H. Baddeley	Hanley
18	4	153827	Hulse, Nixon & Adderley	Longton
19	4	153844	G. L. Ashworth & Bros.	Hanley
25	3	154143–4	E. F. Bodley & Co.	Burslem
30	3	154220	Thos. Fell & Co.	Newcastle upon Tyne
30	4	154221	T. & R. Boote	Burslem
Sept 6	2	154401	Malkin, Walker & Hulse	Longton
11	3	154678	Minton & Co.	Stoke
12	2	154693	Thos. Cooper	Longton

APPENDIX B

Date	Parcel No.	Patent No.	Factory, Retailer Wholesaler, etc	Place
17	6	154812	Hope & Carter	Burslem
22	7	155103	Minton & Co.	Stoke
26	1	155220–2	Hope & Carter	Burslem
Oct 1	7	155263–4	Thos. Fell & Co.	Newcastle upon Tyne
9	3	155550	Hill Pottery	Burslem
15	2	156190	Turner & Tomkinson	Tunstall
23	8	156715–7	Wm. Baker & Co.	Fenton
Nov 11	3	157274	E. F. Bodley & Co.	Burslem
19	5	157547	Geo. Wooliscroft	Tunstall
28	4	157907	Minton & Co.	Stoke
Dec 3	5	158052–3	T. C. Brown–Westhead Moore & Co.	Hanley
5	2	158091	Wm. Brownfield	Cobridge
9	5	158221	Thomas Cooper	Hanley
17	5	158480	The Old Hall Earthenware Co. (Ltd.)	Hanley
18	3	158498	Geo. Jones	Stoke
1863				
Jan 12	6	159083	Davenport, Banks & Co.	Etruria
16	2	159123	Minton & Co.	Stoke
16	8	159153	Liddle, Elliot & Sons	Longport
29	1	159551	Josiah Wedgwood & Sons	Etruria
30	3	159573	T. & R. Boote	Burslem
Feb 2	3	159613	Minton & Co.	Stoke
17	4	159972	T. & R. Boote	Burslem
24	5	160110	James Stiff & Sons	London
Mar 6	2	160319	G. L. Ashworth & Bros.	Hanley
13	2	160456	Hope & Carter	Burslem
13	3	160457	Wilkinson & Sons	Hanley
20	8	160752	Worthington & Green	Hanley
20	9	160753–4	John Pratt & Co.	Fenton
21	2	160759	Beech & Hancock	Tunstall

Date	Parcel No.	Patent No.	Factory, Retailer Wholesaler, etc	Place
21	4	160761	Hulse, Nixon & Adderley	Longton
21	5	160762	James Edwards & Son	Burslem
23	2	160791–2	Bodley & Harrold	Burslem
Apr 11	1	161404	J. Macintyre	Burslem
23	4	161852	T. C. Brown–Westhead Moore & Co.	Hanley
25	1	161861	Beech & Hancock	Tunstall
30	3	162021	Wilkinson & Son	Hanley
May 4	6	162122	Harding & Cotterill	Burton-on-Trent
11	3	162261–2	E. Pearson	Cobridge
12	1	162267	Bodley & Harrold	Burslem
15	10	162304	Harding & Cotterill	Burton-on-Trent
22	4	162618–9	W. T. Copeland	Stoke
26	9	162765	T. C. Brown–Westhead, Moore & Co.	Hanley
June 4	5	162976	The Old Hall Earthenware Co. (Ltd.)	Hanley
8	15	163188	Minton & Co.	Stoke
8	16	163189	Wm. Brownfield	Cobridge
July 14	2	164213	Turner & Tomkinson	Tunstall
15	3	164221	H. Venables	Hanley
20	3	164353	Wm. Brownfield	Cobridge
24	3	164468–9	W. T. Copeland	Stoke
28	6	164635	Minton & Co.	Stoke
Aug 11	3	165045–7	Turner & Tomkinson	Tunstall
12	4	165171	Hancock, Whittingham & Co.	Burslem
21	1	165317	J. Clementson	Hanley
28	5	165448	H. Venables	Hanley
Sept 7	6	165720	T. & R. Boote	Burslem
28	4	166439	H. Venables	Hanley
28	6	166441–2	James Edwards & Son	Longport

APPENDIX B

Date	Parcel No.	Patent No.	Factory, Retailer Wholesaler, etc	Place
Oct 2	5	166625	H. Venables	Hanley
6	5	166775	Thompson Bros.	Burton
14	7	167289	Wm. Brownfield	Cobridge
15	2	167299	F. Brewer & Son	Longton
17	1	167374	T. & R. Boote	Burslem
22	5	167536	Eardley & Hammersley	Tunstall
24	5	167560	Josiah Wedgwood & Sons	Etruria
26	7	167594–5	The Old Hall Earthenware Co. (Ltd.)	Hanley
28	8	167715	George Jones & Co.	Stoke
31	3	167761–3	Edmund T. Wood	Tunstall
Nov 3	5	168132	John Meir & Son	Tunstall
4	7	168188	T. & R. Boote	Burslem
6	1	168234–5	Geo. Jones & Co.	Stoke
16	10	168765	Wm. Kirkham	Stoke
26	12	169553	Wm. Brownfield	Cobridge
27	3	169561	Bodley & Harrold	Burslem
Dec 2	5	169774	J. W. Pankhurst	Hanley
2	6	169775	T. & R. Boote	Burslem
18	4	170294	F. & R. Pratt & Co.	Fenton
23	2	170418	Wm. Brownfield	Cobridge
30	1	170590	T. C. Brown–Westhead Moore & Co.	Hanley
1864				
Jan 5	2	170759	Wm. Brownfield	Cobridge
11	5	170883	Malkin, Walker & Hulse	Longton
Feb 2	5	171421	Josiah Wedgwood & Sons	Etruria
5	5	171520	Hope & Carter	Burslem
6	3	171536	Thos. Goode & Co.	London
13	6	171673	W. T. Copeland	Stoke
22	7	171970	Cork, Edge & Malkin	Burslem
25	6	172060	Liddle, Elliot & Son	Longport
29	6	172183	J. & D. Hampson	Longton
Mar 3	4	172212	Geo. L. Ashworth & Bros.	Hanley

APPENDIX B

Date	Parcel No.	Patent No.	Factory, Retailer Wholesaler, etc	Place
12	5	172559	Cork, Edge & Malkin	Burslem
18	1	172648	T. C. Brown–Westhead, Moore & Co.	Hanley
22	3	172815–6	Minton & Co.	Stoke
23	4	172876	Burgess & Leigh	Burslem
Apr 9	4	173200	Josiah Wedgwood & Sons	Etruria
15	4	173659	Geo. Jones	Stoke
18	5	173671	Minton & Co.	Stoke
21	4	173785	T. C. Brown–Westhead, Moore & Co.	Hanley
21	8	173799	Liddle, Elliot & Son	Longport
23	11	173996	Geo. L. Ashworth & Bros.	Hanley
26	3	174112	Bodley & Harrold	Burslem
27	4	174138	Hope & Carter	Burslem
29	2	174168	Wm. Brownfield	Cobridge
May 9	3	174424	R. T. Boughton & Co.	Burslem
10	5	174455–8	Geo. Jones & Co.	Stoke
11	3	174475	R. H. Grove	Barlaston
18	5	174795	Geo. Ray	Longton
21	1	174817	J. & D. Hampson	Longton
June 9	7	175330	Minton & Co.	Stoke
16	3	175500	Hope & Carter	Burslem
30	4	175927	Wm. Brownfield	Cobridge
30	10	175935	The Worcester Royal Porcelain Co. Ltd.	Worcester
July 2	3	175959	Wood & Sale	Hanley
9	5	176164	Pinder, Bourne & Co.	Burslem
11	8	176235–6	idem	Burslem
18	6	176597	Bodley & Harrold	Burslem
18	7	176598	Evans & Booth	Burslem
19	4	176701	Hope & Carter	Burslem
19	8	176706	Wood & Sale	Hanley
28	4	176916	Holland & Green	Longton
Aug 10	2	177455	James Fellows	W/hmptn
20	10	177912	Geo. Jones & Co.	Stoke

Date	Parcel No.	Patent No.	Factory, Retailer Wholesaler, etc	Place
26	5	178037	T. C. Brown–Westhead Moore & Co.	Hanley
Sept 6	5	178264	W. T. Copeland	Stoke
10	1	178410	Minton & Co.	Stoke
12	2	178433	idem	Stoke
14	4	178521	Bodley & Harrold	Burslem
16	6	178597–8	Geo. L. Ashworth & Bros.	Hanley
19	1	178680–1	Josiah Wedgwood & Sons	Etruria
21	1	178693–4	Minton & Co.	Stoke
22	6	178823–7	Josiah Wedgwood & Sons	Etruria
Oct 4	2	179445	Geo. Jones & Co.	Stoke
12	4	179656	Wm. Brownfield	Cobridge
27	4	180444	Evans & Booth	Burslem
28	2	180449	The Worcester Royal Porcelain Co. Ltd.	Worcester
28	4	180453	Bodley & Harrold	Burslem
28	9	180483	Minton & Co.	Stoke
29	2	180486	Chas. Collinson & Co.	Burslem
31	3	180569	Cork, Edge & Malkin	Burslem
Nov 1	7	180695	W. T. Copeland	Stoke
4	3	180713	Livesley, Powell & Co.	Hanley
10	2	181214–5	Elsmore & Forster	Tunstall
10	3	181296	Hope & Carter	Burslem
10	10	181286	Geo. Jones & Co.	Stoke
24	5	181722	T. C. Brown–Westhead Moore & Co.	Hanley
29	1	181843	Hope & Carter	Burslem
Dec 9	1	182203	Wm. Kirkham	Stoke
10	8	182249	Hope & Carter	Burslem
31	6	182699	Geo. Jones & Co.	Stoke
1865				
Jan 6	3	182806	Hope & Carter	Burslem
6	4	182807	Minton & Co.	Stoke
14	4	183331	Geo. Jones & Co.	Stoke

APPENDIX B

Date	Parcel No.	Patent No.	Factory, Retailer Wholesaler, etc	Place
Feb 1	1	183650–2	Minton & Co.	Stoke
2	4	183706–7	Geo. L. Ashworth & Bros.	Hanley
13	7	183940	F. & R. Pratt & Co.	Fenton
14	4	183945	Liddle, Elliot & Son	Longport
27	4	184220	Livesley, Powell & Co.	Hanley
Mar 31	3	185473	Hope & Carter	Burslem
Apr 1	4	185520	Wm. Brownfield	Cobridge
3	4	185613	Minton & Co.	Stoke
22	5	186266	Thos. Till & Sons	Burslem
22	7	186273	James Edwards & Son	Burslem
26	5	186325	idem	Burslem
28	4	186349	Hope & Carter	Burslem
28	7	186354	Henry Alcock & Co.	Cobridge
29	3	186361	The Worcester Royal Porcelain Co. (Ltd.)	Worcester
May 2	8	186477	Livesley, Powell & Co.	Hanley
15	2	186841	J. T. Hudden	Longton
17	2	186901	Minton & Co.	Stoke
June 6	6	187358–9	J. T. Hudden	Longton
9	4	187403	The Worcester Royal Porcelain Co. (Ltd.)	Worcester
13	5	187533	idem	Worcester
14	6	187574	The Hill Pottery Co. Ltd.	Burslem
15	2	187576	J. T. Hudden	Longton
16	1	187583	Evans & Booth	Burslem
17	5	187633	The Worcester Royal Porcelain Co. (Ltd.)	Worcester
29	2	187847–8	Ed. F. Bodley & Co.	Burslem
30	4	187861	The Hill Pottery Co. Ltd.	Burslem
July 3	7	187972	T. C. Brown–Westhead, Moore & Co.	Hanley
12	3	188167	James Edwards & Son	Burslem
Aug 21	6	189155	J. Furnival & Co.	Cobridge
23	5	189283	Josiah Wedgwood & Sons	Etruria
Sept 11	4	189700	R. T. Boughton & Co.	Burslem

APPENDIX B

Date	Parcel No.	Patent No.	Factory, Retailer Wholesaler, etc	Place
11	5	189701	Thos. Cooper (Excrs of)	Hanley
14	2	189718	T. C. Brown–Westhead, Moore & Co.	Hanley
18	6	189782	Liddle, Elliot & Son	Longport
28	4	190200	Minton & Co.	Stoke
30	4	190656	S. Barker & Son	Swinton
Oct 13	8	190903	T. C. Brown–Westhead, Moore & Co.	Hanley
24	4	191292	Edward Johns	Staffs.
30	4	191407–8	Wm. Brownfield	Cobridge
Nov 10	4	192236	Pinder Bourne & Co. & Anthony Shaw	Burslem
23	10	192793	The Old Hall Earthenware Co. Ltd.	Hanley
29	8	192963	James Edwards & Son	Burslem
Dec 2	3	193061	The Worcester Royal Porcelain Co. (Ltd.)	Worcester
23	3	193844	James Dudson	Hanley
1866				
Jan 2	4	194063	Pratt & Co.	Fenton
3	6	194194	J. T. Close & Co.	Stoke
13	2	194450	Ed. F. Bodley & Co.	Burslem
17	4	194537	Burgess & Leigh	Burslem
24	1	194696	Minton & Co.	Stoke
31	5	194840	James Edwards & Son	Burslem
Feb 2	7	194949	W. T. Copeland	Stoke
Mar 2	2	195644	Ford, Challinor & Co.	Tunstall
10	1	195841	The Old Hall Earthenware Co. (Ltd.)	Hanley
Apr 14	6	196551	Walker & Carter	Longton
14	7	196552–4	Geo. L. Ashworth & Bros.	Hanley
16	8	196619	The Old Hall Earthenware Co. (Ltd.)	Hanley
18	4	196651	James Edwards & Son	Burslem

317

Date	Parcel No.	Patent No.	Factory, Retailer Wholesaler, etc	Place
20	7	196672–3	Wm. Brownfield	Cobridge
May 1	4	196987–8	J. Furnival & Co.	Cobridge
25	1	197705–6	Hope & Carter	Burslem
June 4	4	197857	James Broadhurst	Longton
12	1	198135–7	John Edwards	Fenton
21	4	198383–4	Pinder, Bourne & Co.	Burslem
30	4	198589	Thos. Minshall	Stoke
July 19	5	199186	J. T. Hudden	Longton
25	3	199295	Geo. Jones	Stoke
Aug 17	3	200006	Morgan, Wood & Co.	Burslem
29	4	200324	Ed. F. Bodley & Co.	Burslem
Sept 6	4	200599	F. & R. Pratt & Co.	Fenton
13	9	201040	T. & C. Ford	Hanley
15	8	201089	Geo. L. Ashworth & Bros.	Hanley
20	8	201495	Anthony Keeling	Tunstall
Oct 8	3	202103–5	Minton & Co.	Stoke
13	3	202493	Thos. Furnival	Cobridge
Nov 3	6	203173	Minton & Co.	Stoke
12	3	203538	W. T. Copeland	Stoke
14	8	203817	T. C. Brown–Westhead, Moore & Co.	Hanley
15	4	203912	Geo. Grainger & Co.	Worceste
Dec 13	4	204764	Liddle, Elliot & Son	Longport
14	8	204794	Samuel Barker & Son	Swinton
15	5	204863	T. C. Brown–Westhead, Moore & Co.	Hanley
19	5	205088	John Meir & Son	Tunstall
24	2	205201	J. T. Hudden	Longton
1867				
Jan 8	5	205372	James Edwards & Son	Burslem
17	3	205596	Ed. F. Bodley & Co.	Burslem
23	2	205759	The Worcester Royal Porcelain Co. (Ltd.)	Worceste
Feb 9	1	206033	Ed. F. Bodley & Co.	Burslem

APPENDIX B

Date	Parcel No.	Patent No.	Factory, Retailer Wholesaler, etc	Place
23	5	206275	Worthington & Harrop	Hanley
Mar 2	7	206422	Josiah Wedgwood & Sons	Etruria
4	4	206497	T. C. Brown–Westhead, Moore & Co.	Hanley
5	6	206517	Powell & Bishop	Hanley
6	4	206522	The Old Hall Earthenware Co. (Ltd.)	Hanley
9	3	206564	John Edwards	Fenton
11	2	206662	Josiah Wedgwood & Sons	Etruria
14	1	206718	Davenport Banks & Co.	Etruria
15	7	206762–6	Wm. Brownfield	Cobridge
18	5	206867–8	Cockson & Chetwynd & Co.	Cobridge
19	5	206881	James Edwards & Son	Burslem
20	2	206887	Josiah Wedgwood & Sons	Etruria
21	10	206971	James Edwards & Son	Burslem
25	3	206994	Josiah Wedgwood & Sons	Etruria
26	4	207024–5	Minton & Co.	Stoke
Apr 3	5	207163	idem	Stoke
4	2	207165	Josiah Wedgwood & Sons	Etruria
4	9	207201	Elsmore & Forster	Tunstall
17	1	207564	Chas. Hobson	Burslem
23	3	207616	Adams, Scrivener & Co.	Longton
24	2	207636	W. T. Copeland	Stoke
May 6	3	207938	J. & M. P. Bell & Co.	Glasgow
7	4	207977	John Meir & Son	Tunstall
8	6	208002	T. C. Brown–Westhead Moore & Co.	Hanley
18	7	208394	Wm. McAdam	Glasgow
22	6	208434–5	Clementson Bros.	Hanley
June 6	3	208750	Josiah Wedgwood & Sons	Etruria
11	6	208819	Clementson Bros.	Hanley
11	7	208820	Cockson, Chetwynd & Co.	Cobridge
13	3	208891	W. & J. A. Bailey	Alloa
21	4	209057	Wm. Brownfield	Cobridge

319

Date	Parcel No.	Patent No.	Factory, Retailer Wholesaler, etc	Place
21	8	209062	E. & D. Chetwynd	Hanley
24	4	209087	idem	Hanley
July 1	7	209290	Joseph Ball	Longton
4	5	209362	E. J. Ridgway	Hanley
8	3	209431	Geo. L. Ashworth & Bros.	Hanley
12	5	209530	Geo. Jones	Stoke
15	2	209556	Josiah Wedgwood & Sons	Etruria
17	2	209601	E. & D. Chetwynd	Hanley
25	3	209726	Hope & Carter	Burslem
Aug 28	10	210598	The Worcester Royal Porcelain Co. Ltd.	Worceste
Sept 16	7	211275	Thos. Goode & Co.	London
17	3	211290	Wedgwood & Co.	Tunstall
21	1	211536	Geo. L. Ashworth & Bros.	Hanley
25	9	211873–4	Powell & Bishop	Hanley
Oct 2	1	211995	Minton & Co.	Stoke
3	5	212054	Thompson Bros.	Burton-on-Trent
3	6	212055	Minton & Co.	Stoke
7	4	212078	idem	Stoke
10	1	212194	Thos. Booth	Hanley
24	5	212765	Ford, Challinor & Co.	Tunstall
26	1	212881	W. T. Copeland & Sons	Stoke
28	4	212956	idem	Stoke
29	3	212964	Josiah Wedgwood & Sons	Etruria
30	3	212974	J. T. Hudden	Longton
31	7	213065	Powell & Bishop	Hanley
Nov 6	7	213430	W. & J. A. Bailey	Alloa
7	4	213436	James Edwards & Son	Burslem
18	9	214000	Ford, Challinor & Co.	Tunstall
Dec 3	3	214618	W. T. Copeland & Sons	Stoke
12	6	214981	F. & R. Pratt & Co.	Fenton
20	3	215085	Josiah Wedgwood & Sons	Etruria
27	1	215314	J. & J. B. Bebbington	Hanley

APPENDIX B

Date	Parcel No.	Patent No.	Factory, Retailer Wholesaler, etc	Place
1868				
Jan 3	1	215481	Minton & Co.	Stoke
7	8	215636	Thompson Bros.	Burton-on-Trent
7	11	215642	Cockson, Chetwynd & Co.	Cobridge
8	5	215674	T. & R. Boote	Burslem
9	7	215698	Taylor, Tunnicliffe & Co.	Hanley
10	2	215705	Cork, Edge & Malkin	Burslem
11	2	215725	Wm. Brownfield	Cobridge
13	2	215735	Geo. L. Ashworth & Bros.	Hanley
16	13	215879	The Old Hall Earthenware Co. (Ltd.)	Hanley
25	3	216186	Hope & Carter	Burslem
30	6	216333	J. Furnival & Co.	Cobridge
31	8	216347	Josiah Wedgwood & Sons	Etruria
31	14	216363	T. & R. Boote	Burslem
Feb 5	4	216451	Adams, Scrivener & Co.	Longton
5	8	216470	E. Hodgkinson	Hanley
10	8	216676–8	Minton & Co.	Stoke
12	1	216699	Josiah Wedgwood & Sons	Etruria
14	10	216821	John Mortlock	London
18	1	216895	Josiah Wedgwood & Sons	Etruria
18	2	216896–7	T. C. Brown–Westhead, Moore & Co.	Hanley
20	9	216988	Minton & Co.	Stoke
25	6	217070	John Rose & Co.	Coalport
27	5	217100	Alcock & Digory	Burslem
28	7	217112	W. & J. A. Bailey	Alloa
Mar 5	12	217208	Thos. Goode & Co.	London
5	15	217212	Minton & Co.	Stoke
25	7	217615	W. T. Copeland & Sons	Stoke
25	8	217616–7	The Worcester Royal Porcelain Co. (Ltd.)	Worcester
26	3	217630	Walker & Carter	Longton
Apr 1	6	217727	Minton & Co.	Stoke

Date	Parcel No.	Patent No.	Factory, Retailer Wholesaler, etc	Place
6	6	217938–9	Pinder, Bourne & Co.	Burslem
16	7	218139	Geo. L. Ashworth & Bros.	Hanley
21	6	218285	Beech & Hancock	Tunstall
23	8	218387	R. Hammersley	Tunstall
28	7	218466	T. G. Green	Burton-on-Trent
May 13	1	218664	Adams, Scrivener & Co.	Longton
14	2	218764	Hope & Carter	Burslem
14	6	218773	Philip Brookes	Fenton
26	5	218951	T. C. Brown–Westhead Moore & Co.	Hanley
26	6	218952	Pinder, Bourne & Co.	Burslem
28	3	218967	Holdcroft & Wood	Tunstall
28	5	218969–71	Minton & Co.	Stoke
28	7	218973	J. & T. Bevington	Hanley
30	4	219042	T. & R. Boote	Burslem
June 8	4	219174	Burgess & Leigh	Burslem
12	5	219316–7	Wm. Brownfield	Cobridge
16	4	219344	W. P. & G. Phillips	London
22	5	219484	Minton & Co.	Stoke
July 10	3	219756	Josiah Wedgwood & Sons	Etruria
16	3	219833	Hackney & Co.	Longton
20	2	219942–3	Hope & Carter	Burslem
24	4	219997	W. T. Copeland & Sons	Stoke
30	6	220183	Adams, Scrivener & Co.	Longton
Aug 1	5	220236–7	T. & R. Boote	Burslem
13	1	220772	Josiah Wedgwood & Sons	Etruria
15	8	220821–4	James Edwards & Son	Burslem
17	2	220828	Ed. F. Bodley & Co.	Burslem
21	2	220906	Ralph Malkin	Fenton
31	7	221124	T. & R. Boote	Burslem
Sept 1	1	221125–6	James Wardle	Hanley
4	6	221203–4	Gelson Bros.	Hanley
5	3	221214	T. C. Brown–Westhead, Moore & Co.	Hanley

322

APPENDIX B

Date	Parcel No.	Patent No.	Factory, Retailer Wholesaler, etc	Place
5	6	221217–9	McBirney & Armstrong	Belleek
9	4	221311	Hope & Carter	Burslem
9	5	221312	F. Jones & Co.	Longton
9	6	221313	Wedgwood & Co.	Tunstall
9	9	221316	J. & T. Bevington	Hanley
12	3	221521–2	Minton & Co.	Stoke
14	4	221548	Thos. Booth & Co.	Burslem
17	4	221688	T. C. Sambrook & Co.	Burslem
21	4	221814–7	George Ash	Hanley
25	4	221881–2	Minton & Co.	Stoke
25	13	222083–4	T. C. Brown–Westhead, Moore & Co.	Hanley
Oct 8	7	222460	Minton & Co.	Stoke
9	2	222476	J. Holdcroft	Stoke
9	3	222477	Hope & Carter	Burslem
9	5	222482–4	Davenports & Co.	Longport
14	8	222736	Geo. Jones	Stoke
17	4	223063	Minton & Co.	Stoke
21	8	223308	W. P. & G. Phillips	London
22	1	223309	McBirney & Armstrong	Belleek
22	5	223314–5	James Edwards & Son	Burslem
Nov 3	5	223817–8	Minton & Co.	Stoke
3	6	223819	T. C. Brown–Westhead, Moore & Co.	Hanley
6	13	224090	Powell & Bishop	Hanley
9	5	224172	Josiah Wedgwood & Sons	Etruria
16	3	224382	Knapper & Blackhurst	Tunstall
17	1	224389	Moore Bros.	Cobridge
21	5	224539	Minton & Co.	Stoke
24	5	224645	T. C. Brown–Westhead, Moore & Co.	Hanley
25	4	224724	Cork, Edge & Malkin	Burslem
Dec 1	4	224953	T. C. Brown–Westhead, Moore & Co.	Hanley

323

Date		Parcel No.	Patent No.	Factory, Retailer Wholesaler, etc	Place
	3	5	225073–4	The Worcester Royal Porcelain Co. (Ltd.)	Worcester
	11	5	225410	Ed. T. Bodley & Co.	Burslem
	12	4	225425	Wm. Brownfield	Cobridge
	14	7	225441	Cockson, Chetwynd & Co.	Cobridge
	23	5	225734	Minton & Co.	Stoke
	23	6	225735	The Worcester Royal Porcelain Co. (Ltd.)	Worcester
	31	6	225993	Geo. L. Ashworth & Bros.	Hanley
	31	7	225994	R. Hammersley	Tunstall
1869					
Jan	1	8	226051	Geo. Jones	Stoke
	4	4	226098	Minton & Co.	Stoke
	7	6	226131	Thos. Goode & Co.	London
	21	6	226527–8	Minton & Co.	Stoke
	22	5	226570	Gelson Bros.	Hanley
	22	13	226581	T. C. Brown–Westhead, Moore & Co.	Hanley
	25	3	226625	Worthington & Son	Hanley
	28	5	226738	Minton & Co.	Stoke
	28	10	226747–8	George Ash	Hanley
Feb	1	7	226910	T. C. Brown–Westhead, Moore & Co.	Hanley
	2	4	226928	Geo. Yearsley	Longton
	9	5	227219	Minton & Co.	Stoke
	11	10	227277	Geo. Jones	Stoke
	15	1	227307	Thos. Booth & Co.	Burslem
	19	2	227345	Josiah Wedgwood & Sons	Etruria
	22	6	227403	idem	Etruria
	22	11	227409	McBirney & Armstrong	Belleek
	22	13	227411	Pinder, Bourne & Co.	Burslem
	27	5	227518	Josiah Wedgwood & Sons	Etruria
Mar	1	8	227556–8	Worthington & Son	Hanley
	3	8	227619	Thos. Till & Sons	Burslem

APPENDIX B

Date	Parcel No.	Patent No.	Factory, Retailer Wholesaler, etc	Place
6	8	227668	F. Primavesi	Cardiff
8	6	227696	F. & R. Pratt & Co.	Fenton
9	1	227743–4	Geo. Jones	Stoke
9	3	227746	idem	Stoke
10	10	227823	F. Primavesi	Cardiff
24	1	228141	J. F. Wileman	Fenton
Apr 1	1	228290	Wood & Pigott	Tunstall
2	6	228377	Wm. Brownfield	Cobridge
2	7	228378	Minton & Co.	Stoke
6	3	228430	Baker & Chetwynd	Burslem
7	2	228455	Minton & Co.	Stoke
7	4	228457	The Worcester Royal Porcelain Co. (Ltd.)	Worcester
12	4	228572	Taylor, Tunnicliffe & Co.	Hanley
12	5	228573	Liddle, Elliot & Son	Longport
20	5	228764	idem	Longport
28	13	228937	J. & T. Bevington	Hanley
May 11	1	229319	Adams, Scrivener & Co.	Longton
13	16	229405	James Edwards & Son	Burslem
21	1	229523	Worthington & Son	Hanley
26	4	229627	Thos. Booth	Hanley
27	8	229642–4	Davenport & Co.	Longport
June 3	6	229837	McBirney & Armstrong	Belleek
8	7	229959	W. P. & G. Phillips & Pearce	London
19	5	230183–4	Wm. Brownfield	Cobridge
25	4	230429	James Edwards & Son	Burslem
26	9	230455	Minton & Co.	Stoke
July 3	9	230707–8	Josiah Wedgwood & Sons	Etruria
6	3	230739	John Meir & Son	Tunstall
19	8	231101	James Wardle	Hanley
20	2	231124	Josiah Wedgwood & Sons	Etruria
21	6	231153–4	George Ash	Hanley
23	6	231215	Minton & Co.	Stoke
24	4	231222	W. T. Copeland & Sons	Stoke

APPENDIX B

Date	Parcel No.	Patent No.	Factory, Retailer Wholesaler, etc	Place
26	4	231241	Leveson Hill (Excrs of)	Stoke
27	4	231256	J. T. Hudden	Longton
Aug 2	6	231504	W. T. Copeland	Stoke
3	5	231602	John Edwards	Fenton
4	4	231613	Tomkinson Bros. & Co.	Hanley
11	13	231812	W. P. & G. Phillips & Pearce	London
19	6	232307	W. T. Copeland & Sons	Stoke
26	6	232474	idem	Stoke
31	6	232586–7	John Pratt & Co.	Lane Delph
31	12	232598	W. T. Copeland & Sons	Stoke
Sept 4	3	232822	Minton & Co.	Stoke
8	5	232878	W. T. Copeland & Sons	Stoke
8	6	232879	Pinder, Bourne & Co.	Burslem
9	3	232890	John Pratt & Co.	Lane Delph
10	4	232903	Minton & Co.	Stoke
21	7	233411	Gelson Bros.	Hanley
22	10	233527	W. & J. A. Bailey	Alloa
30	8	233864–6	T. C. Brown–Westhead Moore & Co.	Hanley
Oct 1	3	233923–4	Minton & Co.	Stoke
4	6	234016	idem	Stoke
14	3	234465	McBirney & Armstrong	Belleek
15	6	234486	Geo. Jones	Stoke
23	4	235012	idem	Stoke
26	2	235158	James Ellis & Son	Hanley
27	5	235168	McBirney & Armstrong	Belleek
29	3	235399–400	Minton & Co.	Stoke
29	4	235401–2	Powell & Bishop	Hanley
Nov 2	12	235589	Ed. Clarke	Tunstall
3	12	235691	T. C. Brown–Westhead, Moore & Co.	Hanley

Date	Parcel No.	Patent No.	Factory, Retailer Wholesaler, etc	Place
8	1	235827–9	McBirney & Armstrong	Belleek
8	2	235830	T. C. Brown–Westhead, Moore & Co.	Hanley
9	11	235966	Tams & Lowe	Longton
10	3	235974	Wm. Brownfield	Cobridge
13	5	236184–5	McBirney & Armstrong	Belleek
15	8	236203–7	Liddle, Elliot & Son	Longport
18	5	236435	Alcock & Digory	Burslem
19	12	236478	The Worcester Royal Porcelain Co. (Ltd.)	Worcester
20	8	236533	Thos. Goode & Co.	London
20	9	236534	John Mortlock	London
23	1	236585	McBirney & Armstrong	Belleek
24	4	236628	Minton & Co.	Stoke
26	3	236653	idem	Stoke
Dec 1	3	236756	Geo. Jones	Stoke
3	9	236829	Wm. Brownfield	Cobridge
17	7	237224	Minton & Co.	Stoke
18	2	237229	Powell & Bishop	Hanley
18	3	237230	McBirney & Armstrong	Belleek
20	8	237358	George Ash	Hanley
22	7	237500	Geo. Jones	Stoke
24	1	237552	Gelson Bros.	Hanley
28	2	237565	John Pratt & Co.	Lane Delph
31	2	237644	Minton & Co.	Stoke
1870				
Jan 1	5	237691	T. C. Brown–Westhead, Moore & Co.	Hanley
3	4	237742	Geo. Jones	Stoke
7	9	237899	Pellatt & Co.	London
15	12	238147–8	Liddle, Elliot & Son	Longport
27	8	238388	Chas. Hobson	Burslem
29	3	238436	Minton & Co.	Stoke

APPENDIX B

Date	Parcel No.	Patent No.	Factory, Retailer Wholesaler, etc	Place
Feb 1	6	238527–8	T. C. Brown–Westhead, Moore & Co.	Hanley
3	13	238595–6	idem	Hanley
4	7	238603	Powell & Bishop	Hanley
7	5	238627	Wiltshaw, Wood & Co.	Burslem
7	6	238628	W. & J. A. Bailey	Alloa
9	2	238663	Josiah Wedgwood & Sons	Etruria
10	8	238688	Minton & Co.	Stoke
11	12	238761–2	W. P. & G. Phillips & Pearce	London
15	6	238898–9	T. C. Brown–Westhead Moore & Co.	Hanley
25	2	239139	Minton & Co.	Stoke
28	6	239239	idem	Stoke
Mar 2	4	239304	idem	Stoke
7	6	239422	Chas. Hobson	Burslem
8	1	239424–6	Geo. Jones	Stoke
10	1	239474	idem	Stoke
10	9	239510	Powell & Bishop	Hanley
11	8	239528	Leveson Hill (Excrs of)	Stoke
14	4	239548	T. C. Brown–Westhead, Moore & Co.	Hanley
15	6	239585	Thos. Till & Sons	Burslem
16	2	239590–1	Minton & Co.	Stoke
17	4	239610–1	McBirney & Armstrong	Belleek
17	7	239622	The Worcester Royal Porcelain Co. (Ltd.)	Worcester
17	9	239628	J. Mortlock	London
18	6	239642	Minton & Co.	Stoke
23	9	239793–4	J. Blackshaw & Co.	Stoke
25	4	239968	Hope & Carter	Burslem
25	5	239969–70	Minton & Co.	Stoke
26	1	240000–1	idem	Stoke
26	2	240002	Worthington & Son	Hanley

APPENDIX B

Date		Parcel No.	Patent No.	Factory, Retailer Wholesaler, etc	Place
28		9	240079	The Old Hall Earthenware Co. Ltd.	Hanley
r 7		9	240383	Cork, Edge & Malkin	Burslem
7		10	240384–5	Baker & Co.	Fenton
7		11	240386	Harvey Adams & Co.	Longton
9		1	240458	Minton & Co.	Stoke
11		3	240493	The Worcester Royal Porcelain Co. Ltd.	Worcester
13		4	240516	Thos. Goode & Co.	London
14		7	240570	Minton & Co.	Stoke
ay 5		1	241231	James Oldham & Co.	Hanley
6		5	241264–5	McBirney & Armstrong	Belleek
10		4	241367–8	George Ash	Hanley
13		8	241474	T. C. Brown–Westhead, Moore & Co.	Hanley
17		7	241544	idem	Hanley
18		6	241567–8	Bates, Elliott & Co.	Longport
21		6	241649	The Old Hall Earthenware Co. Ltd.	Hanley
21		12	241666	James Edwards & Son	Burslem
25		7	241754	idem	Burslem
26		5	241960	Minton & Co.	Stoke
30		15	242077	Geo. Jones	Stoke
ne 3		8	242154	F. & R. Pratt & Co.	Fenton
7		15	242233	Hope & Carter	Burslem
7		16	242234	Thos. Booth	Hanley
9		3	242391	T. C. Brown–Westhead, Moore & Co.	Hanley
10		1	242392–4	Wm. Brownfield	Cobridge
11		3	242439	James Edwards & Son	Burslem
17		7	242503–8	Minton, Hollins & Co.	Stoke
22		1	242634–5	Harvey Adams & Co.	Longton
22		3	242637–8	Minton, Hollins & Co.	Stoke
22		4	242639	The Worcester Royal Porcelain Co. Ltd.	Worcester

329

APPENDIX B

Date	Parcel No.	Patent No.	Factory, Retailer Wholesaler, etc	Place
27	1	242715	Geo. Jones	Stoke
July 5	5	242859	Baker & Co.	Fenton
8	7	243049–50	James Wardle	Hanley
13	8	243176	James Edwards & Son	Burslem
14	9	243197–9	Minton, Hollins & Co.	Stoke
14	10	243200	The Worcester Royal Porcelain Co. Ltd.	Worceste
15	1	243207	W. T. Copeland & Sons	Stoke
16	2	243235	James Wardle	Hanley
19	6	243352	F. & R. Pratt & Co.	Fenton
20	5	243368	Thos. Booth	Hanley
21	1	243378	idem	Hanley
22	1	243385	Cork, Edge & Malkin	Burslem
27	1	243480	Beech, Unwin & Co.	Longton
Aug 1	2	243555	R. G. Scrivener & Co.	Hanley
4	4	243646	James Wardle	Hanley
4	5	243647–8	J. Broadhurst	Longton
9	2	243807	Wm. Brownfield	Cobridge
22	4	244137–8	T. & R. Boote	Burslem
23	6	244173	Geo. Jones	Stoke
25	5	244223	T. & R. Boote	Burslem
Sept 7	7	244703	Bailey & Cooke	Hanley
10	9	244741	Minton & Co.	Stoke
16	5	244961	idem	Stoke
19	2	244976	Wm. Brownfield	Cobridge
27	4	245227	Elsmore, Forster & Co.	Tunstall
27	6	245229	W. P. & G. Phillips & D. Pearce	London
28	11	245265	Gelson Bros.	Hanley
Oct 4	7	245463	Joseph Holdcroft	Longton
4	8	245464	Minton & Co.	Stoke
6	4	245604	idem	Stoke
6	5	245605	James Broadhurst	Longton
7	3	245620	Minton & Co.	Stoke
8	9	245668	Powell & Bishop	Hanley

APPENDIX B

Date		Parcel No.	Patent No.	Factory, Retailer Wholesaler, etc	Place
	19	2	245985–6	Geo. Jones	Stoke
	22	2	246149	Wm. Brownfield	Cobridge
	25	6	246181	T. C. Brown–Westhead, Moore & Co.	Hanley
Nov	4	9	246927	idem	Hanley
	9	8	247047	John Meir & Son	Tunstall
	9	9	247048	Pellatt & Co.	London
	10	5	247071–3	Minton & Co.	Stoke
	10	10	247079–80	Wm. Brownfield	Cobridge
	12	3	247248	McBirney & Armstrong	Belleek
	12	8	247255	Minton, Hollins & Co.	Stoke
	22	3	247944	Geo. Jones	Stoke
	24	3	248041	Minton & Co.	Stoke
	24	8	248049	Bates, Elliott & Co.	Longport
	25	1	248051	Minton & Co.	Stoke
	25	2	248052	Turner, Goddard & Co.	Tunstall
	26	9	248114–6	T. & R. Boote	Burslem
Dec	1	7	248242	Wm. Brownfield	Cobridge
	2	11	248294	T. C. Brown–Westhead, Moore & Co.	Hanley
	5	4	248309–15	Minton, Hollins & Co.	Stoke
	16	5	248869	Bates, Elliott & Co.	Longport
	17	11	248899	idem	Longport
	19	9	248953	Harvey, Adams & Co.	Longton
	27	4	249104	James Edwards & Son	Burslem
1871					
Jan	2	2	249235	Gelson Bros.	Hanley
	6	3	249331	Minton & Co.	Stoke
	7	8	249356	Bates, Elliott & Co.	Longport
	9	4	249388–93	McBirney & Armstrong	Belleek
	10	7	249439	Geo. Jones	Stoke
	11	4	249464	J. Mortlock	London
	12	7	249479	McBirney & Armstrong	Belleek
	12	12	249490	Soane & Smith	London

APPENDIX B

Date	Parcel No.	Patent No.	Factory, Retailer Wholesaler, etc	Place
24	4	249811	idem	London
26	8	249903–6	Minton, Hollins & Co.	Stoke
27	9	249927	The Worcester Royal Porcelain Co. Ltd.	Worceste
30	2	249972	Gelson Bros.	Hanley
Feb 2	3	250020	James Edwards & Son	Burslem
6	5	250168–71	McBirney & Armstrong	Belleek
8	9	250231	James Macintyre & Co.	Burslem
11	9	250291	T. C. Brown–Westhead, Moore & Co.	Hanley
13	6	250366	Edge, Malkin & Co.	Burslem
13	7	250367	Worthington & Son	Hanley
13	9	250369	Powell & Bishop	Hanley
13	10	250370	Ed. F. Bodley & Co.	Burslem
15	7	250416–8	Powell & Bishop	Hanley
17	7	250440–1	Thos. Peake	Tunstall
20	2	250478–9	Elsmore & Forster	Tunstall
28	8	250657	The Watcombe Terra Cotta Clay Co. Ltd.	Devon
Mar 9	4	250865	J. & T. Bevington	Hanley
14	4	250954	John Pratt & Co.	Lane Delph
15	10	251013	Bates, Elliott & Co.	Longport
27	1	251246	Wm. Brownfield & Son	Cobridge
29	1	251329	Thos. Furnival & Son	Cobridge
Apr 4	4	251453	McBirney & Armstrong	Belleek
22	4	251966	John Pratt & Co.	Stoke
24	4	251988	Josiah Wedgwood & Sons	Etruria
26	12	252068	Minton, Hollins & Co.	Stoke
27	7	252093–4	Wood & Clarke	Burslem
27	8	252095–7	W. P. & G. Phillips & Pearce	London
28	1	252128	Wood & Clarke	Burslem
29	6	252156	idem	Burslem
29	7	252157	James Edwards & Son	Burslem

APPENDIX B

Date	Parcel No.	Patent No.	Factory, Retailer Wholesaler, etc	Place
May 1	9	252171–3	T. C. Brown–Westhead, Moore & Co.	Hanley
2	3	252176	Ambrose Bevington	Hanley
2	4	252177–80	Wm. Brownfield & Son	Cobridge
3	4	252188	John Jackson & Co.	Rother'm
6	1	252258	W. P. & G. Phillips & Pearce	London
9	9	252387	Liddle, Elliott & Co.	Longport
11	13	252487	Powell & Bishop	Hanley
13	6	252503	Elsmore & Forster	Tunstall
22	9	252709	McBirney & Armstrong	Belleek
24	10	252756	John Meir & Son	Tunstall
June 2	4	253017	T. C. Brown–Westhead, Moore & Co.	Hanley
7	7	253069	Grove & Stark	Longton
16	9	253335	John Twigg	Rother'm
17	3	253339–40	Minton & Co.	Stoke
19	9	253378–9	Pinder, Bourne & Co.	Burslem
22	1	253472	Thos. Till & Sons	Burslem
23	9	253571	Bates, Elliott & Co.	Longport
July 4	8	253796–8	W. T. Copeland	Stoke
14	6	254013	Taylor, Tunnicliffe & Co.	Hanley
15	2	254030	Thos. Booth	Hanley
19	2	254074	Ambrose Bevington	Hanley
22	8	254130–3	Haviland & Co.	London and Limoges
25	12	254239	Bates, Elliott & Co.	Longport
29	6	254344	Hope & Carter	Burslem
Aug 2	3	254429	Robinson & Leadbeater	Stoke
9	7	254757	Bates, Elliott & Co.	Longport
18	10	254899	Pratt & Co.	Fenton
28	5	255267	James Wardle	Hanley
29	2	255274	Geo. Jones	Stoke
30	4	255320	Thos. Barlow	Longton

Date	Parcel No.	Patent No.	Factory, Retailer Wholesaler, etc	Place
31	9	255333	J. H. & J. Davis	Hanley
Sept 15	7	255821	J. Bevington & Co.	Hanley
15	10	255825	Thos. Barlow	Longton
19	2	255849	Minton & Co.	Stoke
25	8	256079	T. C. Brown–Westhead, Moore & Co.	Hanley
28	5	256215	Thos. Booth & Co.	Tunstall
Oct 4	7	256357–60	Minton & Co.	Stoke
4	9	256362	Pinder, Bourne & Co.	Burslem
6	6	256427–9	Moore & Son	Longton
9	8	256538	E. J. Ridgway & Son	Hanley
10	3	256582	J. T. Hudden	Longton
10	6	256586	T. C. Brown–Westhead, Moore & Co.	Hanley
11	4	256598	McBirney & Armstrong	Belleek
14	6	256687	Thos. Booth & Co.	Tunstall
14	7	256688	Josiah Wedgwood & Sons	Etruria
14	8	256689	McBirney & Armstrong	Belleek
18	4	256853	Moore & Son	Longton
19	6	256907	W. T. Copeland & Sons	Stoke
24	3	257126	Robert Cooke	Hanley
31	5	257258	Minton & Co.	Stoke
31	6	257259	Edge, Hill & Palmer	Longton
Nov 3	4	257364–5	R. G. Scrivener & Co.	Hanley
3	5	257366	J. F. Wileman	Fenton
15	4	257728	John Thomson & Sons	Glasgow
23	6	257944–6	Thos. Ford	Hanley
Dec 1	6	258095	Geo. Jones	Stoke
15	5	258773	Robinson & Leadbeater	Stoke
16	7	258816	McBirney & Armstrong	Belleek
22	6	258949	F. & R. Pratt	Fenton
23	3	258956–7	Geo. Jones	Stoke
29	10	259053	T. C. Brown–Westhead, Moore & Co.	Hanley

APPENDIX B

Date	Parcel No.	Patent No.	Factory, Retailer Wholesaler, etc	Place
1872				
Jan 1	5	259076	Moore & Son	Longton
1	6	259077	Edge Malkin & Co.	Burslem
5	3	259264	McBirney & Armstrong	Belleek
6	1	259271	Minton & Co.	Stoke
18	6	259801	The Worcester Royal Porcelain Co. Ltd.	Worcester
20	6	259854	Geo. Jones	Stoke
30	7	260081	W. T. Copeland & Sons	Stoke
Feb 2	2	260187	Moore & Son	Longton
2	11	260240–1	Turner & Tomkinson	Tunstall
3	4	260255–6	Geo. Jones	Stoke
7	3	260297	Ambrose Bevington	Hanley
15	3	260463	Powell & Bishop	Hanley
16	6	260503	McBirney & Armstrong	Belleek
16	7	260504–6	Geo. Jones	Stoke
19	6	260565	Wm. H. Goss	Stoke
20	4	260578	The Worcester Royal Porcelain Co. Ltd.	Worcester
22	3	260640	Minton & Co.	Stoke
Mar 4	3	260868	Geo. Jones	Stoke
4	4	260869–70	Minton & Co.	Stoke
4	6	260872	Minton, Hollins & Co.	Stoke
7	7	260992–3	Harvey, Adams & Co.	Longton
7	10	260998	Bates, Elliott & Co.	Burslem
8	5	261006–8	Minton, Hollins & Co.	Stoke
9	1	261016	McBirney & Armstrong	Belleek
13	8	261120	Minton, Hollins & Co.	Stoke
16	6	261190	Minton & Co.	Stoke
18	6	261207	idem	Stoke
20	10	261325	The Worcester Royal Porcelain Co. Ltd.	Worcester
21	14	261379	R. M. Taylor	Fenton
22	5	261391	J. Holdcroft	Longton

APPENDIX B

Date	Parcel No.	Patent No.	Factory, Retailer Wholesaler, etc	Place
22	8	261394	T. C. Brown–Westhead, Moore & Co.	Hanley
26	3	261453–4	Robinson & Leadbeater	Stoke
26	6	261458	Phillips & Pearce	London
Apr 5	4	261638	Wedgwood & Co.	Tunstall
5	5	261639	Minton & Co.	Stoke
6	1	261646–7	J. Holdcroft	Longton
9	6	261724	T. C. Brown–Westhead, Moore & Co.	Hanley
10	11	261749	Thos. Furnival & Son	Cobridge
17	13	261976	E. J. Ridgway & Son	Hanley
19	5	262013	Minton, Hollins & Co.	Stoke
24	5	262203	John Pratt & Co. Ltd.	Lane Delph
27	9	262354	Moore & Son	Longton
May 2	9	262425–6	Harvey Adams & Co.	Longton
2	11	262428–9	Thos. Furnival & Son	Cobridge
3	9	262471–2	Minton & Co.	Stoke
3	11	262474	Bates, Elliott & Co.	Burslem
6	3	262483–5	Moore & Son	Longton
6	8	262493	Bates, Elliott & Co.	Burslem
6	9	262494–5	Minton, Hollins & Co.	Stoke
10	1	262651	Moore & Son	Longton
11	4	262672	Thos. Booth & Sons	Hanley
27	1	262951	Geo. Jones	Stoke
27	3	262953	Minton, Hollins & Co.	Stoke
29	2	262990	Geo. Jones	Stoke
29	5	262993–4	Geo. Grainger & Co.	Worcester
30	1	262999–3000	Minton & Co.	Stoke
June 3	6	263106	The Watcombe Terra Cotta Clay Co. Ltd.	Devon
5	3	263134	Hope & Carter	Burslem
6	6	263162	Wm. Brownfield & Son	Cobridge
7	4	263191	Minton, Hollins & Co.	Stoke

336

APPENDIX B

Date	Parcel No.	Patent No.	Factory, Retailer Wholesaler, etc	Place
11	5	263315	Josiah Wedgwood & Sons	Etruria
11	12	263348	W. T. Copeland & Sons	Stoke
18	3	263496–7	Geo. L. Ashworth & Bros.	Hanley
18	4	263498–9	Minton, Hollins & Co.	Stoke
21	7	263541–2	idem	Stoke
22	5	263561	Minton & Co.	Stoke
22	8	263565	Wm. Brownfield & Son	Cobridge
27	1	263771	T. C. Brown–Westhead, Moore & Co.	Hanley
July 2	2	263883–4	Robinson & Leadbeater	Stoke
2	3	263885	Josiah Wedgwood & Sons	Etruria
13	5	264081	Gelson Bros.	Hanley
15	4	264194	Robinson & Leadbeater	Stoke
16	5	264206–7	Minton, Hollins & Co.	Stoke
19	5	264299–303	R. M. Taylor	Fenton
20	3	264306–7	Geo. Jones	Stoke
24	2	264490	W. & T. Adams	Tunstall
29	7	264613	J. Dimmock & Co.	Hanley
31	3	264636–7	Minton & Co.	Stoke
Aug 2	1	264685–6	E. J. Ridgway & Son	Stoke
14	4	265105	T. Booth & Co.	Tunstall
16	1	265167–8	Wm. Brownfield & Sons	Cobridge
19	4	265254	W. E. Cartlidge	Hanley
19	5	265255	W. & J. A. Bailey	Alloa
Sept 2	3	265666	McBirney & Armstrong	Belleek
2	8	265687	Bates, Elliott & Co.	Burslem
12	6	265969	Minton, Hollins & Co.	Stoke
25	9	266628–31	Minton, Hollins & Co.	Stoke
26	2	266633	F. Jones	Longton
26	5	266636	W. E. Cartlidge	Hanley
Oct 7	7	266959	T. C. Brown–Westhead, Moore & Co.	Hanley
11	5	267060–4	Josiah Wedgwood & Sons	Etruria
12	10	267103–4	Bates, Elliott & Co.	Burslem

Date	Parcel No.	Patent No.	Factory, Retailer Wholesaler, etc	Place
14	4	267112	Minton, Hollins & Co.	Stoke
17	8	267265	Josiah Wedgwood & Sons	Etruria
18	5	267317–9	Geo. Jones	Stoke
30	2	267523	J. F. Wileman	Fenton
30	5	267527	The Brownhills Pottery	Tunstall
30	9	267534	Maw & Co.	Broseley
Nov 2	6	267588–91	The Worcester Royal Porcelain Co. Ltd.	Worcester
4	3	267618	Geo. Grainger & Co.	Worcester
11	2	267806	W. E. Cartlidge	Hanley
12	4	267839	Minton & Co.	Stoke
14	13	267893–5	Wm. Brownfield & Son	Cobridge
14	14	267896	Moore Bros.	Longton
18	3	267972	Holland & Green	Longton
30	8	268309	Belfield & Co.	Preston-pans
Dec 2	5	268322	T. C. Brown–Westhead, Moore & Co.	Hanley
4	3	268388	John Pratt & Co. Ltd.	Lane Delph
10	2	268724–5	Minton & Co.	Stoke
11	8	268748–9	The Old Hall Earthenware Co. Ltd.	Hanley
14	5	268806–7	Wm. Brownfield & Son	Cobridge
24	1	269197	Cockson & Chetwynd	Cobridge
27	4	269269	John Adams (Excrs of)	Longton
27	5	269270	R. G. Scrivener & Co.	Hanley
27	8	269275	John Meir & Son	Tunstall
1873				
Jan 10	1	269585	Geo. Jones	Stoke
13	4	269621	W. T. Copeland & Sons	Stoke
14	8	269686	J. Defries	London
15	2	269690	Worthington & Son	Hanley

APPENDIX B

Date	Parcel No.	Patent No.	Factory, Retailer Wholesaler, etc	Place
29	1	269993–70001	Minton, Hollins & Co.	Stoke
29	2	270002–4	Moore Bros.	Longton
Feb 1	1	270042–50	Minton, Hollins & Co.	Stoke
10	2	270298	W. & J. A. Bailey	Alloa
12	4	270354	Bates, Elliott & Co.	Burslem
15	1	270385	Minton & Co.	Stoke
19	14	270600–1	J. & T. Bevington	Hanley
25	6	270700	Geo. Jones	Stoke
27	4	270751	Thos. Till & Sons	Burslem
27	8	270755	Minton, Hollins & Co.	Stoke
Mar 6	1	271031–2	Minton & Co.	Stoke
6	9	271057	The Brownhills Pottery Co.	Tunstall
26	6	271561–2	Geo. Jones	Stoke
Apr 3	6	271851	Minton & Co.	Stoke
15	4	272091	Taylor, Tunnicliffe & Co.	Hanley
19	2	272206	Minton & Co.	Stoke
23	6	272293	Gelson Bros.	Hanley
28	5	272364–5	Powell & Bishop	Hanley
29	3	272384–5	Geo. Jones	Stoke
May 3	2	272637	Thos. Till & Sons	Burslem
3	7	272642–6	Wm. Brownfield & Son	Cobridge
3	8	272647–8	Minton & Co.	Stoke
6	2	272662	idem	Stoke
12	8	272835	T. C. Brown–Westhead, Moore & Co.	Hanley
14	7	272896–7	Moore Bros.	Longton
16	6	272983	Minton, Hollins & Co.	Stoke
17	4	272988–90	John L. Johnson & Co.	Longton
22	5	273089	Worthington & Son	Hanley
26	7	273158–9	Moore Bros.	Longton
26	8	273160	Soane & Smith	London
29	4	273246	Worthington & Son	Hanley
29	8	273251	Thos. Ford	Hanley

Date	Parcel No.	Patent No.	Factory, Retailer Wholesaler, etc	Place
30	15	273376	T. C. Brown–Westhead, Moore & Co.	Hanley
June 11	4	273662–3	Bates, Elliott & Co.	Burslem
17	3	273736–7	Taylor, Tunnicliffe & Co.	Hanley
19	3	273804	Pinder & Bourne & Co.	Burslem
28	4	274047	Thos. Goode & Co.	London
30	3	274054–5	Minton, Hollins & Co.	Stoke
July 3	9	274162	Minton, Hollins & Co.	Stoke
4	7	274183	T. C. Brown–Westhead, Moore & Co.	Hanley
28	2	274663	Chas. Hobson	Burslem
28	8	274701	John Meir & Sons	Tunstall
29	3	274704	McBirney & Armstrong	Belleek
31	1	274725–6	Mintons	Stoke
Aug 5	2	274804	Baker & Chetwynd	Burslem
14	10	275050	T. C. Brown–Westhead, Moore & Co.	Hanley
25	1	275514–5	Geo. Jones	Stoke
27	1	275600	The Worcester Royal Porcelain Co. Ltd.	Worcester
30	2	275661	T. C. Brown–Westhead, Moore & Co.	Hanley
Sept 2	8	275755	Edge, Malkin & Co.	Burslem
4	3	275816	Mintons	Stoke
10	7	275994	Powell & Bishop	Hanley
15	3	276151	T. C. Brown–Westhead, Moore & Co.	Hanley
16	4	276159	idem	Hanley
17	8	276213	The Worcester Royal Porcelain Co. Ltd.	Worcester
19	4	276338	T. C. Brown–Westhead, Moore & Co.	Hanley
25	8	276517	Harvey, Adams & Co.	Longton
25	10	276522	Jane Beech	Burslem
29	2	276566	Wm. Brownfield & Son	Cobridge

APPENDIX B

Date	Parcel No.	Patent No.	Factory, Retailer Wholesaler, etc	Place
Oct 4	3	276796–8	Moore Bros.	Longton
4	4	276799	Heath & Blackhurst	Burslem
6	6	276816–7	T. C. Brown–Westhead, Moore & Co.	Hanley
11	6	277136	Mintons	Stoke
13	3	277148–9	Geo. Jones	Stoke
22	6	277385	Mintons	Stoke
Nov 3	3	277844	Hope & Carter	Burslem
3	4	277845–7	Geo. Jones	Stoke
6	6	277969	Wedgwood & Co.	Tunstall
10	7	278169	T. C. Brown-Westhead, Moore & Co.	Hanley
12	3	278185	Worthington & Son	Hanley
Dec 2	6	278769–70	Taylor, Tunnicliffe & Co.	Hanley
4	6	278821	The Old Hall Earthenware Co. Ltd.	Hanley
5	1	278822	Harvey, Adams & Co.	Longton
5	8	278867	Wm. Brownfield & Son	Cobridge
10	12	279180	Geo. Jones & Sons	Stoke
27	7	279437	idem	Stoke
1874				
Jan 1	3	279476–7	Bates, Elliott & Co.	Burslem
10	15	279655–6	Davenports & Co.	London (and Longport)
20	3	279938	Powell & Bishop	Hanley
21	7	279964	W. T. Copeland & Sons	Stoke
23	5	280010	John Meir & Son	Tunstall
30	4	280153–6	Haviland & Co.	Limoges and London
Feb 9	4	280343	The Worcester Royal Porcelain Co. Ltd.	Worcester
9	5	280344	Bodley & Co.	Burslem

341

Date	Parcel No.	Patent No.	Factory, Retailer Wholesaler, etc	Place
11	2	280350	Thos. Booth & Sons	Hanley
14	9	280492	Worthington & Son	Hanley
19	1	280609	Geo. Jones & Sons	Stoke
25	6	280785	Robinson & Leadbeater	Stoke
25	7	280786	Geo. Jones & Sons	Stoke
26	7	280802–4	Minton, Hollins & Co.	Stoke
Mar 2	1	280853	McBirney & Armstrong	Belleek
3	4	280907	Geo. Jones & Sons	Stoke
4	3	280919	Mintons	Stoke
4	8	280925	The Worcester Royal Porcelian Co. Ltd.	Worcester
13	6	281106	J. Dimmock & Co.	Hanley
14	2	281129	Mintons	Stoke
17	5	281190	Powell & Bishop	Hanley
21	5	281301	idem	Hanley
24	4	281319	Mintons	Stoke
27	2	281404	Worthington & Son	Hanley
28	3	281429–30	Geo. Jones & Sons	Stoke
30	1	281437	Worthington & Son	Hanley
Apr 7	4	281639	The Worcester Royal Porcelain Co. Ltd.	Worcester
14	4	281776	A. Bevington	Hanley
15	7	281822	Mintons	Stoke
20	7	281871–80	Minton, Hollins & Co.	Stoke
21	8	281899	Geo. Jones & Sons	Stoke
22	1	281902	Wm. Brownfield & Son	Cobridge
23	8	281954	T. C. Brown–Westhead, Moore & Co.	Hanley
25	2	281984	Geo. Jones & Sons	Stoke
29	7	282088	Ridgway, Sparks & Ridgway	Hanley
29	9	282091	T. Furnival & Son	Cobridge
30	2	282098	Thos. Booth & Sons	Hanley
May 5	3	282134	Bates, Elliott & Co.	Burslem
9	3	282218–9	Geo. Jones & Sons	Stoke

APPENDIX B

Date	Parcel No.	Patent No.	Factory, Retailer Wholesaler, etc	Place
11	2	282249–51	Moore Bros.	Longton
11	3	282252	J. Thomson & Sons	Glasgow
11	4	282253	Holland & Green	Longton
20	11	282497	Bates, Elliott & Co.	Burslem
21	5	282526	Mintons	Stoke
22	8	282555	idem	Stoke
23	4	282567–8	Geo. Jones & Sons	Stoke
June 1	7	282662	The Worcester Royal Porcelain Co. Ltd.	Worcester
6	2	282799–802	Wm. Brownfield & Son	Cobridge
6	5	282806	Chas. Ford	Hanley
16	6	282982	Cockson & Chetwynd	Cobridge
17	7	283041	Edge, Malkin & Co.	Burslem
18	1	283050	Mintons	Stoke
23	3	283201	Williamson & Son	Longton
23	7	283208	The Worcester Royal Porcelain Co. Ltd.	Worcester
25	5	283266–8	Thos. Ford	Hanley
26	4	283275	Pinder, Bourne & Co.	Burslem
July 10	2	283547	Mintons	Stoke
13	6	283570–1	T. C. Brown–Westhead, Moore & Co.	Hanley
27	1	283980	Hulse & Adderley	Longton
30	5	284053	Minton, Hollins & Co.	Stoke
Aug 1	8	284131–5	Mintons	Stoke
1	9	284136	Cockson & Chetwynd	Cobridge
6	7	284204	T. C. Brown–Westhead, Moore & Co.	Hanley
8	2	284254–5	Wm. Brownfield & Son	Cobridge
15	4	284417	Bates, Elliott & Co.	Burlsem
22	6	284562	J. T. Hudden	Longton
28	4	284699–700	Geo. Jones & Sons	Stoke
31	6	284779	T. J. & J. Emberton	Tunstall

Date	Parcel No.	Patent No.	Factory, Retailer Wholesaler, etc	Place
Sept 1	3	284791	Thos. Till & Sons	Burslem
3	11	284883	Geo. Adler	Saxony and London
3	12	284884–5	Cockson & Chetwynd	Cobridge
4	3	284897	Mintons	Stoke
5	4	284916–7	The Worcester Royal Porcelain Co. Ltd.	Worcester
5	7	284920	Furnival & Son	Cobridge
7	3	284936–7	Thos. Booth & Sons	Hanley
10	3	285013	Wm. Brownfield & Son	Cobridge
12	1	285181	Mintons	Stoke
15	2	285281	Geo. Jones & Sons	Stoke
16	7	285304	M. Bucholz	London
17	4	285322	R. Britton & Sons	Leeds
30	4	285776	Wm. Brownfield & Son	Cobridge
Oct 2	5	285826–8	Geo. Grainger & Co.	Worcester
3	4	285841–4	Moore Bros.	Longton
6	3	286000	Mintons	Stoke
6	4	286001	Grove & Stark	Longton
10	4	286134	Mintons	Stoke
12	2	286171	Powell & Bishop	Hanley
17	8	286359–60	Bates, Elliott & Co.	Burslem
21	8	286424	Geo. Jones & Sons	Stoke
24	3	286504–5	Robinson & Leadbeater	Stoke
27	1	286530	George Ash	Hanley
28	9	286563	Pinder, Bourne & Co.	Burslem
Nov 2	3	286715	James Edwards & Son	Burslem
3	4	286720–2	W. & E. Corn	Burslem
6	3	286759	Wm. Brownfield & Son	Cobridge
7	4	286774–80	Thos. Ford	Hanley
10	3	286794	Geo. Jones & Sons	Stoke
12	3	286931	Mintons	Stoke
12	12	286942	Bates, Elliott & Co.	Burslem
20	12	287317	F. & R. Pratt & Co.	Fenton

Date	Parcel No.	Patent No.	Factory, Retailer Wholesaler, etc	Place
25	7	287438–9	Minton, Hollins & Co.	Stoke
ec 1	5	287598	W. T. Copeland & Sons	Stoke
4	6	287638	Thos. Barlow	Longton
5	4	287676	Holmes & Plant	Burslem
7	8	287694–7	T. C. Brown–Westhead, Moore & Co.	Hanley
8	2	287699	Geo. Jones & Sons	Stoke
10	4	287731	Pinder, Bourne & Co.	Burslem
10	11	287752–6	The Worcester Royal Porcelain Co. Ltd.	Worcester
12	3	287776	Geo. Jones & Sons	Stoke
12	5	287785	Port Dundas Pottery Co.	Port Dundas
18	6	287982	Geo. Jones & Sons	Stoke
18	7	287983	Ambrose Bevington	Hanley
18	9	287985	Geo. Grainger & Co.	Worcester
18	11	287990–7	Minton, Hollins & Co.	Stoke
75				
n 2	4	288241–2	T. C. Brown–Westhead, Moore & Co.	Hanley
6	3	288276–8	Minton, Hollins & Co.	Stoke
12	3	288366	The Worcester Royal Porcelain Co. Ltd.	Worcester
16	9	288502	The Brownhills Pottery Co.	Tunstall
18	8	288521	T. C. Brown–Westhead, Moore & Co.	Hanley
20	3	288552	Robinson & Leadbeater	Stoke
20	4	288553–6	Wm. Brownfield & Son	Cobridge
21	2	288682	Geo. Jones & Sons	Stoke
23	9	288755–8	T. C. Brown–Westhead, Moore & Co.	Hanley
28	5	288830	Mintons	Stoke
29	1	288861–2	Worthington & Son	Hanley
eb 3	7	288972	Chas. Ford	Hanley

Date		Parcel No.	Patent No.	Factory, Retailer Wholesaler, etc	Place
	5	5	289076	T. & R. Boote	Burslem
	6	2	289083	Moore Bros.	Longton
	9	1	289172	Pinder, Bourne & Co.	Burslem
	9	2	289173	Geo. Jones & Sons	Stoke
	12	6	289280	J. Maddock & Sons	Burslem
	15	2	289310	Moore Bros.	Longton
	17	7	289334	Mintons	Stoke
	23	5	289503	J. Maddock & Sons	Burslem
	23	6	289504	Geo. Jones & Sons	Stoke
	23	8	289507–8	George Ash	Hanley
	24	3	289535	Stephen Clive	Tunstall
Mar	5	2	289769	Wm. Brownfield & Son	Cobridge
	12	5	289874–6	Geo. Jones & Sons	Stoke
	24	13	290153	Minton, Hollins & Co.	Stoke
	24	14	290154–5	T. C. Brown–Westhead, Moore & Co.	Hanley
	30	1	290186	Thos. Booth & Sons	Hanley
	31	5	290209–10	Wm. Brownfield & Son	Cobridge
Apr	3	7	290259	J. Dimmock & Co.	Hanley
	3	9	290261–2	E. F. Bodley & Son	Burslem
	7	3	290352	Mintons	Stoke
	9	6	290393–4	Wm. Brownfield & Son	Cobridge
	10	7	290407–8	Powell & Bishop	Hanley
	15	5	290500	R. Malkin	Fenton
	17	1	290738	Pinder, Bourne & Co.	Burslem
	20	1	290787	J. Dimmock & Co.	Hanley
	20	2	290788	Mintons	Stoke
	21	5	290812	Stephen Clive	Tunstall
	22	3	290841–2	W. P. & G. Phillips	London
	22	4	290843–6	Minton, Hollins & Co.	Stoke
May	3	8	290998	Soane & Smith	London
	7	7	291109	Geo. Jones & Sons	Stoke
	7	8	291110	Burgess & Leigh	Burslem
	11	6	291229	Thos. Goode & Co.	London
	20	1	291440	Bates, Elliott & Co.	Burslem

APPENDIX B

Date	Parcel No.	Patent No.	Factory, Retailer Wholesaler, etc	Place
20	3	291444	J. Dimmock & Co.	Hanley
22	1	291458	Holland & Green	Longton
26	6	291518–20	T. C. Brown–Westhead, Moore & Co.	Hanley
28	10	291556	Campbellfield Pottery Co.	Glasgow
28	12	291558	J. Mortlock	London
31	8	291568	Geo. Jones & Sons	Stoke
31	18	291611	Ridgway, Sparks & Ridgway	Hanley
ne 2	9	291749–51	Minton, Hollins & Co.	Stoke
5	7	291870–1	W. P. & G. Phillips	London
7	3	291882	W. & T. Adams	Tunstall
8	4	291911	The Worcester Royal Porcelain Co. (Ltd.)	Worcester
10	6	292005	Wm. Brownfield & Son	Cobridge
12	5	292034	Chas. Stevenson	Greenock
12	6	292035	Maddock & Gater	Burslem
12	10	292042	Thos. Furnival & Son	Stoke
15	5	292080	Josiah Wedgwood & Sons	Etruria
19	6	292184	Thos. Till & Sons	Burslem
26	2	292367–70	Geo. Jones & Sons	Stoke
ly 5	1	292542	Wm. Brownfield & Son	Cobridge
7	8	292579–80	Moore Bros.	Longton
8	5	292620	idem	Longton
20	4	292985	E. J. D. Bodley	Burslem
23	10	293035	T. C. Brown–Westhead, Moore & Co.	Hanley
27	5	293114	F. W. Grove & J. Stark	Longton
28	7	293129	Minton, Hollins & Co.	Stoke
ug 19	7	293748	F. W. Grove & J. Stark	Longton
28	6	294038–9	W. P. & G. Phillips	London
ept 2	3	294147	T. Elsmore & Son	Tunstall
13	2	294434–5	Geo. Jones & Sons	Stoke
14	9	294514	Minton, Hollins & Co.	Stoke
18	2	294571–2	Geo. Jones & Sons	Stoke

347

Date	Parcel No.	Patent No.	Factory, Retailer Wholesaler, etc	Place
21	1	294595	R. Cochran & Co.	Glasgow
24	2	294657	H. Aynsley & Co.	Longton
25	3	294662	F. W. Grove & J. Stark	Longton
28	6	294768–9	T. C. Brown–Westhead, Moore & Co.	Hanley
30	4	294825–7	John Edwards	Fenton
Oct 2	6	294906	Josiah Wedgwood & Sons	Etruria
6	4	294936	R. Cooke	Hanley
11	4	295001	Powell & Bishop	Hanley
11	10	295014–5	The Brownhills Pottery Co.	Tunstall
16	8	295131	Burgess, Leigh & Co.	Burslem
28	3	295443	Minton, Hollins & Co.	Stoke
30	9	295473–4	W. P. & G. Phillips	London
Nov 5	3	295551–3	Geo. Jones & Sons	Stoke
8	4	295792–8	Minton, Hollins & Co.	Stoke
8	8	295803	W. T. Copeland & Sons	Stoke
12	1	295908	Geo. Jones & Sons	Stoke
12	2	295909	Burgess, Leigh & Co.	Burslem
13	8	295933	The Worcester Royal Porcelain Co. Ltd.	Worcester
Dec 1	2	296475	Wm. Brownfield & Son	Cobridge
1	9	296508	Gelson Bros.	Hanley
3	4	296531	Geo. Jones & Sons	Stoke
6	8	296644	John Meir & Son	Tunstall
10	3	296770	Mintons	Stoke
11	5	296813	F. W. Grove & J. Stark	Longton
11	8	296818	Soane & Smith	London
13	8	296834–49	Minton, Hollins & Co.	Stoke
15	2	296939–40	Mintons China Works	Stoke
15	3	296941–5	Mintons	Stoke
24	4	297217–8	Chas. Ford	Hanley
24	6	297221	Bates, Walker & Co.	Burslem
29	5	297245	Edge, Malkin & Co.	Burslem
29	6	297246–7	T. C. Brown–Westhead, Moore & Co.	Hanley

APPENDIX B

Date	Parcel No.	Patent No.	Factory, Retailer Wholesaler, etc	Place
30	2	297250	Mintons	Stoke
30	8	297276	Mintons, Hollins & Co.	Stoke

1876

Date	Parcel No.	Patent No.	Factory, Retailer Wholesaler, etc	Place
Jan 4	4	297343	Mintons	Stoke
6	2	297471	Moore Bros.	Longton
11	7	297587	E. J. D. Bodley	Burslem
21	13	297791	Bale & Co.	Etruria
22	6	297809–11	Geo. Jones & Sons	Stoke
22	8	297813	Chas. Ford	Hanley
24	1	297817	Mintons	Stoke
24	4	297845	J. Friedrich	London
24	6	297863–4	Bates, Walker & Co.	Burslem
26	2	297977	Edge, Malkin & Co.	Burslem
26	3	297978	Powell & Bishop	Hanley
28	8	298018	James Edwards & Son	Burslem
29	3	298027–9	Wm. Brownfield & Son	Cobridge
Feb 1	2	298049	idem	Cobridge
2	7	298063	Josiah Wedgwood & Sons	Etruria
2	12	298069	Ridgway, Sparks & Ridgway	Hanley
3	5	298077	Powell & Bishop	Hanley
4	6	298103	Mintons	Stoke
4	12	298141–2	The Worcester Royal Porcelain Co. Ltd.	Worcester
8	9	298235	Bates, Walker & Co.	Burslem
19	5	298458	Geo. Jones & Sons	Stoke
21	4	298473	The Worcester Royal Porcelain Co. Ltd.	Worcester
22	3	298480–3	Minton, Hollins & Co.	Stoke
29	9	298693	J. Dimmock & Co.	Hanley
Mar 2	8	298821–4	T. Gelson & Co.	Hanley
2	11	298832	The Brownhills Pottery Co.	Tunstall
10	8	299076–8	Minton, Hollins & Co.	Stoke

349

Date	Parcel No.	Patent No.	Factory, Retailer Wholesaler, etc	Place
14	5	299177	T. C. Brown–Westhead, Moore & Co.	Hanley
17	5	299236	Mintons	Stoke
18	3	299246	Robinson & Chapman	Longton
23	8	299366	E. J. D. Bodley	Burslem
24	7	299380	Bates, Walker & Co.	Burslem
28	8	299474	W. E. Withinshaw	Burslem
30	4	299497–9	Geo. Jones & Sons	Stoke
Apr 8	6	299773	Bates, Walker & Co.	Burslem
11	4	299819	Thos. Gelson & Co.	Hanley
12	4	299830	Powell & Bishop	Hanley
12	11	299852	J. Dimmock & Co.	Hanley
21	7	300020	Minton, Hollins & Co.	Stoke
21	10	300037–8	Furnival & Son	Cobridge
22	5	300105	The Worcester Royal Porcelain Co. Ltd.	Worcester
27	3	300260	Mintons	Stoke
May 8	7	300421–3	T. C. Brown–Westhead, Moore & Co.	Hanley
10	3	300463	Geo. Jones & Sons	Stoke
11	9	300491	F. & R. Pratt & Co.	Fenton
16	7	300603–4	Mintons	Stoke
22	3	300682	Moore Bros.	Longton
22	4	300683–5	Josiah Wedgwood & Sons	Etruria
23	7	300734–7	Haviland & Co.	Limoges and London
24	3	300746	Mintons	Stoke
25	6	300779	Moore Bros.	Longton
29	8	300809–10	Geo. Jones & Sons	Stoke
June 3	2	301030	Mintons	Stoke
3	5	301035–7	E. J. D. Bodley	Burslem
7	1	301087	Thos. Gelson & Co.	Hanley
8	4	301099	Mintons	Stoke
9	6	301164	W. T. Copeland & Sons	Stoke

APPENDIX B

Date	Parcel No.	Patent No.	Factory, Retailer Wholesaler, etc	Place
15	1	301254	Henry Meir & Son	Tunstall
15	9	301267–9	Minton, Hollins & Co.	Stoke
19	2	301302	Josiah Wedgwood & Sons	Etruria
19	9	301310	J. Holdcroft	Longton
21	4	301330	Mintons	Stoke
22	4	301342	Thos. Gelson & Co.	Hanley
23	5	301402	Mintons	Stoke
26	6	301443–4	Minton, Hollins & Co.	Stoke
28	8	301543	J. Aynsley	Longton
uly 1	3	301589–90	Mintons	Stoke
1	4	301591	John Tams	Longton
3	2	301596	Ford & Challinor	Tunstall
5	1	301619	Thos. Till & Sons	Burslem
5	7	301641	W. T. Copeland & Sons	Stoke
10	3	301877	Thos. Gelson & Co.	Hanley
12	2	301926	E. J. D. Bodley	Burslem
18	3	301984	Soane & Smith	London
26	3	302125	Geo. Jones & Sons	Stoke
28	10	302178	Thos. Gelson & Co.	Hanley
28	11	302179	Powell & Bishop	Hanley
31	8	302220	G. Grainger & Co.	Worcester
ug 8	1	302384	Robinson & Chapman	Longton
25	8	302901	F. & R. Pratt & Co.	Fenton
ept 5	5	303289–90	Bates & Walker & Co.	Burslem
6	9	303308	Pinder & Bourne & Co.	Burslem
6	10	303309	Wm. Brownfield & Sons	Cobridge
9	8	303455	Worthington & Son	Hanley
9	9	303456–7	T. C. Brown–Westhead, Moore & Co.	Hanley
11	1	303459	E. J. D. Bodley	Burslem
12	6	303522–3	Geo. Jones & Sons	Stoke
18	10	303677	G. L. Ashworth & Bros.	Hanley
20	3	303731–2	Hollinshead & Kirkham	Burslem
22	3	303757	Powell & Bishop	Hanley
26	5	303853	Hope & Carter	Burslem

APPENDIX B

Date		Parcel No.	Patent No.	Factory, Retailer Wholesaler, etc	Place
	26	10	303918	T. C. Brown–Westhead, Moore & Co.	Hanley
	28	2	303926–7	Moore Bros.	Longton
	28	10	303942	Hope & Carter	Burslem
Oct	7	2	304128	Wm. Harrop	Hanley
	7	3	304129–31	Wm. Brownfield & Sons	Cobridge
	7	4	304132–3	Josiah Wedgwood & Sons	Etruria
	7	6	304144–5	Wm. Adams	Tunstall
	9	1	304149–50	Geo. Jones & Sons	Stoke
	12	8	304321	Ambrose Bevington	Hanley
	17	4	304376	T. C. Brown–Westhead, Moore & Co.	Hanley
	17	9	304383	Wardle & Co.	Hanley
	19	3	304428	Burgess, Leigh & Co.	Burslem
	20	2	304454–66	Mintons	Stoke
	21	3	304473	Edge, Malkin & Co.	Burslem
	23	2	304489	Mintons	Stoke
	31	2	304910–4	Wm. Brownfield & Sons	Cobridge
Nov	1	2	304926	Moore Bros.	Longton
	7	3	305065	Robert Jones	Hanley
	8	3	305080	Geo. Jones & Sons	Stoke
	8	9	305090	Wm. Brownfield & Sons	Cobridge
	9	10	305150	Belfield & Co.	Preston-pans
	11	9	305173	Moore Bros.	Longton
	13	3	305181	Mintons	Stoke
	14	2	305189	Josiah Wedgwood & Sons	Etruria
	14	8	305195	Clementson Bros.	Hanley
	17	3	305222	Banks & Thorley	Hanley
	18	3	305233	Minton, Hollins & Co.	Stoke
	18	7	305264	Minton, Hollins & Co.	Stoke
	18	9	305266	The Worcester Royal Porcelain Co. Ltd.	Worcester
	23	5	305312	Wm. Adams	Tunstall
	24	15	305461–2	Thos. Furnival & Sons	Cobridge

APPENDIX B

Date	Parcel No.	Patent No.	Factory, Retailer Wholesaler, etc	Place
28	2	305510	W. Hudson & Son	Longton
29	11	305568	Thos. Furnival & Sons	Cobridge
Dec 5	2	305684	Wedgwood & Co.	Tunstall
11	2	305829	John Tams	Longton
12	11	305885	The Campbell Brick & Tile Co.	Stoke
14	1	305934	Harvey Adams & Co.	Longton
14	11	305973	J. Dimmock & Co.	Hanley
18	9	306100	James Beech	Longton
20	7	306184	J. & T. Bevington	Hanley
21	2	306202	F. W. Grove & J. Stark	Longton
23	5	306282	Chas. Ford	Hanley
27	15	306341	The Campbell Brick & Tile Co.	Stoke
28	6	306367	Harvey Adams & Co.	Longton
1877				
Jan 4	10	306564	The Campbellfield Pottery Co.	Glasgow
17	5	306953	The Worcester Royal Porcelain Co. Ltd.	Worcester
20	2	307028	F. W. Grove & J. Stark	Longton
24	10	307213	Wm. Brownfield & Sons	Cobridge
25	6	307236	Wood & Co.	Burslem
25	7	307237–9	Geo. Jones & Sons	Stoke
26	3	307258	Mintons	Stoke
26	4	307259	Powell & Bishop	Hanley
Feb 1	6	307432	James Edwards & Son	Burslem
2	7	307495–7	The Worcester Royal Porcelain Co. Ltd.	Worcester
3	4	307506–7	Minton, Hollins & Co.	Stoke
5	2	307525–7	McBirney & Armstrong	Belleek
7	3	307551	Holland & Green	Longton
7	7	307570–2	Wm. Brownfield & Sons	Cobridge
9	7	307603	Robinson & Co.	Longton

APPENDIX B

Date	Parcel No.	Patent No.	Factory, Retailer Wholesaler, etc	Place
9	11	307613	T. C. Brown–Westhead, Moore & Co.	Hanley
12	3	307646	James Beech	Longton
14	16	307782	The Worcester Royal Porcelain Co. Ltd.	Worceste
15	10	307794	Minton, Hollins & Co.	Stoke
16	9	307866	John Rose & Co.	Coalport
19	2	307877	Wm. Brownfield & Sons	Cobridge
20	8	307892	G. Grainger & Co.	Worceste
21	6	307906	Mintons	Stoke
21	9	307909	W. T. Copeland & Sons	Stoke
24	3	307983	Thos. Hughes	Burslem
27	2	308010	Mintons	Stoke
Mar 1	4	308116–21	Hallam, Johnson & Co.	Longton
8	14	308329	W. T. Copeland & Sons	Stoke
10	7	308357	Geo. Jones & Sons	Stoke
14	9	308493	The Campbell Brick & Tile Co.	Stoke
20	3	308650–2	Clementson Bros.	Hanley
20	8	308662	J. Dimmock & Co.	Hanley
22	14	308718	E. J. D. Bodley	Burslem
24	1	308781–2	Powell & Bishop	Hanley
31	7	308916	E. F. Bodley & Co.	Burslem
Apr 3	1	308918	Powell & Bishop	Hanley
4	5	308932	J. Mortlock	London
5	2	308934	Ford, Challinor & Co.	Tunstall
12	11	309233	J. Dimmock & Co.	Hanley
23	4	309617	John Tams	Longton
26	2	309680	J. & T. Bevington	Hanley
26	7	309696	The Worcester Royal Porcelain Co. Ltd.	Worceste
27	10	309746	John Rose & Co.	Coalport
May 2	2	309818–21	Geo. Jones & Sons	Stoke
4	13	309917	The Old Hall Earthenware Co. Ltd.	Hanley

354

APPENDIX B

Date	Parcel No.	Patent No.	Factory, Retailer Wholesaler, etc	Place
5	4	309922	Josiah Wedgwood & Sons	Etruria
12	7	310034	Thos. Furnival & Sons	Cobridge
16	5	310175	Wm. Brownfield & Sons	Cobridge
18	6	310267	Josiah Wedgwood & Sons	Etruria
22	5	310359–61	Wm. Brownfield & Sons	Cobridge
24	8	310448	T. C. Brown–Westhead, Moore & Co.	Hanley
30	13	310556	T. Furnival & Sons	Cobridge
une 1	2	310599	J. & R. Hammersley	Hanley
5	6	310670	E. J. D. Bodley	Burslem
7	1	310709	idem	Burslem
7	2	310710	Joseph Holdcroft	Longton
8	7	310761–4	Minton, Hollins & Co.	Stoke
9	3	310775–6	Baker & Co.	Fenton
13	2	310909	idem	Fenton
15	7	310972	Ridgway, Sparks & Ridgway	Hanley
19	4	311031	Ford & Challinor	Tunstall
19	6	311033	Murray & Co.	Glasgow
22	3	311141	Walker & Carter	Stoke
22	13	311181–6	Steele & Wood	Stoke
22	14	311187	E. F. Bodley & Co.	Burslem
26	11	311366	T. Furnival & Sons	Cobridge
28	9	311423	idem	Cobridge
29	10	311448–9	Sherwin & Cotton	Hanley
uly 2	3	311523	W. T. Copeland & Sons	Stoke
6	2	311626	Mintons	Stoke
7	4	311684	Ridge, Meigh & Co.	Longton
9	2	311711	Minton, Hollins & Co.	Stoke
14	2	311883–4	John Tams	Longton
17	9	312019–21	James Edwards & Son	Burslem
20	7	312062–4	Haviland & Co.	London and Limoges
20	15	312113	Taylor, Tunnicliffe & Co.	Hanley

APPENDIX B

Date	Parcel No.	Patent No.	Factory, Retailer Wholesaler, etc	Place
23	2	312125	John Edwards	Fenton
25	5	312187	Ford, Challinor & Co.	Tunstall
26	6	312311–4	Minton, Hollins & Co.	Stoke
31	1	312421	McBirney & Armstrong	Belleek
31	2	312422	Minton & Hollins & Co.	Stoke
Aug 1	4	312434	Holmes, Stonier & Hollinshead	Hanley
3	14	312521	The Campbell Brick & Tile Co.	Stoke
13	5	312909	Haviland & Co.	London and Limoges
15	7	313009	The Campbell Brick & Tile Co.	Stoke
17	11	313080	Ridgway, Sparks & Ridgway	Stoke
18	6	313099–101	Minton, Hollins & Co.	Stoke
18	7	313102	Furnival & Son	Cobridge
23	6	313280	W. Hudson & Son	Longton
25	2	313324	Wm. Wood & Co.	Burslem
25	3	313325–9	Minton, Hollins & Co.	Stoke
28	9	313381	T. C. Brown–Westhead, Moore & Co.	Hanley
Sept 11	3	314046	G. W. Turner & Sons	Tunstall
19	5	314292	Minton, Hollins & Co.	Stoke
20	3	314385	Josiah Wedgwood & Sons	Etruria
22	7	314470–1	Mintons	Stoke
22	13	314480	Minton, Hollins & Co.	Stoke
25	5	314548	Mintons	Stoke
28	9	314675	J. Holdcroft	Longton
Oct 2	7	314890	Bates, Walker & Co.	Burslem
3	2	314896	Robinson & Leadbeater	Stoke
4	4	314906–7	J. & T. Bevington	Hanley
10	3	315102	John Edwards	Fenton

APPENDIX B

Date	Parcel No.	Patent No.	Factory, Retailer Wholesaler, etc	Place
10	5	315104–5	Wm. Brownfield & Sons	Cobridge
15	2	315271–2	Geo. Jones & Sons	Stoke
16	6	315400–1	Powell & Bishop	Hanley
19	8	315473	Minton, Hollins & Co.	Stoke
19	13	315479	T. C. Brown–Westhead, Moore & Co.	Hanley
24	10	315565	F. W. Grove & J. Stark	Longton
24	14	315574	F. & R. Pratt & Co.	Fenton
30	7	315684	Wedgwood & Co.	Tunstall
31	6	315765	Geo. Jones & Sons	Stoke
Nov 5	4	315918	Powell & Bishop	Hanley
6	11	315954–6	Wm. Brownfield & Sons	Cobridge
7	1	316087–9	E. J. D. Bodley	Burslem
7	2	316090	Mintons	Stoke
7	10	316101	Pinder, Bourne & Co.	Burslem
9	8	316122	Taylor, Tunnicliffe & Co.	Hanley
15	12	316309	T. C. Brown–Westhead, Moore & Co.	Hanley
20	9	316502	James Edwards & Sons	Burslem
21	8	316526	Davenports & Co.	Longport
22	1	316542–3	The Old Hall Earthenware Co. Ltd.	Hanley
22	13	316560	B. & S. Hancock	Stoke
24	7	316605	J. Dimmock & Co.	Hanley
29	3	316723	J. Holdcroft	Longton
Dec 1	5	316763	J. Holdcroft	Longton
1	6	316764	Oakes, Clare & Chadwick	Burslem
5	2	316842	E. J. D. Bodley	Burslem
6	4	316863	Mintons	Stoke
7	14	316912	J. Unwin	Longton
14	1	317112	J. Dimmock & Co.	Hanley
15	10	317203	The Worcester Royal Porcelain Co. Ltd.	Worcester
21	6	317404	Mintons	Stoke

Date		Parcel No.	Patent No.	Factory, Retailer Wholesaler, etc	Place
	21	10	317410	T. Furnival & Sons	Cobridge
	22	5	317427–8	Wm. Brownfield & Sons	Cobridge
	29	6	317494	T. C. Brown–Westhead, Moore & Co.	Hanley
1878					
Jan	3	4	317537–9	Minton, Hollins & Co.	Stoke
	9	4	317692–4	The Brownhills Pottery Co.	Tunstall
	10	12	317733	J. Mortlock & Co.	London
	14	1	317756	J. Maddock & Sons	Burslem
	14	2	317757	Cotton & Rigby	Burslem
	14	3	317758	Wm. Adams	Tunstall
	14	6	317763	Minton, Hollins & Co.	Stoke
	15	5	317780	Josiah Wedgwood & Sons	Etruria
	18	5	317826	Taylor, Tunnicliffe & Co.	Hanley
	22	6	317940	J. Dimmock & Co.	Hanley
	24	6	318041	W. T. Copeland & Sons	Stoke
	25	9	318107–8	Wm. Brownfield & Sons	Cobridge
	28	11	318141	T. C. Brown–Westhead, Moore & Co.	Hanley
	30	3	318158–9	Geo. Jones	Stoke
	30	15	318189–90	The Brownhills Pottery Co.	Tunstall
	31	1	318210	B. & S. Hancock	Stoke
Feb	1	4	318239	Geo. Jones & Sons	Stoke
	1	11	318265–6	Minton, Hollins & Co.	Stoke
	1	16	318275–9	The Derby Crown Porcelain Co. Ltd.	Derby
	5	5	318397	The Campbell Brick & Tile Co.	Stoke
	9	6	318469	J. Dimmock & Co.	Hanley
	11	5	318543–4	T. C. Brown–Westhead, Moore & Co.	Hanley
	12	5	318556–63	Derby Crown Porcelain Co. Ltd.	Derby
	20	6	318800	Minton, Hollins & Co.	Stoke

APPENDIX B

Date	Parcel No.	Patent No.	Factory, Retailer Wholesaler, etc	Place
20	7	318801	The Worcester Royal Porcelain Co. Ltd.	Worcester
21	10	318821	W. E. Cartlidge	Burslem
22	8	318843	The Campbell Brick & Tile Co.	Stoke
28	3	319041	Dunn, Bennett & Co.	Hanley
Mar 5	2	319190	F. W. Grove & J. Stark	Longton
6	5	319201	Minton, Hollins & Co.	Stoke
7	4	319219	John Edwards	Fenton
9	1	319278–9	The Brownhills Pottery Co.	Tunstall
9	8	319293	Moore Bros.	Longton
9	11	319296	Powell & Bishop	Hanley
11	1	319310–1	Taylor, Tunnicliffe & Co.	Hanley
13	1	319370	Mintons	Stoke
13	7	319387	J. & T. Bevington	Hanley
13	10	319394	W. T. Copeland & Sons	Stoke
15	10	319507	John Rose & Co.	Coalport
23	8	319634–6	Derby Crown Porcelain Co. Ltd.	Derby
25	9	319679	F. J. Emery	Burslem
27	6	319725–6	G. W. Turner & Sons	Tunstall
27	15	319867–72	Minton, Hollins & Co.	Stoke
Apr 2	6	320030	Belfield & Co.	Preston-pans
10	4	320281	Mintons	Stoke
13	9	320373	McBirney & Armstrong	Belleek
17	4	320482	Mintons	Stoke
17	14	320568–9	Ridgway, Sparks & Ridgway	Stoke
20	2	320606	Thos. Furnival & Sons	Cobridge
20	6	320616	The Worcester Royal Porcelain Co. Ltd.	Worcester
24	2	320669	Wm. Brownfield & Sons	Cobridge
27	12	320793	McBirney & Armstrong	Belleek
30	7	320874–5	Josiah Wedgwood & Sons	Etruria

359

APPENDIX B

Date	Parcel No.	Patent No.	Factory, Retailer Wholesaler, etc	Place
May 3	2	321028	Josiah Wedgwood & Sons	Etruria
3	9	321163	Robinson & Leadbeater	Stoke
8	9	321231–2	Bates & Bennett	Cobridge
14	6	321361	Elsmore & Son	Tunstall
17	12	321575	J. Dimmock & Co.	Hanley
20	9	321632–4	Derby Crown Porcelain Co. Ltd.	Derby
21	11	321693	Banks & Thorley	Hanley
23	3	321704	Josiah Wedgwood & Sons	Etruria
23	4	321705	Moore Bros.	Longton
24	2	321726	Josiah Wedgwood & Sons	Etruria
27	20	322007	E. J. D. Bodley	Burslem
29	9	322039	Minton, Hollins & Co.	Stoke
June 1	5	322130	J. Mortlock & Co.	London
4	9	322168	F. Furnival & Sons	Cobridge
5	14	322223–4	W. T. Copeland & Sons	Stoke
7	1	322309	Geo. Jones & Sons	Stoke
8	8	322390	Wm. Wood & Co.	Burslem
12	10	322471	Harvey Adams & Co.	Longton
13	2	322476	John Tams	Longton
13	3	322477	McBirney & Armstrong	Belleek
19	7	322597–8	E. F. Bodley & Co.	Burslem
21	8	322662	Allen & Green	Fenton
27	7	322931–2	Josiah Wedgwood & Sons	Etruria
29	1	322948	Wood, Son & Co.	Cobridge
July 1	1	322971	Burgess & Leigh	Burslem
3	2	323132	Mintons	Stoke
6	7	323315–20	Joseph Cliff & Sons	Leeds
8	6	323396	Josiah Wedgwood & Sons	Etruria
9	8	323434	Mintons	Stoke
9	9	323435	Josiah Wedgwood & Sons	Etruria
9	10	323436	J. Dimmock & Co.	Hanley
10	14	323508	Bates & Bennett	Cobridge
11	1	323521	Soane & Smith	London
11	11	323596	W. & J. A. Bailey	Alloa

APPENDIX B

Date	Parcel No.	Patent No.	Factory, Retailer Wholesaler, etc	Place
12	4	323604	Josiah Wedgwood & Sons	Etruria
12	13	323626	Samuel Lear	Hanley
12	15	323628	T. C. Brown–Westhead, Moore & Co.	Hanley
15	1	323650–1	Pratt & Simpson	Fenton
17	9	323774–5	Wm. Adams	Tunstall
18	2	323778	Ambrose Bevington	Hanley
20	1	323847	J. Bevington	Hanley
20	6	323893	John Meir & Son	Tunstall
20	11	323910–1	E. J. D. Bodley	Burslem
26	3	324177	Josiah Wedgwood & Sons	Etruria
30	2	324324	idem	Etruria
30	6	324336	Powell, Bishop & Stonier	Hanley
30	12	324347	E. Clarke	Longport
31	8	324383	Mintons	Stoke
31	13	324388	James Edwards & Son	Burslem
Aug 6	3	324576	Moore Bros.	Longton
7	3	324730	Thos. Hughes	Burslem
9	10	324848	Derby Crown Porcelain Co. Ltd.	Derby
9	12	324870–2	Craven, Dunnill & Co. Ltd.	Jackfield
14	4	325029–34	S. H. Sharp	Leeds
16	9	325094	The Campbell Brick & Tile Co.	Stoke
23	1	325278	Moore Bros.	Longton
23	7	325319	J. Dimmock & Co.	Hanley
Sept 3	12	325612	G. & L. Wohlauer	Dresden
5	3	325716	Moore Bros.	Longton
9	5	325992–4	Wm. Brownfield & Sons	Cobridge
10	2	326006	Josiah Wedgwood & Sons	Etruria
12	6	326146	J. Bevington	Hanley
13	5	326155	G. L. Ashworth & Bros.	Hanley

APPENDIX B

Date		Parcel No.	Patent No.	Factory, Retailer Wholesaler, etc	Place
	13	16	326198	The Worcester Royal Porcelain Co. Ltd.	Worcester
	20	19	326482	R. Wotherspoon & Co.	Glasgow
	24	3	326785	T. Bevington	Hanley
	28	5	326970–1	Minton, Hollins & Co.	Stoke
	30	1	327000	Mintons	Stoke
Oct	2	2	327035	Mintons	Stoke
	3	8	327110	J. T. Hudden	Longton
	4	8	327227	F. & R. Pratt & Co.	Fenton
	5	4	327235	Jones Bros. & Co.	W/hmptn
	5	13	327271	The Worcester Royal Porcelain Co. Ltd.	Worcester
	8	6	327359	Moore Bros.	Longton
	8	7	327360	Bates, Gildea & Walker	Burslem
	9	9	327392	Josiah Wedgwood	Etruria
	11	8	327556	Minton, Hollins & Co.	Stoke
	14	8	327625–6	W. T. Copeland & Sons	Stoke
	23	1	328018	The Brownhills Pottery Co.	Tunstall
	23	11	328144–5	Pinder & Bourne & Co.	Burslem
	24	1	328146	T. Furnival & Sons	Cobridge
	24	2	328147	J. Dimmock & Co.	Hanley
	24	13	328274	The Worcester Royal Porcelain Co. Ltd.	Worcester
	26	4	328320	Wm. Brownfield & Sons	Cobridge
	30	3	328436–7	Minton, Hollins & Co.	Stoke
	30	5	328439–40	Mintons	Stoke
Nov	1	3	328620	J. Bevington	Hanley
	4	1	328699	Edge, Malkin & Co.	Burslem
	5	11	328774	H. Burgess	Burslem
	5	17	328790–2	E. J. D. Bodley	Burslem
	6	3	328795	Samuel Lear	Hanley
	13	13	329075	John Rose & Co.	Coalport
	15	1	329108	Craven, Dunnill & Co. Ltd.	Jackfield
	15	11	329147	F. & R. Pratt & Co.	Fenton
	16	5	329157	J. Dimmock & Co.	Hanley

Date	Parcel No.	Patent No.	Factory, Retailer Wholesaler, etc	Place
20	13	329378	Cliff & Tomlin	Leeds
23	2	329456	E. & C. Challinor	Fenton
26	14	329673	T. & R. Boote	Burslem
27	9	329709	J. McIntyre & Co.	Burslem
29	14	329782–3	W. & E. Corn	Burslem
Dec 2	7	329901	T. C. Brown–Westhead, Moore & Co.	Hanley
2	8	329902	J. F. Meakin	London
3	9	329922	J. McIntyre & Co.	Burslem
4	2	329939	Wm. Brownfield & Sons	Cobridge
6	3	330061	Mintons	Stoke
7	2	330097	A. Shaw	Burslem
19	8	330485	Thos. Hughes	Burslem
27	13	330677	T. & R. Boote	Burslem
28	4	330687	J. Gaskell, Son & Co.	Burslem
1879				
Jan 7	7	330920	W. T. Copeland & Sons	Stoke
8	11	330965–6	Minton, Hollins & Co.	Stoke
9	8	330997–8	Wm. Brownfield & Sons	Cobridge
14	5	331152	The New Wharf Pottery Co.	Burslem
14	6	331153	The Campbell Brick & Tile Co.	Stoke
16	3	331228	B. & S. Hancock	Stoke
16	13	331342	F. & R. Pratt & Co.	Fenton
20	15	331418–9	Derby Crown Porcelain Co. Ltd.	Derby
22	4	331458	Dunn, Bennett & Co.	Hanley
28	11	331597	W. T. Copeland & Sons	Stoke
29	2	331600	T. Furnival & Sons	Cobridge
29	3	331601	T. Bevington	Hanley
29	15	331677	E. J. D. Bodley	Burslem
1	13	331775	Clementson Bros.	Hanley
3	1	331777	Josiah Wedgwood & Sons	Etruria

Date	Parcel No.	Patent No.	Factory, Retailer Wholesaler, etc	Place
5	7	331892–3	Mintons	Stoke
8	1	332030	Mintons	Stoke
14	4	332251	T. Furnival & Sons	Cobridge
15	2	332266	The Campbell Brick & Tile Co.	Stoke
17	6	332296	McBirney & Armstrong	Belleek
24	2	332606	W. P. Jervis	Stoke
24	3	332607–9	W. & T. Adams	Tunstall
25	4	332642	Mintons	Stoke
28	1	332823	E. Chetwynd	Stoke
28	7	332831	Clementson Bros.	Hanley
Mar 1	1	332837	T. Furnival & Sons	Cobridge
4	4	332938	F. W. Grove & J. Stark	Longton
6	10	333047	Powell, Bishop & Stonier	Hanley
12	4	333210	Edge, Malkin & Co.	Burslem
12	12	333235–6	W. T. Copeland & Sons	Stoke
13	1	333241–4	Wm. Davenport & Co.	Longport
13	14	333301	Clementson Bros.	Hanley
14	9	333319	E. Clarke	Longport
17	2	333368	Powell, Bishop & Stonier	Hanley
18	1	333431	Josiah Wedgwood & Sons	Etruria
19	2	333485	J. Hawthorn	Cobridge
26	17	333751–2	The Worcester Royal Porcelain Co. Ltd.	Worcester
28	6	333801	Clementson Bros.	Hanley
29	4	333813	Beck, Blair & Co.	Longton
Apr 3	9	334030	T. C. Brown–Westhead, Moore & Co.	Hanley
4	12	334052–3	Pinder, Bourne & Co.	Burslem
9	5	334137	H. Alcock & Co.	Cobridge
10	12	334200	T. C. Brown–Westhead, Moore & Co.	Hanley
12	1	334206	The Worcester Royal Porcelain Co. Ltd.	Worcester

APPENDIX B

Date	Parcel No.	Patent No.	Factory, Retailer Wholesaler, etc	Place
15	6	334241–2	T. C. Brown–Westhead, Moore & Co.	Hanley
23	8	334508	T. C. Brown–Westhead, Moore & Co.	Hanley
24	3	334531	Josiah Wedgwood & Sons	Etruria
May 2	5	334803	A. Bevington	Hanley
5	1	334860–1	T. Furnival & Sons	Cobridge
5	6	334897	Bates, Gildea & Walker	Burslem
6	7	334923–5	Sampson Bridgwood & Son	Longton
7	11	334978	The Worcester Royal Porcelain Co. Ltd.	Worcester
9	15	335057	idem	Worcester
13	4	335148–51	Pinder & Bourne & Co.	Burslem
13	8	335167–8	Clementson Bros.	Hanley
14	9	335182	T. C. Brown–Westhead, Moore & Co.	Hanley
14	13	335187–8	E. J. D. Bodley	Burslem
19	1	335308–9	Wm. Brownfield & Sons	Cobridge
21	5	335496	Harvey Adams & Co.	Longton
23	2	335551–2	Sampson Bridgwood & Son	Longton
23	14	335608	Harvey Adams & Co.	Longton
29	2	335715	John Tams	Longton
29	12	335739–40	Pinder, Bourne & Co.	Burslem
30	3	335744	McBirney & Armstrong	Belleek
30	10	335791	J. Dimmock & Co.	Hanley
30	12	335793	F. W. Grove & J. Stark	Longton
31	4	335805	Minton, Hollins & Co.	Stoke
June 10	4	336030	T. Furnival & Sons	Cobridge
11	8	336075	Thos. Till & Sons	Burslem
13	13	336132	T. C. Brown–Westhead, Moore & Co.	Hanley
18	4	336185	F. W. Grove & J. Stark	Longton
24	11	336415	Josiah Wedgwood & Sons	Etruria
25	1	336417	Clementson Bros.	Hanley

APPENDIX B

Date	Parcel No.	Patent No.	Factory, Retailer Wholesaler, etc	Place
26	13	336471–4	Haviland & Co.	Limoges and London
27	11	336496	Shorter & Boulton	Stoke
30	12	336586–7	Birks Bros. & Seddon	Cobridge
July 2	2	336676	Josiah Wedgwood & Sons	Etruria
7	2	336917	J. F. Wileman	Fenton
8	1	336930	Mintons	Stoke
8	16	336967–8	T. C. Brown–Westhead, Moore & Co.	Hanley
9	12	337058	idem	Hanley
10	2	337060	T. Bevington	Hanley
10	3	337061	Moore Bros.	Longton
16	4	337157–8	A. Bevington & Co.	Hanley
16	14	337177	T. C. Brown–Westhead, Moore & Co.	Hanley
25	4	337497	Mintons	Stoke
26	6	337536	Minton, Hollins & Co.	Stoke
31	2	337660	Mintons	Stoke
Aug 2	2	337814	H. M. Williamson & Sons	Longton
5	12	337945–7	J. Mortlock & Co.	London
6	6	337958	Wardle & Co.	Hanley
13	2	338135	F. W. Grove & J. Stark	Longton
22	4	338559	McBirney & Armstrong	Belleek
27	13	338872	Bates, Gildea & Walker	Burslem
Sept 4	6	339193	T. C. Brown–Westhead, Moore & Co.	Hanley
10	13	339373	idem	Hanley
17	4	339685–6	Wm. Brownfield & Sons	Cobridge
18	10	339979	T. C. Brown–Westhead, Moore & Co.	Hanley
26	4	340431	J. T. Hudden	Longton
29	3	340569	Edge, Malkin & Co.	Burslem
Oct 9	6	341137	Bates, Gildea & Walker	Burslem

Date	Parcel No.	Patent No.	Factory, Retailer Wholesaler, etc	Place
10	2	341151	T. C. Brown–Westhead, Moore & Co.	Hanley
11	5	341229–30	E. J. D. Bodley	Burslem
15	1	341347	Mintons	Stoke
16	5	341466	J. Roth	London
16	16	341500	Minton, Hollins & Co.	Stoke
17	2	341502	G. L. Ashworth & Bros.	Hanley
18	3	341629	Josiah Wedgwood & Sons	Etruria
23	12	341864	C. Pillivuyt & Co.	London
24	4	341882–3	The Campbell Brick & Tile Co.	Stoke
27	9	341997	E. F. Bodley & Co.	Burslem
29	5	342098	Mintons	Stoke
29	7	342100	Clementson Bros.	Hanley
29	15	342152	F. D. Bradley	Longton
30	4	342158	Mintons	Stoke
Nov 3	12	342396	Minton, Hollins & Co.	Stoke
3	14	342398	Tundley, Rhodes & Procter	Burslem
6	2	342461	Josiah Wedgwood & Sons	Etruria
6	3	342462–3	Moore Bros.	Longton
6	4	342464–72	Burmantofts (Wilcock & Co.)	Leeds
12	11	342769	The Worcester Royal Porcelain Co. Ltd.	Worcester
15	12	342921	C. Ford	Hanley
15	16	342925–7	W. T. Copeland & Sons	Stoke
17	2	342929	Powell, Bishop & Stonier	Hanley
19	5	343017	idem	Hanley
20	4	343070–1	Elsmore & Son	Tunstall
21	6	343148	Mintons	Stoke
21	14	343166	Soane & Smith	London
22	7	343219	The Worcester Royal Porcelain Co. Ltd.	Worcester
28	5	343530	Wm. Brownfield & Sons	Cobridge

Date	Parcel No.	Patent No.	Factory, Retailer Wholesaler, etc	Place
28	6	343531	A. Bevington & Co.	Hanley
29	3	343585	Mintons	Stoke
29	4	343586	T. C. Brown–Westhead, Moore & Co.	Hanley
Dec 1	2	343618	J. Holdcroft	Longton
2	4	343652–3	T. C. Brown–Westhead, Moore & Co.	Hanley
2	5	343654	Elsmore & Son	Tunstall
2	17	343716	J. Aynsley & Sons	Longton
6	2	343815–6	T. & R. Boote	Burslem
10	14	344077	Clementson Bros.	Hanley
11	4	344082–4	Moore Bros.	Longton
17	11	344387	Ridgways	Stoke
19	1	344452	Clementson Bros.	Hanley
19	3	344454	Burmantofts (Wilcock & Co.)	Leeds
20	5	344478	Josiah Wedgwood & Sons	Etruria
22	2	344503	Mintons	Stoke
24	2	344568	Sherwin & Cotton	Hanley
1880				
Jan 3	1	344838	Sherwin & Cotton	Hanley
7	3	344961–2	T. Bevington	Hanley
7	4	344963	T. & R. Boote	Burslem
7	5	344964–9	Soane & Smith	London
7	8	344972	Minton, Hollins & Co.	Stoke
8	9	344997	The Old Hall Earthenware Co. Ltd.	Hanley
9	3	345003	Sherwin & Cotton	Hanley
9	12	345045	T. G. Allen	London
13	1	345131	T. C. Brown–Westhead, Moore & Co.	Hanley
14	11	345184–5	The Worcester Royal Porcelain Co. Ltd.	Worcester
16	8	345288	S. Fielding & Co.	Stoke

APPENDIX B

Date	Parcel No.	Patent No.	Factory, Retailer Wholesaler, etc	Place
16	14	345299	Brockwell & Son	London
21	7	345469–71	Pinder, Bourne & Co.	Burslem
22	2	345481	Mintons	Stoke
22	8	345493–4	Minton, Hollins & Co.	Stoke
23	5	345511	Mintons	Stoke
26	11	345719	Wm. Brownfield & Sons	Cobridge
27	13	345798	Wardle & Co.	Hanley
28	3	345801	T. C. Brown–Westhead, Moore & Co.	Hanley
28	4	345802	J. Aynsley & Sons	Longton
28	12	345833	Powell, Bishop & Stonier	Hanley
29	9	345860–1	E. J. D. Bodley	Burslem
30	2	345864	Taylor, Tunnicliffe & Co.	Hanley
Feb 3	11	345952	Powell, Bishop & Stonier	Hanley
9	18	346202	Whittingham, Ford & Riley	Burslem
10	4	346208–10	Mintons	Stoke
11	10	346344	T. Bevington	Hanley
12	4	346360	W. A. Adderley	Longton
12	7	346363	Wm. Brownfield & Sons	Cobridge
14	14	346467	Bates, Gildea & Walker	Burslem
18	12	346594	The Derby Crown Porcelain Co. Ltd.	Derby
24	2	346832	Mintons	Stoke
24	11	346870	Wm. Harrop & Co.	Hanley
25	18	346920	Clementson Bros.	Hanley
25	23	346945	Sherwin & Cotton	Hanley
26	6	346952–3	Minton, Hollins & Co.	Stoke
26	7	346954	Moore Bros.	Longton
Mar 3	6	347138	J. Holdcroft	Longton
4	8	347203	Soane & Smith	London
8	4	347344	T. Furnival & Sons	Cobridge
8	10	347360	W. Harrop & Co.	Hanley
12	4	347476	W. A. Adderley	Longton
16	3	347599	J. F. Wileman & Co.	Fenton
16	11	347645	Sherwin & Cotton	Hanley

Date	Parcel No.	Patent No.	Factory, Retailer Wholesaler, etc	Place
16	12	347646–7	J. Macintyre & Co.	Burslem
17	6	347660	Josiah Wedgwood & Sons	Etruria
18	3	347690–6	Moore Bros.	Longton
22	4	347838	Powell, Bishop & Stonier	Hanley
23	4	347872	Taylor, Tunnicliffe & Co.	Hanley
25	6	348018	Mintons	Stoke
30	4	348110	Sherwin & Cotton	Hanley
31	3	348114	Thos. Peake	Tunstall
Apr 12	6	348606–8	Bates, Gildea & Walker	Burslem
15	11	348761	Ridgways	Stoke
19	11	348911–3	The Worcester Royal Porcelain Co. Ltd.	Worcester
22	11	349025–6	Sherwin & Cotton	Hanley
22	5	349027	W. H. Grindley & Co.	Tunstall
26	1	349221	T. Furnival & Sons	Cobridge
27	11	349239–41	Moore Bros.	Longton
27	13	349318–23	The Worcester Royal Porcelain Co. Ltd.	Worcester
29	4	349340–1	Mintons	Stoke
30	6	349380	T. Furnival & Sons	Cobridge
May 3	3	349438–43	Wm. Brownfield & Sons	Cobridge
5	13	349528	S. Fielding & Co.	Stoke
10	6	349693	Powell, Bishop & Stonier	Hanley
11	15	349791	Soane & Smith	London
13	8	349852–3	Mintons	Stoke
13	15	349869	Minton, Hollins & Co.	Stoke
14	26	349939	Bates, Gildea & Walker	Burslem
25	4	350098	Wm. Brownfield & Sons	Cobridge
26	6	350142	Mintons	Stoke
June 1	4	350251	Mintons	Stoke
2	3	350353	Sherwin & Cotton	Hanley
7	6	350476	J. Dimmock & Co.	Hanley
8	1	350477	Geo. Jones & Sons	Stoke
10	3	350554	Sherwin & Cotton	Hanley
10	4	350555	E. J. D. Bodley	Burslem

Date	Parcel No.	Patent No.	Factory, Retailer Wholesaler, etc	Place
10	12	350613	J. Dimmock & Co.	Hanley
11	3	350616	Josiah Wedgwood & Sons	Etruria
14	12	350842	J. Roth	London
15	4	350848	Buckley, Wood & Co.	Burslem
16	3	350972	Wedgwood & Co.	Tunstall
17	4	351025	Samuel Lear	Hanley
17	15	351058	Ridgways	Stoke
17	16	351059	J. Macintyre & Co.	Burslem
17	20	351063	The Crystal Porcelain Co.	Hanley
17	21	351064	J. Dimmock & Co.	Hanley
19	11	351186	Josiah Wedgwood & Sons	Etruria
19	15	351190	J. Roth	London
22	1	351259	W. H. Grindley & Co.	Tunstall
26	13	351496–7	The Worcester Royal Porcelain Co. Ltd.	Worcester
July 5	11	351866	Westwood & Moore	Brierley Hill
7	4	351909	Sherwin & Cotton	Hanley
7	5	351910	Mintons	Stoke
7	15	351928	F. J. Emery	Burslem
12	4	352094	Mintons	Stoke
13	12	352138	Thos. Barlow	Longton
15	3	352192	Dunn, Bennett & Co.	Hanley
15	4	352193	F. W. Grove & J. Stark	Longton
16	9	352224	Sherwin & Cotton	Hanley
16	10	352225	Moore Bros.	Longton
16	19	352278	S. Fielding & Co.	Stoke
28	2	352872	The Brownhills Pottery Co.	Tunstall
31	8	353079	The Old Hall Earthenware Co. Ltd.	Hanley
Aug 4	3	353108	Pinder, Bourne & Co.	Burslem
11	14	353543	Clementson Bros.	Hanley
14	12	353713–4	Wm. Davenport & Co.	Longport
17	6	353746	Sherwin & Cotton	Hanley
18	3	353818	Josiah Wedgwood & Sons	Etruria

371

APPENDIX B

Date	Parcel No.	Patent No.	Factory, Retailer Wholesaler, etc	Place
21	2	354026	Sherwin & Cotton	Hanley
21	10	354081	W. A. Adderley	Longton
23	5	354092	Jackson & Gosling	Longton
23	6	354093–4	T. C. Brown–Westhead, Moore & Co.	Hanley
24	10	354154	E. J. D. Bodley	Burslem
Sept 3	3	354639	T. C. Brown–Westhead, Moore & Co.	Hanley
4	7	354766–7	J. Beech & Son	Longton
11	3	355091–100	Wm. Brownfield & Sons	Cobridge
14	6	355169	Mintons	Stoke
15	6	355231	G. L. Ashworth & Bros.	Hanley
15	12	355255–7	Minton, Hollins & Co.	Stoke
23	3	355575	Ambrose Wood	Hanley
25	6	355651–4	Minton, Hollins & Co.	Stoke
27	5	355745–6	John Marshall & Co.	Bo'ness, Scotland
29	3	355947–8	The Brownhills Pottery Co.	Tunstall
30	4	355987	The Worcester Royal Porcelain Co. Ltd.	Worcester
Oct 1	3	356014	Wade & Colclough	Burslem
6	4	356163	Josiah Wedgwood & Sons	Etruria
12	4	356514	Mintons	Stoke
13	5	356532	Josiah Wedgwood & Sons	Etruria
20	10	356970	Burgess & Leigh	Burslem
21	13	357033–5	The Worcester Royal Porcelain Co. Ltd.	Worcester
22	4	357039	E. F. Bodley & Son	Burslem
22	12	357088	J. Aynsley & Sons	Longton
26	13	357298–9	Minton, Hollins & Co.	Stoke
27	5	357305	Taylor, Tunnicliffe & Co.	Hanley
27	20	357429	J. Tams	Longton
27	21	357430	G. Woolliscroft & Son	Etruria
28	2	357466	Sherwin & Cotton	Hanley

372

Date	Parcel No.	Patent No.	Factory, Retailer Wholesaler, etc	Place
30	6	357560	Jones & Hopkinson	Hanley
Nov 2	2	357609	W. H. Grindley & Co.	Tunstall
4	4	357656–7	W. & T. Adams	Tunstall
4	15	357724–5	Minton, Hollins & Co.	Stoke
9	4	357954	Josiah Wedgwood & Sons	Etruria
10	2	358062–3	Wilcock & Co. (Burmantofts)	Leeds
10	13	358141	Bednall & Heath	Hanley
18	3	358466	S. Radford	Longton
18	14	358500	Mintons	Stoke
19	15	358552	The Crown Derby Porcelain Co. Ltd.	Derby
24	4	358747	F. W. Grove & J. Stark	Longton
24	5	358748	Bates, Gildea & Walker	Burslem
Dec 6	2	359292	Powell, Bishop & Stonier	Hanley
7	10	359321–6	Pinder, Bourne & Co.	Burslem
8	5	359342–3	Wittmann & Roth	London
15	15	359668–71	Wm. Brownfield & Sons	Cobridge
18	2	359784	Bates, Gildea & Walker	Burslem
24	8	359997	T. C. Brown–Westhead, Moore & Co.	Hanley
29	7	360042–4	Doulton & Co.	Lambeth
31	1	360100	The Old Hall Earthenware Co. Ltd.	Hanley
31	4	360103–5	Sherwin & Cotton	Hanley
1881				
Jan 5	7	360326	J. Roth	London
6	2	360331	B. & S. Hancock	Stoke
6	8	360355	F. D. Bradley	Longton
7	13	360484	Sherwin & Cotton	Hanley
12	5	360633	idem	Hanley
14	10	360747	The Worcester Royal Porcelain Co. Ltd.	Worcester
14	18	360799	E. J. D. Bodley	Burslem

APPENDIX B

Date	Parcel No.	Patent No.	Factory, Retailer Wholesaler, etc	Place
15	4	360806–7	Holmes, Stonier & Hollinshead	Hanley
20	3	360900	Mintons	Stoke
21	11	360954	W. & T. Adams	Tunstall
26	4	361116–7	Minton, Hollins & Co.	Stoke
27	15	361151	The Worcester Royal Porcelain Co. Ltd.	Worcester
28	3	361170	G. Woolliscroft & Son	Hanley
Feb 8	5	361537	F. W. Grove & J. Stark	Longton
8	6	361538–41	Wm. Brownfield & Sons	Cobridge
11	10	361668	F. J. Emery	Burslem
15	6	361748	W. A. Adderley	Longton
16	3	361784	F. D. Bradley	Longton
17	2	361813	Murray & Co.	Glasgow
18	3	361868	S. Radford	Longton
19	15	361927	S. S. Bold	Hanley
21	4	361937	Taylor, Waine & Bates	Longton
24	8	362086	Wm. Harrop & Co.	Hanley
25	14	362166	J. Macintyre & Co.	Burslem
28	9	362242	E. J. D. Bodley	Burslem
Mar 3	5	362423	J. Dimmock & Co.	Hanley
7	11	362545	J. Aynsley & Sons	Longton
8	3	362548	F. W. Grove & J. Stark	Longton
14	1	362815	E. J. D. Bodley	Burslem
17	9	362992	Shorter & Boulton	Stoke
19	4	363026–7	Mintons	Stoke
23	4	363157	Mintons	Stoke
24	2	363206–7	T. S. Pinder	Burslem
24	3	363208	W. A. Adderley	Longton
29	6	363421	T. A. Simpson	Hanley
31	2	363461	J. T. Hudden	Longton
Apr 7	2	363720	Sherwin & Cotton	Hanley
7	9	363732	The Old Hall Earthenware Co. Ltd.	Hanley
8	2	363738	W. Harrop & Co.	Hanley

APPENDIX B

Date	Parcel No.	Patent No.	Factory, Retailer Wholesaler, etc	Place
8	3	363739	Wedgwood & Co.	Tunstall
8	14	363785	The Worcester Royal Porcelain Co. Ltd.	Worcester
9	5	363793	R. H. Plant & Co.	Longton
11	1	363800	A. Bevington & Co.	Hanley
12	4	363849–50	Mintons	Stoke
14	10	363975	Mintons	Stoke
16	17	364110	J. Marshall & Co.	Bo'ness, Scotland
19	3	364116	Sherwin & Cotton	Hanley
19	5	364118	T. & R. Boote	Burslem
21	4	364172	Sherwin & Cotton	Hanley
21	5	364173–4	E. J. D. Bodley	Burslem
23	7	364238	J. F. Wileman	Fenton
28	12	364488	W. T. Copeland & Sons	Stoke
30	3	364528	Trubshaw, Hand & Co.	Longton
30	4	364529	Josiah Wedgwood & Sons	Etruria
May 3	4	364604	Wm. Wood & Co.	Burslem
3	5	364605	Sherwin & Cotton	Hanley
4	2	364624	idem	Hanley
4	3	364625–7	Wm. Brownfield & Sons	Cobridge
5	2	364648	W. & T. Adams	Tunstall
6	4	364736	R. H. Plant & Co.	Longton
11	3	364941	J. Tams	Longton
13	2	365005	Mintons	Stoke
16	2	365066	Josiah Wedgwood & Sons	Etruria
17	9	365134–5	J. Mortlock & Co.	London
20	11	365206	W. A. Adderley	Longton
21	3	365211	Powell, Bishop & Stonier	Hanley
24	5	365391	G. L. Ashworth & Bros.	Hanley
24	6	365392–3	Mintons	Stoke
24	7	365394	F. J. Emery	Burslem
25	3	365424	Powell, Bishop & Stonier	Hanley
25	9	365442–4	The Worcester Royal Porcelain Co. Ltd.	Worcester

APPENDIX B

Date	Parcel No.	Patent No.	Factory, Retailer Wholesaler, etc	Place
25	10	365445–6	Josiah Wedgwood & Sons	Etruria
26	7	365461	G. Woolliscroft & Son	Hanley
30	1	365539	T. Furnival & Sons	Cobridge
30	2	365540	The Decorative Art Tile Co.	Hanley
June 1	3	365730	Mintons	Stoke
1	13	365793	J. Mortlock & Co.	London
3	4	365827	S. P. Ledward	Cobridge
4	3	365852	T. Furnival & Sons	Cobridge
4	4	365853	The Decorative Art Tile Co.	Hanley
7	3	365875	E. F. Bodley & Son	Burslem
7	4	365876–7	The Decorative Art Tile Co.	Hanley
7	17	365914–6	The Worcester Royal Porcelain Co. Ltd.	Worceste
8	6	365955	The Crystal Porcelain Co.	Hanley
13	1	366015	S. Lear	Hanley
16	8	366078–9	S. Fielding & Co.	Stoke
18	1	366093	Jackson & Gosling	Longton
21	13	366220–2	Birks Bros. & Seddon	Cobridge
21	20	366246	Gildea & Walker	Burslem
July 2	1	366634	McBirney & Armstrong	Belleek
2	5	366643	T. Furnival & Sons	Cobridge
6	7	366809	Josiah Wedgwood & Sons	Etruria
9	10	366922–3	Wardle & Co.	Hanley
14	6	367133–4	T. C. Brown–Westhead, Moore & Co.	Hanley
15	5	367150	Wm. Corbitt & Co.	Rthrham
16	3	367213	Trubshaw, Hand & Co.	Longton
18	4	367249	G. Hall	Worceste
19	2	367259	The Dalehall Brick & Tile Co.	Burslem
25	2	367418	J. H. Davis	Hanley
28	3	367516	McBirney & Armstrong	Belleek

APPENDIX B

Date	Parcel No.	Patent No.	Factory, Retailer Wholesaler, etc	Place
28	4	367517	A. Wood	Hanley
28	14	367538	Ridgways	Stoke
29	2	367542–3	Sherwin & Cotton	Hanley
29	3	367544	Whittmann & Roth	London
30	3	367549	Sampson Bridgwood & Son	Longton
30	4	367550	Sherwin & Cotton	Hanley
30	5	367551	Mintons	Stoke
30	15	367590	W. T. Copeland & Sons	Stoke
Aug 2	1	367608	E. J. D. Bodley	Burslem
5	12	367892–3	Pinder, Bourne & Co.	Burslem
10	13	368044	The Old Hall Earthenware Co. Ltd.	Hanley
20	11	368686	The Worcester Royal Porcelain Co. Ltd.	Worcester
23	3	368802	F. W. Grove & J. Stark	Longton
24	11	368942	T. & R. Boote	Burslem
27	3	369202	S. Lear	Hanley
27	9	369215–8	Gildea & Walker	Burslem
29	7	369248	W. & T. Adams	Tunstall
Sept 2	4	369389	Dale, Page & Goodwin	Longton
3	11	369526	T. A. Simpson	Hanley
6	1	369538	The Derby Crown Porcelain Co. Ltd.	Derby
7	10	369654	Adams & Sleigh	Burslem
9	11	369731	The Worcester Royal Porcelain Co. Ltd.	Worcester
10	12	369778–81	J. Roth	London
16	10	370093	Geo. Jones & Sons	Stoke
22	9	370400	Bold & Michelson	Hanley
23	21	370470–2	Minton, Hollins & Co.	Stoke
27	9	370611	Pinder, Bourne & Co.	Burslem
28	4	370620	E. J. D. Bodley	Burslem
28	13	370633	Gildea & Walker	Burslem
29	3	370636	Geo. Jones & Sons	Stoke
30	3	370702–3	Davenports Ltd.	Longport

APPENDIX B

Date	Parcel No.	Patent No.	Factory, Retailer Wholesaler, etc	Place
30	15	370725–8	Mintons	Stoke
Oct 4	6	370885	Wm. Brownfield & Sons	Cobridge
6	5	370998	J. & R. Boote	Burslem
6	7	371000	The Campbell Brick & Tile Co.	Stoke
7	27	371098	Mintons	Stoke
8	3	371102	Adams & Sleigh	Burslem
11	16	371247	The Worcester Royal Porcelain Co. Ltd.	Worcester
12	14	371330–1	Mintons	Stoke
13	3	371337	Adderley & Lawson	Longton
13	5	371339	T. & R. Boote	Burslem
20	1	371866	Thos. Begley	Burslem
20	2	371867	Robinson & Chapman	Longton
22	1	371959	Mintons	Stoke
26	8	372138	Mintons	Stoke
26	16	372171	T. C. Brown–Westhead, Moore & Co.	Hanley
27	1	372185	Robinson & Chapman	Longton
29	3	372347	T. & R. Boote	Burslem
29	4	372348	Wm. Brownfield & Sons	Cobridge
29	11	372376	Wardle & Co.	Hanley
29	14	372379	Minton, Hollins & Co.	Stoke
31	11	372464	T. A. Simpson	Hanley
Nov 2	1	372489–90	T. C. Brown–Westhead, Moore & Co.	Hanley
3	12	372613	The Worcester Royal Porcelain Co. Ltd.	Worcester
4	24	372727	idem	Worcester
8	1	372918	T. & R. Boote	Burslem
9	6	372979	F. W. Grove & J. Stark	Longton
9	7	372980–2	E. J. D. Bodley	Burslem
10	2	372995	Brough & Blackhurst	Longton
19	3	373541	Sampson Bridgwood & Son	Longton

378

Date	Parcel No.	Patent No.	Factory, Retailer Wholesaler, etc	Place
19	12	373573	The Worcester Royal Porcelain Co. Ltd.	Worcester
21	1	373575	J. Bevington	Hanley
22	9	373615	J. Tams	Longton
22	17	373647	Ambrose Wood	Hanley
23	13	373707	Shorter & Boulton	Stoke
25	1	373821	Adams & Sleigh	Burslem
25	15	373860	J. Roth	London
29	10	374058	The Worcester Royal Porcelain Co. Ltd.	Worcester
Dec 2	16	374229	J. Roth	London
5	11	374376	John Rose & Co.	Coalport
8	9	374498	Adderley & Lawson	Longton
9	2	374516	E. J. D. Bodley	Burslem
10	7	374579	T. C. Brown–Westhead, Moore & Co.	Hanley
12	12	374628	John Fell	Longton
16	3	374782	Mintons	Stoke
20	9	374948	Bednall & Heath	Hanley
21	3	374955	F. Grosvenor	Glasgow
21	9	374987	The Worcester Royal Porcelain Co. Ltd.	Worcester
24	5	375054	J. Broadhurst	Fenton
1882				
Jan 3	6	375415	Holmes, Plant & Maydew	Burslem
4	2	375426–7	W. T. Copeland & Sons	Stoke
4	7	375439	J. Roth	London
4	9	375444	F. & R. Pratt & Co.	Fenton
7	2	375494	W. H. Grindley & Co.	Tunstall
7	11	375580	Ridgways	Hanley
10	5	375599	S. Lear	Hanley
11	1	375709–12	Minton, Hollins & Co.	Stoke
13	4	375815–6	The Decorative Art Tile Co.	Hanley

APPENDIX B

Date	Parcel No.	Patent No.	Factory, Retailer Wholesaler, etc	Place
18	10	376032	Robinson & Son	Longton
26	5	376425	J. T. Hudden	Longton
26	16	376443	S. Fielding & Co.	Stoke
27	8	376461	Craven, Dunnill & Co. Ltd.	Jackfield
30	2	376528	Hollinshead & Kirkham	Tunstall
30	3	376529	F. W. Grove & J. Stark	Longton
Feb 1	1	376580	Edge, Malkin & Co.	Burslem
3	4	376672–3	T. C. Brown–Westhead, Moore & Co.	Hanley
4	10	376754	Minton, Hollins & Co.	Stoke
6	4	376764–6	The Campbell Tile Co.	Stoke
7	2	376798	Wm. Mills	Hanley
8	7	376839	Wardle & Co.	Hanley
15	4	377048	F. W. Grove & J. Stark	Longton
16	6	377135–7	Mintons	Stoke
18	5	377273	J. F. Wileman & Co.	Fenton
23	17	377488–9	Minton, Hollins & Co.	Stoke
24	3	377492	Taylor, Tunnicliffe & Co.	Hanley
Mar 1	11	377779	The Worcester Royal Porcelain Co. Ltd.	Worcester
1	12	377780	Minton, Hollins & Co.	Stoke
7	7	378051	idem	Stoke
13	3	378252	J. T. Hudden	Longton
15	3	378337	Powell, Bishop & Stonier	Hanley
15	4	378338	Murray & Co.	Glasgow
20	5	378643	W. A. Adderley	Longton
23	2	378739	W. & T. Adams	Tunstall
23	15	378823	T. A. Simpson	Hanley
27	3	378937	D. Chapman	Longton
27	10	378959	Shorter & Boulton	Stoke
28	12	378988	Ambrose Wood	Hanley
28	16	378993–4	A. Bevington & Co.	Hanley
30	13	379076	John Rose & Co.	Coalport
30	17	379080	S. Fielding & Co.	Stoke
31	3	379088	A. Bevington & Co.	Hanley

APPENDIX B

Date	Parcel No.	Patent No.	Factory, Retailer Wholesaler, etc	Place
Apr 4	2	379212-3	Wm. Brownfield & Sons	Cobridge
11	6	379434	Geo. Jones & Sons	Stoke
11	7	379435-6	Minton, Hollins & Co.	Stoke
21	7	379767	Sampson Bridgwood & Son	Longton
27	14	380072	The New Wharf Pottery Co.	Burslem
May 2	5	380194	G. L. Ashworth & Bros.	Hanley
3	1	380199	S. Radford	Longton
5	2	380401	Wood, Hines & Winkle	Hanley
6	5	380418	Powell, Bishop & Stonier	Hanley
6	6	380419-20	Whittaker, Edge & Co.	Hanley
8	18	380549-50	Davenports Ltd.	Longport
9	3	380553-4	H. Alcock & Co.	Cobridge
9	4	380555	Whittaker, Edge & Co.	Hanley
9	7	380558	Wm. Brownfield & Sons	Cobridge
9	11	380564	Minton, Hollins & Co.	Stoke
10	4	380571-2	John Edwards	Fenton
10	14	380676	S. Fielding & Co.	Stoke
13	6	380789	Geo. Jones & Sons	Stoke
17	2	380869-70	E. J. Bodley	Burslem
24	4	381376	Minton, Hollins & Co.	Stoke
24	21	381434	Doulton & Co.	Burslem
25	11	381480	W. A. Adderley	Longton
27	3	381568	Samuel Lear	Hanley
30	5	381611	W. H. Grindley & Co.	Tunstall
June 5	6	381805	Mintons	Stoke
5	7	381806	Wood, Hines & Winkle	Hanley
9	3	381964	Hall & Read	Burslem
9	4	381965-6	W. A. Adderley	Longton
13	11	382126	A. Shaw & Son	Burslem
13	14	382130-1	Wardle & Co.	Hanley
21	4	382406	Wm. Lowe	Longton
21	5	382407-8	Sampson Bridgwood & Son	Longton
21	11	382472	The Old Hall Earthenware & Co. Ltd	Hanley

Date	Parcel No.	Patent No.	Factory, Retailer Wholesaler, etc	Place
23	1	382593–4	Josiah Wedgwood & Sons	Etruria
23	5	382598	Burgess & Leigh	Burslem
28	2	382721	The Derby Crown Porcelain Co.	Derby
July 1	8	382829	Taylor, Tunnicliffe & Co.	Hanley
3	2	382842	Mintons	Stoke
3	3	382843	E. J. D. Bodley	Burslem
4	3	382859	Wright & Rigby	Hanley
6	4	383020–1	Wm. Brownfield & Sons	Cobridge
14	3	383436–7	Geo. Jones & Sons	Stoke
14	10	383468	Wardle & Co.	Hanley
14	14	383482	Beech & Tellwright	Cobridge
17	8	383549	Wood & Son	Burslem
19	7	383641	Wardle & Co.	Hanley
20	1	383694–6	John Edwards	Fenton
22	8	383802	Geo. Jones & Sons	Stoke
25	3	383855	F. Grosvenor	Glasgow
25	9	383869–71	The Brownhills Pottery Co. Ltd.	Tunstall
26	4	383893	Adderley & Lawson	Longton
28	3	384078	Hawley & Co.	Longton
31	2	384160–1	Sampson Bridgwood & Son	Longton
31	9	384171–2	Mintons	Stoke
Aug 5	4	384353–4	Wm. Brownfield & Sons	Cobridge
10	5	384464	Wright & Rigby	Hanley
21	2	385106	John Tams	Longton
21	8	385129	Adams & Bromley	Hanley
25	2	385411	Mintons	Stoke
26	4	385490	Wm. Wood & Co.	Burslem
28	2	385527	Belfield & Co.	Preston-pans
28	9	385544	Mintons	Stoke
29	12	385623	Wm. Brownfield & Sons	Cobridge
30	14	385693	The Worcester Royal Porcelain Co. Ltd.	Worcester

APPENDIX B

Date	Parcel No.	Patent No.	Factory, Retailer Wholesaler, etc	Place
31	3	385701	A. Bevington & Co.	Hanley
Sept 6	2	385954	Hawley & Co.	Longton
8	5	386085–6	Mintons	Stoke
9	3	386126	Taylor, Tunnicliffe & Co.	Hanley
11	4	386178	Adams & Bromley	Hanley
16	2	386388–9	Hulme & Massey	Longton
19	2	386542	W. H. Grindley & Co.	Tunstall
28	4	387147–8	T. C. Brown–Westhead, Moore & Co.	Hanley
28	22	387229	Bridgett & Bates	Longton
29	2	387231–2	The Brownhills Pottery Co.	Tunstall
Oct 6	2	387598–603	Mintons	Stoke
9	3	387771	W. T. Copeland & Sons	Stoke
9	4	387772	Dean, Capper & Dean	Hanley
11	3	387958–60	Sampson Bridgwood & Son	Longton
11	4	387961	Wood & Son	Burslem
12	17	388200	T. Furnival & Sons	Cobridge
16	4	388296	Wood & Son	Burslem
19	4	388395	Lowe, Ratcliffe & Co.	Longton
31	2	389136	Wm. Lowe	Longton
Nov 1	14	389201	Stonier, Hollinshead & Oliver	Hanley
4	19	389390	The Worcester Royal Porcelain Co. Ltd.	Worcester
8	2	389554	Mintons	Stoke
10	10	389793	Ridgways	Stoke
10	12	389795–7	Pratt & Simpson	Fenton
11	2	389801	Powell, Bishop & Stonier	Hanley
13	1	389893	Edge, Malkin & Co.	Burslem
13	2	389894	Sampson Bridgwood & Son	Longton
14	3	389911–2	Ed. Steel	Hanley
15	7	390004–5	S. Fielding & Co.	Stoke
16	3	390023	Taylor, Tunnicliffe & Co.	Hanley
21	4	390255	J. Holdcroft	Longton

APPENDIX B

Date	Parcel No.	Patent No.	Factory, Retailer Wholesaler, etc	Place
21	8	390264	Gildea & Walker	Burslem
22	11	390285	S. Fielding & Co.	Stoke
24	19	390588	Minton, Hollins & Co.	Stoke
27	3	390617	H. Alcock & Co.	Cobridge
27	4	390618	The Derby Crown Porcelain Co. Ltd.	Derby
27	5	390619	J. F. Wileman & Co.	Fenton
Dec 2	8	390976	Minton, Hollins & Co.	Stoke
4	7	390985	A. Bevington & Co.	Hanley
6	2	391068–9	T. C. Brown–Westhead, Moore & Co.	Hanley
13	4	391361–2	Mintons	Stoke
13	5	391363–4	Josiah Wedgwood	Etruria
14	6	391409	S. Lear	Hanley
15	3	391460	The Old Hall Earthenware Co. Ltd.	Hanley
18	9	391596	J. Lockett & Co.	Longton
19	3	391620	H. Kennedy	Glasgow
21	4	391768	E. J. D. Bodley	Burslem
21	5	391769	Wood, Hines & Winkle	Hanley
22	2	391818	F. W. Grove & J. Stark	Longton
22	14	391846	Lorenz Hutschenreuther	Bavaria
23	4	391855	J. F. Wileman	Fenton
23	12	391917	The New Wharf Pottery Co.	Burslem
23	14	391922–7	The Worcester Royal Porcelain Co.	Worcester
27	1	391929	The New Wharf Pottery Co.	Burslem
1883				
Jan 2	2	392166	The Derby Crown Porcelain Co. Ltd.	Derby
3	1	392176	Wm. Hines	Longton
3	14	392362	T. Furnival & Sons	Cobridge

384

APPENDIX B

Date	Parcel No.	Patent No.	Factory, Retailer Wholesaler, etc	Place
3	18	392388–9	John Rose & Co.	Coalport
4	5	392403	T. C. Brown–Westhead, Moore & Co.	Hanley
8	5	392590	W. T. Copeland & Sons	Stoke
8	12	392621	The Worcester Royal Porcelain Co. Ltd.	Worcester
9	3	392626	Powell, Bishop & Stonier	Hanley
9	4	392627	E. F. Bodley & Son	Longport
9	5	392628–30	Hall & Read	Hanley
9	11	392652	Davenports Ltd.	Longport
10	17	392693	Gildea & Walker	Burslem
12	3	392725	Holmes, Plant & Maydew	Burslem
13	6	392760	Moore & Co.	Longton
13	17	392809	T. & R. Boote	Burslem
16	1	392855	Blair & Co.	Longton
17	3	392888	W. H. Grindley & Co.	Tunstall
23	8	393099	E. F. Bodley & Son	Longport
23	10	393102–3	W. T. Copeland & Sons	Stoke
24	1	393107	Sampson Bridgwood & Son	Longton
24	2	393108–9	Wm. Brownfield & Sons	Cobridge
25	3	393177	The Brownhills Pottery Co.	Tunstall
26	8	393258	Wm. Lowe	Longton
27	8	393298	G. W. Turner & Sons	Tunstall
29	6	393310	Wm. Brownfield & Sons	Cobridge
29	7	393311–2	W. H. Grindley & Co.	Tunstall
30	1	393323	E. F. Bodley & Son	Longport
30	12	393362	Wedgwood & Co.	Tunstall
31	14	393413	Minton, Hollins & Co.	Stoke
Feb 1	3	393418	Sampson Bridgwood & Son	Longton
1	17	393474	E. J. D. Bodley	Burslem
2	4	393495	S. Hancock	Stoke
2	17	393539	Wedgwood & Co.	Tunstall
3	3	393548	Mintons	Stoke
5	2	393647	J. Holdcroft	Longton
6	1	393668	Wood, Hines & Winkle	Hanley

APPENDIX B

Date	Parcel No.	Patent No.	Factory, Retailer Wholesaler, etc	Place
7	4	393714	Hawley & Co.	Longton
7	5	393715	Mountford & Thomas	Hanley
9	9	393979	E. J. D. Bodley	Burslem
12	3	394086	Dunn, Bennett & Co.	Hanley
14	3	394185	W. H. Grindley & Co.	Tunstall
15	5	394215	J. H. Davis	Hanley
17	13	394371	G. W. Turner & Sons	Tunstall
19	1	394374	W. A. Adderley	Longton
20	13	394443	Davenports Ltd.	Longport
20	17	394448	Gildea & Walker	Burslem
21	3	394452	Geo. Jones & Sons	Stoke
22	6	394556–61	Hall & Read	Hanley
22	20	394599	The Worcester Royal Porcelain Co. Ltd.	Worcester
22	21	394600	The Old Hall Earthenware Co.	Hanley
24	12	394676	Josiah Wedgwood & Sons	Etruria
24	13	394677	The Worcester Royal Porcelain Co. Ltd.	Worcester
26	6	394687	Williamson & Sons	Longton
28	3	394765	Thos. Till & Sons	Burslem
Mar 8	5	395284	M. Massey	Hanley
8	20	395316–7	E. F. Bodley & Son	Longport
14	3	395560	The Derby Porcelain Co. Ltd.	Derby
15	3	395622	T. Furnival & Sons	Cobridge
16	6	395688	J. Broadhurst	Fenton
17	8	395703	Mintons	Stoke
20	3	395818	E. A. Wood	Hanley
20	4	395819	Josiah Wedgwood & Sons	Etruria
24	3	396056	Sampson Bridgwood & Son	Longton
30	1	396200–1	Mintons	Stoke
30	9	396245	Minton, Hollins & Co.	Stoke
Apr 2	3	396313	T. & E. L. Poulson	Castleford
3	3	396316	E. Warburton	Longton

APPENDIX B

Date	Parcel No.	Patent No.	Factory, Retailer Wholesaler, etc	Place
6	14	396576	G. & J. Hobson	Burslem
10	1	396648	Banks & Thorley	Hanley
19	3	397090	R. H. Plant & Co.	Longton
21	1	397227	J. F. Wileman & Co.	Fenton
24	7	397311	G. L. Ashworth & Bros.	Hanley
25	14	397376	Pratt & Simpson	Fenton
27	17	397512	C. Littler & Co.	Hanley
27	18	397513	J. H. Davis	Hanley
27	19	397514	Powell, Bishop & Stonier	Hanley
May 2	4	397609–11	T. C. Brown–Westhead, Moore & Co.	Hanley
5	4	397751	Whittaker, Edge & Co.	Hanley
7	8	397819	S. Fielding & Co.	Stoke
8	6	397829–30	T. G. & F. Booth	Tunstall
11	5	398059	R. H. Plant & Co.	Longton
16	12	398280	T. A. Simpson	Stoke
22	11	398425	Powell, Bishop & Stonier	Hanley
22	12	398426	Burns, Oates	London
23	7	398436	T. G. & F. Booth	Tunstall
23	8	398437–8	E. A. Wood	Hanley
24	3	398479	The Brownhills Pottery Co.	Tunstall
25	4	398519	W. A. Adderley	Longton
28	2	398577–80	O. G. Blunden	Poling
31	17	398784	Wardle & Co.	Hanley
June 2	9	398849–55	Minton, Hollins & Co.	Stoke
4	8	398877–8	Clementson Bros.	Hanley
8	2	399068	H. Alcock & Co.	Cobridge
9	2	399135–6	Sampson Bridgwood & Son	Longton
9	6	399143	Mintons	Stoke
11	2	399147	F. W. Grove & J. Stark	Longton
11	8	399161	J. Matthews	Westons'-Mare
11	9	399162	idem	Westons'-Mare

APPENDIX B

Date		Parcel No.	Patent No.	Factory, Retailer Wholesaler, etc	Place
	13	3	399319	Belfield & Co.	Preston-pans
	13	7	399336	Pratt & Simpson	Stoke
	14	2	399367–70	F. W. Grove & J. Stark	Longton
	18	11	399554	John Tams	Longton
	18	12	399555–9	Wm. Brownfield & Sons	Cobridge
	20	3	399640	T. & R. Boote	Burslem
	20	4	399641	Mintons	Stoke
	20	16	399675	W. & E. Corn	Burslem
	21	22	399822	Wardle & Co.	Hanley
	23	4	399875	Josiah Wedgwood & Sons	Etruria
	25	5	399891	Ford & Riley	Burslem
	25	10	399897–8	Wm. Brownfield & Sons	Cobridge
July	2	4	400146	Edge, Malkin & Co.	Burslem
	3	3	400176	J. Aynsley & Sons	Longton
	3	4	400177	Moore Bros.	Longton
	4	7	400348	Wm. Brownfield & Sons	Cobridge
	5	6	400367	F. W. Grove & J. Stark	Longton
	5	19	400462	T. Furnival & Sons	Cobridge
	5	21	400464	Owen, Raby & Co.	Longport
	6	2	400467	Blackhurst & Bourne	Burslem
	10	9	400582	Ambrose Wood	Hanley
	10	11	400583–4	J. Macintyre & Co.	Burslem
	11	1	400596	Josiah Wedgwood & Sons	Etruria
	19	4	400941	Davenports Ltd.	Longport
	19	21	400994	Geo. Jones & Sons	Stoke
	20	11	401035	Hollinshead & Kirkham	Tunstall
	21	3	401040	Bridgett & Bates	Longton
	23	3	401087	Josiah Wedgwood & Sons	Etruria
	26	1	401296	W. A. Adderley	Longton
	27	4	401410	T. C. Brown–Westhead, Moore & Co.	Hanley
	27	13	401426–7	Wm. Bennett	Hanley
	30	10	401553	Wm. Brownfield & Sons	Cobridge
	31	3	401593	T. & R. Boote	Burslem

APPENDIX B

Date	Parcel No.	Patent No.	Factory, Retailer Wholesaler, etc	Place
Aug 1	3	401623	Wagstaff & Brunt	Longton
1	4	401624	Geo. Jones & Sons	Stoke
1	9	401653	T. C. Brown–Westhead, Moore & Co.	Hanley
2	3	401663–4	Davenports Ltd.	Longport
3	17	401769	E. J. Bodley	Burslem
8	9	401842	J. & E. Ridgway	Stoke
9	15	401897–9	Haviland & Co.	France and London
17	5	402346	E. J. D. Bodley	Burslem
20	8	402514	The Worcester Royal Porcelain Co. Ltd.	Worcester
22	1	402560–1	The Brownhills Pottery Co.	Tunstall
23	2	402625–6	Grove & Cope	Hanley
24	12	402736	Mountford & Thomas	Hanley
25	11	402839	Wm. Brownfield & Sons	Cobridge
29	3	402950	J. Aynsley & Sons	Longton
31	6	403110	W. & E. Corn	Burslem
31	7	403111	J. F. Wileman & Co.	Fenton
Sept 1	10	403204	S. Fielding & Co.	Stoke
5	3	403298–9	Wm. Brownfield & Sons	Cobridge
7	4	403486	The Derby Crown Porcelain Co. Ltd.	Derby
7	19	403513–4	Powell, Bishop & Stonier	Hanley
11	4	403665	Josiah Wedgwood & Sons	Etruria
13	17	403802–3	H. Aynsley & Co.	Longton
14	1	403805–6	W. & T. Adams	Tunstall
14	2	403807–9	Mintons	Stoke
17	14	403978	The Derby Crown Porcelain Co. Ltd.	Derby
20	12	404171–5	Hall & Read	Hanley
20	13	404176	The Derby Crown Porcelain Co. Ltd.	Derby

389

APPENDIX B

Date		Parcel No.	Patent No.	Factory, Retailer Wholesaler, etc	Place
	21	4	404196	T. C. Brown–Westhead, Moore & Co.	Hanley
	24	9	404317	Jones & Hopkinson	Hanley
	25	4	404328	F. W. Grove & J. Stark	Longton
	25	5	404329–30	Sampson Bridgwood & Son	Longton
	27	21	404466	Meigh & Forester	Longton
	28	4	404473	Blair & Co.	Longton
	28	5	404474	E. J. D. Bodley	Burslem
	29	4	404571	Sampson Bridgwood & Son	Longton
Oct	2	15	404643	Mellor, Taylor & Co.	Burslem
	2	22	404652–3	Meigh & Forester	Longton
	4	4	404745	Sampson Bridgwood & Son	Longton
	4	5	404746	Whittaker, Edge & Co.	Hanley
	4	24	404809	The Worcester Royal Porcelain Co. Ltd.	Worcester
	6	2	404870	W. H. Grindley & Co.	Tunstall
	8	1	404900	Hollinson & Goodall	Longton
	8	2	404901–2	T. G. & F. Booth	Tunstall
	8	3	404903–5	Hall & Read	Hanley
	9	9	405016–8	A. Bevington & Co.	Hanley
	11	2	405215	Wittmann & Roth	London
	12	13	405336	Bridgetts & Bates	Longton
	13	3	405341	Wood & Son	Burslem
	13	11	405363–4	Wm. Brownfield & Sons	Cobridge
	17	5	405466	The New Wharf Pottery Co.	Burslem
	17	6	405467–8	Hall & Read	Hanley
	20	3	405724	W. A. Adderley	Longton
	20	4	405725–9	Wm. Brownfield & Sons	Cobridge
	23	6	405855	J. Dimmock & Co.	Hanley
	24	11	405946–8	Minton, Hollins & Co.	Stoke
	25	17	406032–3	Taylor, Tunnicliffe & Co.	Hanley
	26	7	406043	Jones & Hopkinson	Hanley
	27	1	406046	The Brownhills Pottery Co.	Tunstall

APPENDIX B

Date	Parcel No.	Patent No.	Factory, Retailer Wholesaler, etc	Place
30	2	406140	J. Marshall & Co.	Bo'ness, Scotland
30	3	406141	The New Wharf Pottery Co.	Burslem
30	17	406187	J. Robinson	Burslem
Nov 1	1	406223	A. Bevington & Co.	Hanley
1	25	406370	Wood, Hines & Winkle	Hanley
1	26	406371	S. Fielding & Co.	Stoke
1	27	406372	Davenports Ltd.	Longport
2	19	406464–9	The Worcester Royal Porcelain Co. Ltd.	Worcester
5	13	406511	H. Alcock & Co.	Cobridge
6	3	406516	E. & C. Challinor	Fenton
7	2	406561	W. & E. Corn	Burslem
10	9	406781	Taylor, Tunnicliffe & Co.	Hanley
10	10	406782	Wm. Brownfield & Sons	Cobridge
13	10	406875	T. G. & F. Booth	Tunstall
14	3	406893	Stonier, Hollinshead & Oliver	Hanley
15	17	407063	T. Furnival & Sons	Cobridge
17	2	407155	The Derby Crown Porcelain Co. Ltd.	Derby
21	3	407333	F. J. Emery	Burslem
22	3	407385	S. Fielding & Co.	Stoke
23	7	407587–8	Minton, Hollins & Co.	Stoke
24	3	407601	Powell, Bishop & Stonier	Hanley
26	2	407623	W. A. Adderley	Longton
26	3	407624	Sampson Bridgwood & Son	Longton
28	12	407805–10	The Worcester Royal Porcelain Co. Ltd.	Worcester
Dec 1	3	407913	idem	Worcester
3	10	407943	James Wilson	Longton
5	2	408035	Malkin, Edge & Co.	Burslem
5	3	408036	The Derby Crown Porcelain Co. Ltd.	Derby

APPENDIX B

Date	Parcel No.	Patent No.	Factory, Retailer Wholesaler, etc	Place
8	8	408136	J. F. Wileman & Co.	Fenton
14	4	408288	The Brownhills Pottery Co.	Tunstall
15	13	408356	T. G. & F. Booth	Tunstall
15	14	408357	Hollinson & Goodall	Longton
29	4	408849	Powell, Bishop & Stonier	Hanley

Index

B. B. & I., 273
B. & B./L., 188
B.B. & S., 189
B.B.W. & M., 147, 168
B. & C., 99
B.C.Co., 192
B.C.Co. monogram, 192
B.C.G., 106
B.E. & Co., 97
B. & E., 189
Beardmore & Co., Frank, 135
Beardmore & Edwards, 189
Bednall & Heath, 147
Beech & Hancock, 245
Beech, James, 98
beehive & 'D.B. & Co.', 103
Belgrave China, 190
Bell China, 213
Bell, John, 233
Belleek, 19, 274
Belper Pottery, 21
Benham, Tony, 59
Bennett & Co., G., 225
Bennett & Co. J., 147
Bennett (Hanley) Ltd., William, 147
Benthall, 21
Bentley & Co. Ltd., G.L., 189
Bentley, Wear & Bourne, 221
Beswick Ltd., J., 190
Beswick & Son., 190
Bevington & Co., 272, 273
Bevington & Co., John, 147
Bevington, James & Thomas, 147
Bevington, John, 147
Bevington, Thomas, 148
Bewley Pottery, 134
B.F., 178
B.F. monogram, 54
B.F.B. under crown, 85
B.G., 130

B.G. & W., 98
B. & H., 99, 147, 190, 245
B.H.B. monogram, 50
B. & H./L., 190
Billinge, Thomas, 54
Billingsley, 70
Billingsley, W., 64, 271
Billingham, 21
Billington, Dora, 59
Bilston, 97
Bilton (1912) Ltd., 225
Biltons Tableware Ltd., 225
Bingham, Edward, 28, 29
Bingley, 72
Bingley & Co., T., 80
Birch, E.J., 221
Birch, Whitehead, 148, 221
Birkenhead, 22
Birks, 225
Birks, Brothers & Seddon, 127
Birks & Co., L.A., 225
Birks, Rawlins & Co. Ltd., 226
Bishop & Stonier, 148, 161
Bishops Waltham Pottery, 22
Bisto, 148
B. & K., 135
B. & K.L., 135
B.L., 75
B.L. monogram, 100
B. & L., 100
Black, on shield, 248
Blackhurst & Bourne, 98
Blackhurst & Co. Ltd., J., 127
Blackhurst & Hulme, 190
Blackhurst, Jabez, 245
Blackhurst & Tunnicliffe, 98
Blackman, Audrey, 69
Blades, John, 56
Blair & Co., 190
Blairs China, 190
Blakeney Art Pottery, 282

396

401

407

411

413

416

419

421

426